Christian Social Ethics

Christian Social Ethics

Models, Cases, Controversies

FRED GLENNON

ORBIS BOOKS

Maryknoll, New York 10545

Published by Orbis Books, Box 302, Maryknoll, NY 10545-0302.

Manufactured in the United States of America.
Book design and typesetting by Joan Weber Laflamme.

Library of Congress Cataloging-in-Publication Data

Names: Glennon, Frederick E., author.
Title: Christian social ethics : models, cases, controversies / Fred Glennon.
Description: Maryknoll, NY : Orbis Books, [2021] | Includes bibliographical references and index. | Summary: "A college-level introductory text in Christian social ethics that combines theory, cases, and analysis"— Provided by publisher.
Identifiers: LCCN 2020036192 (print) | LCCN 2020036193 (ebook) | ISBN 9781626984127 (trade paperback) | ISBN 9781608338764 (epub)
Subjects: LCSH: Christian ethics. | Christian sociology.
Classification: LCC BJ1191 .G74 2021 (print) | LCC BJ1191 (ebook) | DDC 241—dc23
LC record available at https://lccn.loc.gov/2020036192
LC ebook record available at https://lccn.loc.gov/2020036193

Contents

Introduction

In the wake of the death of George Floyd at the hands of a Minneapolis police officer in the spring of 2020, many protestors took to the streets calling for an end to systemic racial injustice. People of all colors marched together under the banner of Black Lives Matter. Noticeably, significant numbers of these protestors were members of Christian congregations who were asking themselves, "What would Jesus do?" The answer was that Jesus would call them to seek repentance for their complicity in America's "original sin" and to stand in solidarity with their brothers and sisters of color to change the policies, laws, and institutions that perpetuate these injustices.[1] One congregant, James Blay, writes: "We must call out injustice, we must scream out that it is unacceptable to dehumanize and criminalize black people, LGBTQ people, brown people, and Native American people, we must drown out those who fail to realize that all lives can't matter until black lives matter."[2]

Other Christians disagree. While they affirm that the love of God extends to all persons regardless of race, the Bible also teaches respect for law and civil authorities. "Let every person be subject to the governing authorities; for there is no authority except from God, and those authorities that exist have been instituted by God. Therefore, whoever resists authority resists what God has appointed, and those who resist will incur judgment" (Rom 13:1–2). Some Christians argue that engaging in such protests undermines the authority of the people in charge and goes against God's will. Moreover, many of these protests embrace other policies such as LGBTQ rights and reproductive rights, which violate Christian teaching on homosexuality and the sanctity of all human life.[3]

---

[1] Many church leaders issued statements condemning racial injustice. For example, the presiding bishop of the Episcopal Church, Michael Curry, released this statement: "Opening and changing hearts does not happen overnight. The Christian race is not a sprint; it is a marathon. Our prayers and our work for justice, healing and truth-telling must be unceasing. Let us recommit ourselves to following in the footsteps of Jesus, the way that leads to healing, justice and love." See "Presiding Bishop Curry's Word to the Church," May 30, 2020, https://episcopalchurch.org.

[2] James Blay, "Who Told You?" sermon, College Park Baptist Church, Greensboro, North Carolina, June 13, 2020.

[3] See Kent Dunnington and Ben Wayman, "How Christians Should—and Should Not—Respond to Black Lives Matter," ABC Religion and Ethics website, June 3, 2019.

Ethical debates among Christians on significant social issues are occurring at family gatherings, in the congregational gatherings of churches, in the class-rooms of academia, in the halls of government, and on the streets of our cities. Each position claims that the weight of Christian morality is on its side. Who is right? What would Jesus really do? I wrote this textbook for those seek-ing some clarity on these debates and the Christian social ethics interpretive frameworks that support the differences in their positions. It is my hope that by exploring the concepts and backgrounds of different approaches and the arguments they develop on important social issues, readers will gain a richer understanding of and appreciation for the breadth of Christian social ethics and its relevance for resolving some of the most pressing issues of our day.

DEFINITIONS

Many students who attend my Christian ethics classes, especially those who see themselves as spiritual but not religious, ask some common questions: Is there a difference between morality and ethics? How is the Christian ethics I teach different from the ethics they learned in their required moral philosophy class? Can one be ethical without being Christian or religious?

In terms of the first question, given that many people use the terms *moral-ity* and *ethics* interchangeably, including most of my students, some question whether we should make any distinctions between them. While I am sym-pathetic to their concern, in this book I want to highlight some slight differ-ence between them, like the distinction one might make between theory and practice. Most of my students see themselves as moral persons. What they mean is that when they encounter a situation or engage with people in their lives that calls for some moral response, they draw upon the moral feelings, habits, values, or codes that they learned from their families, their schools, their society, and their personal experiences to discern directions for their behavior and relationships. For example, when a cashier gives them more change than they were supposed to get, instead of pocketing it, they return the money to the cashier because they value honesty, even if they are not conscious of their motivation at the time. This constitutes their morality. Ethics, on the other hand, is a systematic, critical study concerned with the evaluation of human conduct and character; it is more focused on understanding all the elements—the facts of the situation, the values and beliefs, the social location, and the moral reasoning—that underlie our moral choices and behaviors. Ethics is an attempt to bring these elements to light for examination, review, critique, and assessment. In the example above, an ethical analysis would encourage the students to ferret out and reflect on the values that motivated their honest action, discern the source(s) of those values (family, religion, and so on), seek to identify the moral reasoning or principles they used (could it be the Golden Rule, that is, do to others what you want others to do to you?), and assess the appropriateness of this moral framework for this and future moral actions. To engage in this reflective process, of course, students need time and space away from the moment of moral decision making and action.[4] What better place to do this than in the classroom!

Regarding the second question, religious ethics and moral philosophy often overlap. In their philosophy class students are likely to encounter three normative approaches to ethics: those based on laws and duty, those based on the ends sought, and those exploring moral virtues. The first two address norms for moral conduct; the third looks at norms for moral character. All three of these normative approaches can be found in Christian ethics.[5] In response to the basic moral question, "What should I do?" a law- or duty-oriented approach would ask, "What is the relevant rule, principle, or law?" Using our reason, we discern which rule applies in each situation, and we follow the appropriate rule. What makes the action right is that our behavior conforms to the rule. The virtue that is praised here is the virtue of obedience; the actor is obeying the moral law in this situation and fulfilling his or her obligation. This is known as the ethics of deontology (from the Greek word *deon*, meaning "duty").[6] Clearly, this approach to ethics is *nonconsequentialist*, that is, one abides by the rule, law, or principle regardless of the consequences. We can certainly find this approach in some models of Christian ethics. For example, some Catholic and conservative evangelical Christians who oppose abortion often point to the sanctity of human life as a fundamental, God-given principle. From this they derive a basic rule or law: it is morally impermissible to do any action that undermines the sanctity of human life. Abortion violates this principle and is, therefore, an immoral practice. Abortion opponents may agree that having a child may be financially ruinous for the person or the family involved. They may feel sympathy for the woman who does not want the child and offer counseling on adoption. The bottom line, however, is that the consequences for the woman or the family or even society are ultimately immaterial. What matters, abortion opponents argue, is that the child has a fundamental right to life, and we ought to respect that right.

---

[4] See June O'Connor, "On Doing Religious Ethics," *Journal of Religious Ethics* 7/1 (1979): 81–96. O'Connor uses the metaphor of a ladder, where climbing each rung offers a broader view of the elements in ethical practice, from the worldview level (values, beliefs, and so forth) to the epistemological level (raising questions about why one's interpretive framework is appropriate).

[5] Most Christian ethicists are well-versed in moral philosophy; it is part of their education, which is enhanced by their biblical and theological studies. You will see some reference to these in many of the models of Christian ethics discussed in Chapter 1. The next few paragraphs draw from my chapter on religious ethics in Nancy C. Ring, Kathleen S. Nash, Mary N. MacDonald, and Fred Glennon, *Introduction to the Study of Religion*, 2nd ed. (Maryknoll, NY: Orbis Books, 2012), chap. 5.

[6] The moral philosophy of Immanuel Kant is a good example of this approach. See his *Foundations for the Metaphysics of Morals,* ed. Mary Gregor and Jens Timmermann (Cambridge, UK: Cambridge University Press, 2012).

The ethical model that focuses on ends as the basis of ethical obligation is teleology (from the Greek word *telos*, which means "end"). The response an ethics of ends provides to the moral question, "What should I do?" is "What ends am I seeking to achieve? What are the best means for achieving them?" Then the person uses the most efficient or most ethical means for achieving those ends. Unlike law, the moral action has more to do with the actions themselves and their consequences than with the intention of the actions. That is why this approach has been labeled *consequentialism.*[7] No matter how good the intention of the actor is, if the action does not result in the goal or end sought, the morality of the action is called into question. Let's say a person with no medical training stops to help an accident victim and in the process of helping ends up causing more serious injury. We understand and appreciate the intention of the helper, but we judge the actions by their consequences as well. Christian ethics also includes ends as the basis for moral obligation. For example, the Bible advocates the norms of justice and mercy, because they will generate a specific kind of moral community, enabling all members of the community to experience meaningful, fulfilling, and abundant lives. So, visions of community are moral ends that require certain moral actions to achieve them. This understanding was evident in the civil rights movement in the United States. The Rev. Dr. Martin Luther King Jr. advocated nonviolent resistance as the means to achieve his end, the "beloved community." The beloved community entailed the norms of equality, justice, and peace for all regardless of race. To achieve that end using violent means would be destructive of the very community he was hoping to achieve. Thus, participants in the struggle were trained in the principles of nonviolent resistance.

Discussion of moral norms, laws, and ends limits our focus to the actions themselves, the *doing* of ethics. We also make moral judgments about people, however, as when we say someone is a moral or ethical person. When we make these judgments, we are making judgments about character, the *being* of an ethical person or community. Being and doing are obviously related. It is often the case that because a person has a certain type of character, we know that he or she will do a certain type of action. The difference is that the moral judgment of character focuses more on the inner motivations—the traits, habits, or dispositions a person possesses to act a certain way—than on the actions themselves. This third approach to ethics is called *virtue ethics* (from the Latin word *virtus* and the Greek word *arete*, which combined mean "moral excellence"). When we say that someone has excellent moral character, we are declaring that when moral situations arise, that person tends to do the right thing because he or she has a certain way of being in the world and is predisposed to act in moral ways. Often our description of those persons

---

[7] The moral philosophy of utilitarianism described by John Stuart Mill is part of this approach. See Mill's *Utilitarianism,* ed. Oskar Piest (New York: Liberal Arts Press, Bobbs-Merrill Co., 1957).

includes various virtues, such as compassion, wisdom, or courage.[8] A biblical example of this approach is found in Jesus's parable of the Good Samaritan. In this story a man asks Jesus what he needs to achieve salvation. Jesus tells him that salvation is achieved through living out the twofold command to love God and to love one's neighbor. The man responds with a question, seeking to limit his ethical obligations: "Who is my neighbor?" Instead of answering this question, Jesus responds with the story of the good Samaritan, a story that stresses the moral character of the hero over the fulfillment of the commandment. Briefly, three individuals encounter someone who has been robbed and beaten and is lying by the roadside. The Samaritan is the only one who stops to ensure that the victim receives the care and assistance needed to restore him to health. After telling the story, Jesus asks which of the three persons who passed by embodied the virtues of love and care essential to *being* a neighbor. It is the Samaritan who is the neighbor; it flows from his being because he has the covenant written on his heart.

Understanding the overlap between moral philosophy and Christian ethics helps to answer the third question: Can one be moral without being religious? In today's secular society we may not see the intricate connection between religion and morality clearly. We may agree with the so-called new atheists who contend that religion and morality are separate and distinct human endeavors.[9] It may be possible (or, from the perspective of new atheists, preferable) for us to have morality without religion. In support of our view we can point to numerous moral decisions we have made that had nothing to do with our religious beliefs. We tell the truth because we believe that lying undermines the possibility for genuine relationships. We tutor disadvantaged children in reading and math because we think that all children deserve a good education regardless of economic status. What do these actions have to do with religion? The answer may be nothing or everything, depending upon the source of these underlying values.

While it may be possible to have morality without religion, I contend that the reverse is not true. Religions help people find answers to human questions of ultimacy, including questions about morality: What must I do? What kind of person should I be? How should I relate to others and to the nonhuman world? Religions suggest possible answers to these questions based upon their perceptions of the ultimate ordering of life. Thus, what distinguishes secular morality, ethical ideals, or norms without conscious religious support from religious ethics is that the latter are grounded in some perception of that ultimate ordering. Religions provide the norms for both conduct and character for their practitioners. By advocating particular moral principles,

---

[8] A classic example of this approach is Aristotle, *Nicomachean Ethics*, trans. J.A.K. Thompson (London: Penguin Books, 1953). For a more recent example, see Alasdair MacIntyre, *After Virtue: A Study in Moral Theory* (Notre Dame, IN: University of Notre Dame Press, 1981).

[9] See, for example, Christopher Hitchens, *God Is Not Great: How Religion Poisons Everything* (New York: Little, Brown, and Company, 2008).

laws, and virtues, religions prescribe what religious people and communities should do and the kind of people they should become. Thus, they encompass both moral doing and being. Moreover, religions sanction some ways of doing and being as most in keeping with the perceived ultimate ordering in the universe. Religions help their practitioners to believe that their way of living in relationship to one another and to the world is not simply what ought to be but also what is "really real." How many children have been told that the reason they should respect their parents is because this is what the Bible says? By invoking the name of their sacred text, parents declare that this is not simply what they think is good behavior, but also what God wants. The reverse is also true: acting contrary to what the Bible says can bring about divine judgment. Such examples are a part of what sociologists of religion define as religion's *legitimating role,* an explanation and justification of society's moral order.[10] The moral authority that religions assert may be oppressive or liberating or both. Regardless, religions enable people to answer the question of why a particular moral order is in place.

Christian ethical perspectives contend that there is something in the Christian faith—revealed in the Bible, in Christian history, and in its current embodiments—that can and should provide guidance for Christians when it comes to ethical issues.

> He has told you, O mortal, what is good;
>   and what does the LORD require of you
> but to do justice, and to love kindness,
>   and to walk humbly with your God? (Mic 6:8)

"This is my commandment, that you love one another as I have loved you. No one has greater love than this, to lay down one's life for one's friends." (Jn 15:12–13)

Notice, however, that I emphasize perspectives and not just a singular perspective. As will become clear in this text, there are many approaches to Christian ethics. On the one hand, they are shaped by Christian theologians, churches, and communities that develop theological interpretative frameworks on what Christian faith means and apply it to the ethical issues they face. On the other hand, they are also shaped by other social-institutional locations, loyalties, and experiences that influence the lenses through which they see the issues and their solutions. Examples of such influences that we explore in this book include gender, sexual orientation, race, class, and ethnicity.

This text discusses seven models of Christian social ethics. *Models,* as I am using the term here, are both representations of something and examples for imitation; thus, they are descriptive (models *of*) and prescriptive (models

---

[10] See Peter Berger, *The Sacred Canopy: Elements of a Sociological Theory of Religion* (New York: Random House, 1967).

for). These models, which include situation ethics, evangelical ethics (conservative and progressive), natural law ethics, and liberative ethics (feminist, womanist, and Hispanic), are all Christian (models of) because Christian beliefs and insights about the nature of God, humanity, love, and justice ground significant parts of their ethical frameworks, even though they may understand those beliefs differently. They are also descriptive models in the sense that they represent the breadth of Christian social ethical perspectives that have emerged in the field that any text on Christian social ethics should include.[11] Moreover, they are descriptive because I have chosen to use the writings of one person to represent the model in discussing the ethical framework and how that position would address the social issues embodied in the case studies. The models chosen are also prescriptive (models for) for a similar reason. The representatives chosen for each model are worthy of imitation because they embody the best of that approach in terms of careful articulation of the framework, drawing insights not only from theology and philosophy, but also history, literature, and the natural and social sciences; they also use their experiences and vision to engage many of the most pressing issues society faces. Moreover, the choice of models is prescriptive in the sense that I feature three liberative ethics frameworks prominently in the hopes of raising their exposure and solidifying their position as viable alternatives to natural law, evangelical, and situation ethics approaches.

When writing about Christian ethical perspectives, many texts suggest that they all embody four critical sources: scripture, tradition, reason, and experience. These are often referred to as the "Wesleyan quadrilateral," a methodology for theological and ethical reflection that is credited to John Wesley, leader of the Methodist movement in the late eighteenth century.[12] Different Christian ethical approaches emphasize all four of these sources to some degree, although they might accentuate one over the other. For example, the Bible is fundamental for most Protestant evangelical ethics as the primary source of ethical insight and norms. For Catholics and natural law ethics, tradition and church teaching are the most important sources because they reflect the collective wisdom of the church; the Bible is vital, but to a lesser extent (although that has changed some since the Second Vatican Council, 1962–65). All Christian ethical traditions highlight the importance of reason in ethical decision making. While the Bible and tradition are important sources for ethical insight, they require the use of reason both to understand them

---

[11] Some readers will note the omission of two Christian ethical approaches: Gustafson's theocentric ethics and the character/virtue ethics of Stanley Hauerwas. I have two reasons for omitting them. First, these two traditions focus primarily on the Christian community and the moral life of Christians and less on the implications for the social issues this text seeks to engage. Second, their perspectives are represented in some form in the models I do discuss, and so for the sake of space I chose not to include them.

[12] See Albert C. Outler, ed., *John Wesley* (Oxford, UK: Oxford University Press, 1964), iv.

and to apply them in specific contexts and situations. Christians must use their God-given capacity for rational thought to discern the moral action to take. Experience and context, especially the experiences of those who have worked to overcome oppression and marginalization, are critical to most traditions, particularly situation and liberative ethics. Experience often changes an understanding of what counts as biblical truth, questions the traditional views of key moral concepts, or posits the possibility of a different way of moral reasoning. Experience is also the fundamental datum for raising ethical concerns and questions about the patterns and structures that run counter to the ideal of justice and community—the kingdom of God—envisioned by Christianity.

One final definition to consider is what we mean by Christian *social* ethics, which is part of the title of this book. Some Christian ethics focus on the norms that individual Christians should apply to moral situations they face. Should individual Christians participate in a war they consider immoral and to which they conscientiously object? Some treatises on Christian ethics take this individual approach. Christian social ethics looks more at the institutional and structural issues that create problems for society and the collective response likeminded Christians should take to address them. What should Christians do to address the systemic racism, America's original sin, which generates wide disparities and unequal treatment by whites against persons of color in our economic, educational, and criminal justice institutions? It is not that individual and social ethics are separate. As many feminists rightly claim, the personal is political. The point is that in this text we explore these larger social issues—corporate responsibility, immigration, the environment, and so forth—and all the questions and concerns they raise through the lenses of different Christian social ethics models that advocate for collective actions to address them.

METHOD

In this book I combine two different descriptive comparative approaches: conceptual and direct.[13] I use the *conceptual comparative* method to describe key ethical concepts from the models of Christian social ethics mentioned above, as articulated by a significant representative of that model, in a neutral way to inform the reader about the contours of each model without any judgment on my part about which model is best. Where there are criticisms of other models, they emerge from the representatives themselves, because these models are not generated in a vacuum but often in contrast with the other models. It is only natural that some of the criticisms of one another would become evident. The *direct comparative* approach emerges in the case

---

[13] See Mari Rapela Heidt, *Moral Traditions* (Winona, MN: Anselm Academic, 2010), 12.

studies about significant social issues. I develop the responses to the same issue from two different models, which allows readers to explore the similarities and differences between the two and also encourages them to make some comparisons between them. Here again, I make no judgment about which model best addresses the social issue at hand. There are no "straw men" here, in which one sets up a different perspective by developing its weakest views and then knocking them down.[14] Instead, I make room for each position to speak for itself about its perspective on the social issue raised in the strongest light, in the hope that students and professors who use this text can place their own views in dialogue with these other perspectives.

This approach is different from some normative, single-method texts, which take one model of Christian ethics and then use that model's interpretative framework to come to conclusions about the ethical implications of the social issues they address.[15] In my experience with such texts, students often agree or disagree too quickly with the argument without taking the time to comprehend fully why that stance was chosen. Instead, this text's combination of models, cases, and controversies exposes students to a range of assumptions, frameworks, and experiences, and it provides them with opportunities to locate themselves, to "try on" different models to see which model or combination of models fits them best. In my view this more comprehensive representation helps to resist easy ideological pigeonholing.

This book also uses the case study method (CSM) to explore the social ethical issues in the text.[16] Why case studies? Most people who use CSM, regardless of their discipline, do so because they claim that it helps to develop critical thinking skills; encourages reflective practice and deliberate action; helps students understand the complexity of real-life situations where theory and practice may not match; and engages students in their own learning.[17] It seeks to affirm John Dewey's contention that the best learning takes place when students are given something to do, not something to learn.[18] In my years of using case studies as a pedagogical practice to teach Christian ethics, I agree with that assessment. Two of the most common case studies are those that require a decision and those that require an appraisal. In the first,

---

[14] This does not mean I have no perspective on these models or issues. Even the choice of which ethical positions to include and which to exclude provides some hint about my views if the reader is perceptive enough to glean it.

[15] I do draw from some of these single-method texts to articulate the interpretive frameworks of the models of Christian social ethics I discuss.

[16] The case study method (CSM) is generally associated with the series of case studies developed and used at the Harvard Business School that have become a model for other case studies series. See L. B. Barnes, C. R. Christensen, and A. J. Hansen, *Teaching and the Case Method: Text, Cases, and Readings,* 3rd ed. (Boston: Harvard Business School Press, 1994).

[17] Katherine Merseth, *The Case for Cases in Teacher Education* (Washington, DC: American Association of Higher Education, 1991).

[18] John Dewey, *Democracy and Education* (New York: The Free Press, 1966), 154.

students are required to decide about an issue and a course of action. In the second, they must give their assessment of an issue that the case explores, the problems and concerns it raises, and discern possible alternative solutions. In this text I use the second type of case study. These tend to be open-ended, that is, instead of providing a set conclusion, the focus is on the process that students use to judge the case. Thus, they are more student directed.

This does not mean the professor has no role to play. When I use case studies, I may not function as the main source of information, but my expertise in the content of Christian social ethics and skills in moral reasoning provide the basis for helping students come to grips with their difficulties in understanding the complexities of cases and mastering the content of the models. With appropriate interventions, such as providing background materials, raising provocative questions, and illustrating parallels among student responses at opportune times, I can raise discussions to a higher level and lead students to a greater depth of understanding and critical thinking. At the same time, the case method enables me to do this in a more dialogical and engaged fashion, using active learning strategies rather than relying solely on traditional, lecture-oriented pedagogy.[19]

While case study texts hold many advantages, case studies alone present similar educational difficulties to normative presentations of Christian social ethics. In isolation, case studies fail to provide sufficient background for students to appreciate the full range of discourse. Like the response to normative, single-method texts, case study texts tend to reify students' preexisting assumptions. Students read cases like newspaper articles or "hot topics" of casual conversation. Pitted against contrasting readings by other students, once again without sufficient theoretical grounding or contextualization, ethics becomes mere exchange of opinion. At worst, this reductionism lends credence to a creeping nihilism. The leading case method text in Christian ethics attempts to mitigate this problem by providing author analyses of given cases. In my experience, however, students often read these author analyses without recognizing their factual or reasoned underpinnings. An author's analysis of the case becomes simply one more opinion. I contend that frameworks or models are necessary foreground to successful use of CSM. Theoretical models sketch the landscape of the discourse; case studies color in the trees. This combined approach, which introduces theoretical models and then proceeds to case studies and concomitant analysis, bears the advantages of the case method without its evident disadvantages.

---

[19] Karim Rebeiz argues: "When successful, the CSM elevates the interaction of 'teacher-students' and 'students-students' to a higher order of critical thinking and learning in the Bloom's taxonomy than the traditional method of instruction. The ultimate experience is a sustainable learning experience that stays with the students for a long period of time" (Karim Rebeiz, "An Insider Perspective on Implementing the Harvard Case Study Method in Business Teaching," *US-China Education Review* A 5 [2011]: 592).

STRUCTURE OF THE TEXT

From what I have written above, the reader already has a sense of the structure of the book. Chapter 1 outlines the seven models of Christian social ethics developed in the American context, discussing key theological beliefs, ethical principles, modes of moral reasoning, and the contexts deemed central to the development of that model, even though each model may emphasize one starting point for its interpretive framework over another. Each model is represented by a Christian ethicist(s) whose writings are recognized as a significant embodiment of that model and who has contributed to its development. Collectively, these models incorporate some or all the aspects of normative ethics discussed above: nonconsequentialist, consequentialist, and virtue ethics. At the same time they push the boundaries of normative ethics by incorporating the concrete realities of people whose concerns have not been adequately represented in traditional approaches to ethics.

Chapters 2 through 9 discuss cases about social ethical issues that are being currently debated among ethicists, parishioners, politicians, and citizens. These include debates about sexuality and marriage, corporate responsibility, medicine and health care, immigration, the environment, criminal justice, the relationship between church and state, and violence. While there are many possible cases that could have been developed for each social issue, I chose these cases because they represent relatively recent events and because they have been cases my students have been debating in class discussions and on social media. Professors who use this text should certainly supplement these cases with other relevant cases they deem appropriate at the time. The description of each case is followed by a discussion of the relevant ethical issues and concerns the case raises for persons considering the case. These are drawn both from arguments from commentators about the case and from my own musings on what the case involves. These are not meant to be exhaustive, and my hope is that students and professors will raise additional arguments in their own deliberations in the classroom.

Following the issues and concerns are two analyses of the case from the perspective of the representative of the models. The choice of which positions I use on each issue may seem somewhat arbitrary to the reader. Obviously, any of the models could be included to analyze any of the cases for the purposes of comparison. I could even have looked at each case from all the models discussed, but that approach would have made for a much longer and more expensive book! Instead, my goal was to use the models that made sense for that case study or where the representative of that model had specifically addressed the issue. More important, my decision to limit the case analyses to two perspectives was done in the hope that the professors and the students who use this text will assume the challenge to explore the other models as they wrestle with the issues themselves.

I have made every effort to make this text easy to read and easy to use because I know that students arrive at our classrooms with a variety of life experiences. Perhaps many of them fit the mold of traditional late-adolescent, full-time college students, but we also teach part-time students, parents, workers who have been laid off, retired people, former military personnel, and others who have never had a chance to complete a college education. As I wrote I tried to keep all these people, as well as others, in mind. I trust that this book will be useful to college students and to others, such as church groups, who would like to think more systematically about Christian social ethics. As an aid in that endeavor, at the end of each chapter I include some pedagogical resources for use by the professor, students, and church leaders. These include discussion questions, pedagogical activities, readings, and audiovisuals. The questions seek to draw student attention to the content of the chapter as well as invite them to consider the implications for their own ethical frameworks. Students may pursue the pedagogical activities on their own to demonstrate their learning or professors can assign one or more as class activities. Many of these activities are research based, and many of them culminate in a public presentation of some sort. I expect that professors and students who use this book will select supplementary readings from these lists or other texts that they find helpful. Given the fact that many students are visual learners, the suggested audiovisuals could provide a different medium for exploring the issues and their ethical implications. Here again, my goal in including them in this book is for everyone who uses this text to continue the ethical conversations that the cases and their analyses have begun.

ACKNOWLEDGMENTS

Although I am the final author of this book, and thus I take full responsibility for any errors or omissions, I have not been alone in this process. The initial idea for the book came from a former colleague, Dr. Jane Hicks, who left to teach at St. John Fisher College in Rochester, New York. Even though she decided not to pursue the project with me, I give her credit for getting me interested in it and for devising much of the book's structure. I also want to thank Dr. Dianne Oliver, dean of Arts and Sciences at Nazareth College in Rochester. She was a coauthor at one point and wrote the substantive parts of the feminist and womanist liberative ethics models in Chapter 1. Alas, her move to administration severely constrained her time and availability to complete the project. Yet evidence of her wisdom from our conversations about the project run through most of the text. I appreciate the feedback I received from Dr. Terry Reeder, my colleague at Le Moyne College for the past two years, who used drafts of the models in her class on Christian social ethics. All my colleagues, past and present, in the Department of Religious Studies at Le Moyne College have supported me in my scholarly and pedagogical endeavors, the fruits of which are evident in this text. So is the insight I received from the thousands of students who have bravely entered my ethics classrooms and allowed me to experiment on them with the content and the pedagogy in this book. They have helped me to see more clearly what works and does not work in an introduction to Christian social ethics. My appreciation extends also to the Research and Development Committee of the Faculty Senate at Le Moyne College for recommending my sabbatical leave to the provost in spring 2020, which allowed me to complete the project. Thanks also to the editorial team at Orbis Books, especially Jill Brennan O'Brien, for sticking with the project, holding me to a firm deadline, and making recommendations about which cases to include.

Finally, I dedicate this book to my wife of over forty years, Lindy Glennon, who has been my life partner in every endeavor I have undertaken in my professional career. Her labors as a social worker, first with the victims of child abuse, and for the past twenty-five years in community-action agencies serving poor and at-risk families—building coalitions to address their emotional, educational, and economic needs; and building bridges out of poverty—has inspired me to work diligently to ensure that students who walk into my classroom understand that the ethical responsibility for promoting justice and the well-being of "the least of these" rests with each of us individually and collectively, regardless of our political or religious persuasion.

Reference Abbreviations

"Beloved"   Emilie Townes, "To Be Called Beloved: Womanist Ontology in Postmodern Refraction," in *Womanist Theological Ethics: A Reader,* ed. Katie Cannon et al., 183–202 (Louisville, KY: Westminster John Knox Press, 2011)

Cakeshop   *Masterpiece Cakeshop, Ltd. v. Colorado Civil Rights Commission,* 584 U. S. 1–8 (2018)

"Consciousness"   Emilie Townes, "Black Womanist Consciousness: Economic and Border Thoughts," *Interpretation* 74/1 (2020): 9–14

CPE   Emilie Townes, *Womanist Ethics and the Cultural Production of Evil* (New York: Palgrave Macmillan, 2006)

"Defense"   Jean Porter, "In Defense of Living Nature," in *The Ideal of Nature,* ed. Gregory Kaebnick, 17–28 (Baltimore: Johns Hopkins, 2011)

DEM   Miguel De La Torre, *Doing Ethics from the Margins,* 2nd ed. (Maryknoll, NY: Orbis Books, 2014)

EE3/EE4   John Jefferson Davis, *Evangelical Ethics,* 3rd and 4th eds. (Philipsburg, NJ: P&R Publishing, 2004, 2015)

"Embryo"   Jean Porter, "Is the Embryo a Person?" *Commonweal* (February 8, 2002): 8–10

HH   Joseph Fletcher, *Humanhood: Essays in Biomedical Ethics* (Buffalo, NY: Prometheus Books, 1979)

"Human Need"   Jean Porter, "Human Need and Natural Law," in *Infertility: A Crossroad of Faith, Medicine, and Technology,* ed. Kevin Wm. Wildes, SJ (Dordrecht, The Netherlands: Kluwer Academic Publishing, 1997), 93–106

"Immigration" President Donald J. Trump, "Statement from President Donald J. Trump: Immigration," Statements and Releases, September 5, 2017

JM Beverly W. Harrison, *Justice in the Making: Feminist Social Ethics* (Louisville, KY: Westminster John Knox Press, 2004)

KE Glen Stassen and David Gushee, *Kingdom Ethics: Following Jesus in Contemporary Context* (Downers Grove, IL: InterVarsity Press, 2003)

KE2 Glen Stassen and David Gushee, *Kingdom Ethics*, 2nd ed. (Grand Rapids, MI: Eerdmans, 2016)

LSE Miguel De La Torre, *Latina/o Social Ethics* (Waco, TX: Baylor University Press, 2010)

MC Carol S. Robb, ed. *Making the Connections: Essays in Feminist Social Ethics* (Boston: Beacon Press, 1985)

MR Joseph Fletcher, *Moral Responsibility: Situation Ethics at Work* (Philadelphia: Westminster Press, 1967)

NDL Jean Porter, *Natural and Divine Law: Reclaiming the Tradition for Christian Ethics* (Grand Rapids, MI: Eerdmans, 1999)

NR Jean Porter, *Nature as Reason: A Thomistic Theory of the Natural Law* (Grand Rapids, MI: Eerdmans, 2005)

OH *Obergefell v. Hodges*, 576 US 20 (2015)

RC Beverly W. Harrison, *Our Right to Choose: Toward a New Ethic of Abortion* (Eugene, OR: Wipf and Stock Publishers, 2011)

SE Joseph Fletcher, *Situation Ethics: The New Morality* (Philadelphia: Westminster Press, 1966)

SED Harvey Cox, ed., *The Situation Ethics Debate* (Philadelphia: Westminster Press, 1968)

"Souls"   Emilie M. Townes, "Ethics as an Art of Doing the Work
                   Our Souls Must Have," in *Womanist Theological Ethics:*
                   A Reader (Louisville, KY: Westminster John Knox Press,
                   2011)

TEP   Miguel De La Torre, *The US Immigration Crisis: Toward*
                   an Ethics of Place (Eugene, OR: Cascade Books, 2016)

"Torture"   Jean Porter, "Torture and the Christian Conscience: A
                   Response to Jeremy Waldron," *Scottish Journal of Theol-*
                   ogy 61/3: 340–58

1

Models of Christian Social Ethics

SITUATION ETHICS

Christian ethicist James Gustafson contends that there are four base points that all Christian social ethics should touch upon, even though they may begin with or emphasize one more than the others. These base points include accurate situational analysis, basic theological affirmations, moral principles, and a conception of human moral agency.[1] Those Christian ethicists named as *contextual* or *situational,* Gustafson rightly notes, "all have a special concern that the place of moral responsibility be understood to be highly specific and concrete, and that Christian ethics attend more to acting responsibly in a given place than it has done in those times and persons that seem satisfied with broad moral generalizations."[2] Part of the reason for this increased emphasis on context is the complexity of the world in which we find ourselves. Rapid social change, technological advancements, and the move toward a global society call into question what once seemed to be settled moral perspectives. Moreover, the rise of postmodern thought, with its emphasis on particular cultures and the social construction of moral norms within those cultures, has cast doubt upon the validity of universal moral principles and contributed to the rise of relativism in ethics in general.

Christian ethicist James Nelson identifies a number of ideas associated with Christian situational ethics.[3] First, Christian ethics is more analytical than prescriptive. We can no longer prescribe in advance what appropriate moral decisions should be in all circumstances. Given that the emphasis on

---

[1] James M. Gustafson, *Protestant and Roman Catholic Ethics* (Chicago: University of Chicago Press, 1978), 140.

[2] James M. Gustafson, "Context versus Principles: A Misplaced Debate in Christian Ethics," *Harvard Theological Review* 58/2 (April 1965): 185.

[3] James B. Nelson, "Contextualism and the Ethical Triad," in *The Situation Ethics Debate*, ed. Harvey Cox, 171–86 (Philadelphia: Westminster Press, 1968). (*The Situation Ethics Debate* is hereafter cited as *SED*.)

accurate situational analysis is central to situation ethics, the prior question to "What should I do?" is "What is going on in this situation?" The moral agent does not find a solution, identify a moral rule or principle, and then apply it to a particular ethical dilemma, but rather engages fully the situation that calls for ethical decision-making. Rules or principles in this approach are guides and not prescriptions. The response is to the situation, with the guidance of those principles as much as they are applicable. Nelson also notes that Christian situation ethics emphasize a relational value theory: positive values are related to the needs of persons or other beings in relation to some center of value, which for Christians is God or Christ. The moral agent in this ethical triad is dialogical; the moral self is enmeshed in relationship with other persons in the situation and with the transcendent. That is why Nelson defines situationalism as a method of "disciplined reflection upon the meaning of the relationships among God, the self, and the neighbor."[4] Christians respond to the divine intent and to the neighbor's need. This requires that the moral agent know who the neighbor is and what the neighbor's needs are. God's revelation in Christ reveals authentic human need.

Many Christian ethicists have been labeled as *situationalist* in recent years.[5] For the purposes of this book we focus on the writings of Joseph Fletcher and his discussion of situation ethics. While his work was more prominent in the 1960s and 1970s, the resurgence of key themes in his understanding of situation ethics among today's college students and social policymakers give his views renewed relevance.[6] In particular, many of today's youth are questioning the legalism and rigidity of religious traditions, especially in the face of the rise of various fundamentalisms. They are seeking more freedom and autonomy for themselves and others in making ethical decisions and doing so with a more pragmatic bent. Moreover, considering the stalemate among ideologues in social policy debate, where the word *compromise* (for the sake of the greater good) seems to be a dirty word, there is a renewed interest in the utilitarian formula of the greatest good for the greatest number. Finally, given this text's case-centered approach to ethical issues, inclusion of an internally consistent and clearly articulated case-centered Christian ethical method is appropriate.

Fletcher describes his method, which he says is not systematic, as follows:[7]

---

[4] *SED*, 186.

[5] The most notable of these include H. R. Niebuhr, Gustafson, Paul Lehman, and Nelson, among others.

[6] According to a recent Pew Research Center religious landscape study (2019), 85 percent of religiously unaffiliated millennials contend that right or wrong depends on the situation.

[7] The bulk of the discussion that follows draws from two crucial texts Fletcher authored to discuss situation ethics: *Situation Ethics: The New Morality* (Philadelphia: Westminster Press, 1966) (hereafter cited as *SE*); and *Moral Responsibility: Situation Ethics at Work* (Philadelphia: Westminster Press, 1967) (hereafter cited as *MR*).

We may say that Christian situationism is a method that proceeds, so to speak, from (1) its one and only law, *agapé* (love), to (2) the *sophia* (wisdom) of the church and culture, containing many "general rules" of more or less reliability, to (3) the *kairos* (moment of decision, the fullness of time) in which *the responsible self in the situation* decides whether the *sophia* can serve love there or not. (*SE* 33)

As the reader can see, Fletcher's method does incorporate the other base points mentioned by Gustafson that a Christian social ethic should include: it affirms moral principles, especially the law of love, generated by the church and culture; and it has a view of the moral agent as a free and responsible person. Some would claim that situation ethics is not very theological or Christian. Fletcher would agree that people can be situationists who are not Christian. But he would contend that his approach is Christian because the law of love, the only law he accepts, is universal and is founded upon a basic theological presupposition: God is love. "In . . . Christian ethics, there is no way to reach the key category of love, of *agape* as the primordial or axiomatic value, the *summum bonum*, except by an act of faith which says 'yea' to the faith proposition that 'God is love' and therefore to the value proposition that love is good" (*SE* 13). This love of God is manifest most fully in the incarnation of God's love in Christ. Thus, Fletcher refers to his ethics as "Christological" or "Christonomic," the Christian's grateful response to what God has done in Christ.

However, as with all situationalists the key base point for Fletcher is the concrete situation or objective set of circumstances in which ethical decisions are made. Before one can know whether one has done the right thing, the good thing, or the loving thing, one must understand the situation at hand in all its complexity. Fletcher rejects legalism of any sort, whether the legalism of natural law or scripture, which deduces certain rules or prescriptions that are universal and therefore must be applied in all cases. For example, in a situation involving whether to lie, the legalist would deduce the relevant rule or principle—Do not lie—and apply it in that situation without regard to the context or consequences. Fletcher would contend that while having such principles drawn from one's church or culture is important, it is the situation or context that determines the right course of action. The principles or rules may have a voice, but they do not have veto power. The right thing to do is the loving thing after one has a clear sense of all the factors involved in the situation.

Fletcher suggests that there are four presuppositions in his situation ethics. First, it is inspired by American *pragmatism*, along the lines advocated by William James and John Dewey. Pragmatism is a method by which one discerns what works for the ends or purposes one has in mind. For the Christian, the end against which one's actions will be judged is love. A second presupposition is that situation ethics is relativistic in tactics. Fletcher contends that the norm of *agape* love "relativizes the absolute, it does not absolutize the relative!" (*SE* 45). What he means is that this approach makes the law of love relative to each situation. Only love is the constant; everything else is a variable. There is a sense of humility implicit here—one can never know anything with full certainty. Human knowledge is finite, limited; we cannot assume we know it all. At the same time, we must be willing to be responsible for our actions. A third presupposition is the theological positivism noted above, that God is love: "Thus Christian ethics 'posits' faith in God and *reasons* out what obedience to his commandment to love requires in any situation. . . . Any moral or value judgment in ethics, like a theologian's faith proposition, is a *decision*—not a conclusion" (*SE* 47). It is a choice one makes, not a deduction of reason and logic. Reason is part of it, but one cannot always know that one is right. In this way Fletcher affirms the chasm that exists between "is" and "ought." Our ethical decisions seek justification, not verification, because there is no way to verify them. By saying yes to the theological assertion that "God is love," one also affirms that love is the highest value or highest good (*SE* 49). The final presupposition is personalism, which for Fletcher means that "people are at the center of concern, not things" (*SE* 50). When we treat people as ends, and not as things, then we are acting ethically.

Fletcher fleshes out these presuppositions in the six propositions he articulates for his situation ethics:

> Only one thing is intrinsically good, namely, love: nothing
>   else;
> The ultimate norm of Christian decisions is love:
>   nothing else;
> Love and justice are the same, for justice is love
>   distributed;
> Love wills the neighbor's good whether we like him
>   or not;
> Only the end justifies the means: nothing else; and
> Decisions ought to be made situationally, not
>   prescriptively. (*MR* 14–27)

Fletcher defines Christian love or *agape* as "being goodwill at work in partnership with reason" (*SE* 69). Christian love is an attitude, a matter of will, and not of feeling; it is a freely given love that is nonreciprocal and neighbor regarding (*SE* 79). While he understands love as intrinsically good and absolute, it is not a substantive principle but a formal principle;[8] it is not something

---

[8] *Formal* ethical principles, like the principle of equality, provide a general framework for how we should treat others. *Substantive* ethical principles go beyond recognizing the basic equality of everyone to discerning the differences that exist between people to ensure that the goal of equality is achieved in spite of those differences. For example, equal opportunity (formal equality) can only be achievable when the barriers to such opportunity are overcome, which may mean providing unequal resources to some to overcome those barriers (substantive equality).

we *have* but something we *do* (*SE* 61). Love is substantive only in God (*SE* 62). He contends that the opposite of love is indifference because it treats the other as a thing and not as a person (*SE* 63). Not caring is worse than hate.

Fletcher disagrees with those ethicists who want to talk about love as personal and justice as social, or love as perfect and justice as approximations of the perfect in this world. Instead, he equates the two. "Prudence, careful calculation, gives love the care-fulness it needs; with proper care, love does more than take justice into account, it *becomes* justice" (*SE* 88). The calculating element of this equation is what connects situation ethics to teleology in general and utilitarianism in particular.

> Justice is *agape* working out its problems. Justice is Christian love using its head—calculating its duties. The Christian love ethic, searching seriously for a social policy, forms a coalition with the utilitarian principle of the "greatest good for the greatest number." Of course, it reshapes it into the "most love for the most neighbors." Faith provides the value principle of love and rejects utilitarianism's hedonistic value, using only its *procedural* principle, its method. There is obviously a risk that love may be thinned out by calculation, but this is the "calculated risk" that all-inclusive love is bound to take. (*MR* 19)

In other words, justice is love distributed. Fletcher illustrates this with the example of a doctor choosing to give the last unit of plasma to a mother of three over a man on skid row. To those for whom justice is nonpreferential, it is not clear why one would choose the mother over the man. But where love and justice are the same, there is some discernment about the most loving action, which in this case would give preference to the mother over the man, and this would be just.

Clearly, Fletcher adopts a relational theory of value: "Good and evil are extrinsic. Right and wrong *depend upon the situation*" (*MR* 14). There is nothing that is either intrinsically good or evil. The moral worth of any action depends upon the ends one is seeking, the means one uses, the motive for one's actions, and the consequences. If the end is love, or the most loving thing for the most neighbors; if the means are also loving in the context of that situation even if tragic; if the motive is to bring about love; and if the consequences of the action are that the most good for the most neighbors occurs, then the action is moral. There is also a center of value here: for Fletcher it is the law of love demonstrated in Christ; only love is absolute value. In other words, there is no separation between the right and the good. Such a separationist view rests on the concept that some things are intrinsically good or evil, right or wrong. For example, Catholic social teaching contends that abortion is an intrinsic evil. A situationist would argue that abortion in and of itself is neither good nor evil; it all depends upon the situation and the ends, the motives, the means, and the consequences of the action. If a woman aborts a fetus because she believes that doing so would produce the most loving consequences in that situation (such as stopping the excruciating pain and suffering a fetus would experience because of a genetic disorder like Tay-Sachs disease), then her decision and the means used may be tragic but they are not evil, immoral, or the lesser of two evils; they are right and good.

Fletcher's conception of the moral agent affirms that the self is both personal and social and that the communities, traditions, and circumstances in which a person is raised do shape that person's moral sensibilities, often in the guise of moral rules or principles. However, these principles are guides and not prescriptions for actions. Fletcher rejects the desire for the constants of a legalism that emphasizes order and conformity and seeks to fit reality to rules in a neurotic and infantile desire for security. Instead, Fletcher contends that because of the complexity and ambiguity of ethical problems and decisions today, situation ethics places a premium on the ability of moral agents to act freely and lovingly in each situation, recognizing that in doing so they widen the scope of responsibility, the other side of freedom's coin. "The Christian is called to be mature, to live by grace and freedom, to *respond* to life, to be responsible" (*SE* 82).

Fletcher summarizes his position in the following manner: "Christian ethics . . . is not a scheme of living according to a code but a continuous effort to relate love to a world of relativities through a casuistry obedient to love; its constant task is to work out the strategy and tactics of love for Christ's sake" (*SE* 158). This is not an easy method. It demands attentiveness to what is going on in the world. It demands strong effort to discern what the loving thing to do would be in that situation. It demands that one make that decision in freedom and responsibility. Where one fails, it is a cognitive failure, never a moral one, if one is seeking to do the loving thing. The only time when one has a moral failure is when one refuses to do the loving thing or acts with indifference toward the needs of neighbors.

EVANGELICAL ETHICS

The word *evangelical* is a contested term. There is a variety of ideas associated with it and a plurality of individuals and groups who call themselves by that name. The same is true in the field of Christian ethics. Evangelical ethics covers a broad range on the ideological and political spectrum from conservative (right-center) to progressive (center-left or "new evangelicals," as some refer to themselves).[9] In spite of their diversity, Reuschling suggests that they all have common commitments "to the authority of scripture, the necessity of a vibrant, growing personal faith commitment to Jesus Christ, and a sense of purpose and mission in the world communicated in both word and

---

[9] See Gary Dorrien, *The Remaking of Evangelical Theology* (Louisville, KY: Westminster John Knox Press, 1998), 2–3. The "new evangelicals" is a recent phenomenon initiated by David Gushee.

deed."[10] One might add to these commitments the acceptance of Protestant orthodoxy (the sovereignty of God, the Trinity, the incarnation, the death and resurrection of Jesus, and the transforming power of the Holy Spirit).

In order to do justice to the evangelical ethical tradition, we include discussion of a conservative evangelical ethicist, John Jefferson Davis, and two progressive evangelical ethicists, Glen Stassen and David Gushee. Part of the reason for their inclusion is that both traditions are important for understanding the range of evangelical ethics today. Further, these ethicists have written books that articulate not only their basic ethical convictions but also apply their theories to many of the specific ethical concerns and cases we address in this book. Thus, they provide a developed source for understanding each case we address from their evangelical perspectives.

Conservative

Following Gustafson's base points, some have argued that in Davis's book *Evangelical Ethics*[11] the author emphasizes moral rules or principles as the primary point from which to begin discussion of Christian ethics. He affirms that his approach to Christian ethics is fundamentally "prescriptive and deontological." Christians must discern the will of God in a specific situation and act according to the duties that follow from it. "Evangelical ethics is concerned not with personal preferences and feelings, but with obligations that command the conscience" (*EE3* 16). He appreciates fully the importance of concrete experience and specific situations in moral decision-making—knowing the facts of what is going on in what he calls the "empirical-deliberative" dimension with the help of the natural and social sciences. However, his basic conviction, like most evangelicals, is that the Bible, which for him is the "very Word of God" and "the only infallible and inerrant rule of faith and practice," is the "final court of appeals for ethics." He argues, "Human reason, church, tradition, and the natural and social sciences, may aid moral reflection, but divine revelation, found in the canonical Scriptures of the Old and New Testaments, constitutes the 'bottom line' of the decision-making process" (*EE3* 15).

---

[10] Wyndy Corbin Reuschling, *Reviving Evangelical Ethics* (Grand Rapids, MI: Brazos Press, 2008), 16. George Marsden suggests that the term *evangelicalism* refers to a conceptual unity for Christians who emphasize "1) the Reformation doctrine of the final authority of Scripture; 2) the real, historical character of God's saving work recorded in Scripture; 3) eternal salvation only through personal trust in Christ; 4) the importance of evangelism and missions; and 5) the importance of a spiritually transformed life." George Marsden, *Evangelism and Modern America* (Grand Rapids, MI: Eerdmans, 1984), ix–x.

[11] John Jefferson Davis, *Evangelical Ethics*, 3rd and 4th eds. (Philipsburg, NJ: P&R Publishing, 2004, 2015) (hereafter cited as *EE3* and *EE4*, respectively).

For Davis, then, the reasoning power of the moral agent does play a role in ethical decision-making. While the Bible provides the laws and principles, human reason helps the individual to discern which circumstances are analogous but not addressed in the Bible, and to make appropriate decisions. "Good principles and good facts are both necessary for sound decision making" (*EE3* 17). He gives the example of a civil judge who in the cases brought before him must apply existing law and precedents in ways that serve the principle of justice. However, because of the sinfulness of humanity, the role that reason plays is circumscribed. "Human reason, being impaired by sin, is not to serve as a separate norm as over against Scripture, but rather as the servant of divine revelation in the application of biblical truth" (*EE3* 17). The Bible provides the lens through which the Christian can see what is truly in the long-term interests of humanity. Moreover, in the process of discernment, moral agents are not left to their own devices but have the help and guidance of the Holy Spirit to make appropriate analogies (*EE3* 18).

Davis's view of the limits of human reason also leads him to reject situation ethics and its emphasis on doing the loving thing because we cannot always know what the loving thing to do is. It is often simply one's personal preferences. "Apart from the abiding norms of divine revelation, the moral agent is left to the vagaries of personal preference and the constantly changing 'spirit of the age' to discern the 'loving' thing" (*EE3* 19). Moreover, in contrast to Fletcher, Davis sees no separation between law and love; in his reading of scripture the two go together. It is out of love for God that we obey God's law. "The love of God shed abroad in the heart of the believer is indeed the dynamic motivation of Christian behavior, but this love demonstrates itself in harmony with, and not apart from, the specific commands and precepts of Holy Scripture" (*EE3* 10).

Based on the foundational convictions noted above, Davis calls his approach to Christian ethics "contextual absolutism" (*EE3* 20). There are many moral absolutes in the Bible, not just the law of love, and he identifies several of them within the Decalogue or Ten Commandments. Some require very little discernment in their application, such as the rules against committing murder (killing of innocents) and adultery. Others require the Christian to use reason, guided by biblical truth and the Holy Spirit, to judge how a divine command applies to the situation. But what happens if the moral absolutes conflict in a situation, and no matter which course of action one takes, one engages in sin? Like Fletcher, Davis rejects the lesser-of-two-evils notion. But his reasoning is quite different. Instead of accepting that the loving thing is always the right thing, he believes that divine laws and principles will never conflict. "Contextual absolutism holds that in each and every ethical situation, no matter how extreme, there is a course of action that is morally right and free of sin" (*EE4* 8). The divine obligation may lead to suffering or even martyrdom, which may be part of "the cost of discipleship," much like the example set by Jesus Christ. Moreover, he differentiates between prima facie duties and actual duties when all things are taken into consideration (*EE4* 9).

The higher obligation will always trump the lower one. He gives reference to the duty to obey God over one's normal obligation to obey government. "When the laws of God conflict with the laws of men, human laws must yield to the higher authority of God" (*EE4* 9).

Finally, when it comes to the relationship between Christian ethics and the public order, Davis believes that God's rule includes all human beings, whether they believe in God or not. Thus, like the view of natural law ethics, Christian morality as revealed in scripture is prevalent in the created order; all people live in the moral order created by God, which is often exemplified in general revelation and reason (*EE4* 12). "Where Scripture indicates that unbelievers can have moral awareness on a given issue through *general revelation*, then it may be appropriate for Christians to press for legislation in that area" (*EE4* 13). For example, two areas of legislation, which he draws from scripture, are concerned with killing innocent human life and forbidding homosexuality as a way of life. In those instances unbelievers *ought* to know better (*EE4* 13). But Christians should not have utopian visions for what it possible through civil law; rather, they should be practical in their social action, pushing for legislation in areas that are more urgent, more life and death, such as abortion. "Civil laws that are consistent with the teachings of Scripture point society to a higher standard of righteousness, which is fulfilled only in Jesus Christ. Such laws remain a worthy object of Christian concern and social action" (*EE4* 15).

Progressive

In *Kingdom Ethics*[12] Stassen and Gushee approach Christian ethics from a "Baptist evangelical" framework, which includes elements of the evangelical label, especially "authority of Scripture" and "the tenets of orthodox Christian faith" (*KE* xv). They understand both through the lens of Jesus's life and teaching, found in the Gospels in general and in the Sermon on the Mount in particular. In their view, acknowledging the influence of the black church tradition, true Christian ethics is an "incarnational" ethic of discipleship: Christians must become Christlike in person and action, faithful disciples to the kingdom ethic embodied in the life, ministry, and sacrifice of the living Jesus Christ.

As noted in the Introduction to this text, many Christian ethicists suggest that there are three approaches to moral decision-making. Thus far, we have emphasized the teleological (Fletcher) and deontological (Davis) strains in Christian ethics. Stassen and Gushee incorporate a third approach, virtue ethics, into their ethical framework, which they call "holistic character ethics." They seek to challenge the narrow individualism prevalent in ethics today

---

[12] Glen Stassen and David Gushee, *Kingdom Ethics: Following Jesus in Contemporary Context* (Downers Grove, IL: InterVarsity Press, 2003) (hereafter cited as *KE*).

that focuses only on right and wrong decisions and loses sight of the forces that shape the character of those who make such decisions. They prefer the term *character* over *virtues* because the virtues are only one component of the various elements that shape our moral agency. First are the specific practices, such as coming to the aid of people in need, drawn from one's family, church, or communities that engage in such practices. Second are the virtues that demonstrate good character, such as mercy or compassion. Third is the belief that character is always shaped in community; we need communities that mold the moral character of their members. Finally, Christian character and community are participants in God's larger drama as revealed and embodied in the life, words, and ministry of Jesus. "Ethics as incarnational discipleship points to the *incarnate Jesus, who taught the Sermon on the Mount and the kingdom of God, in the tradition of the prophets of Israel, embodied it in his practices and called us to embody it in our practices of discipleship. This Jesus is our Lord*" (*KE* 58–59). Jesus manifests the kind of character (and resulting actions) that Christians should imitate if they are serious about being Christian and participating in God's reign. In this way Stassen and Gushee believe their approach to Christian ethics embodies all three strands of Christian ethics: deontological, teleological, and the virtues.

Stassen and Gushee's approach incorporates four dimensions they see as essential to good ethical decision-making and part of the ethic espoused by Jesus and the Bible. These dimensions include a way of seeing, a way of reasoning, loyalties and passions, and basic convictions. While all four dimensions shape the kind of characters we become and the moral actions we engage in, the basic-convictions level is fundamental to their view; it is their primary base point. "We are claiming that Christian ethics must be self-consciously grounded in well-conceived theological convictions, fundamentally the vision of the reign of God" (*KE* 61). Like Fletcher, they agree that understanding the situation in all its complexity is important and that cases cannot be decided simply by the uncompromising application of rules. However, because of human sinfulness and ignorance, they confirm the appropriateness of rules and norms, particularly those affirmed by Jesus. These should only be abandoned as a last resort. These rules should not devolve into a kind of legalism that they believe Davis espouses, where rules are absolute and universal for all cases. While Stassen and Gushee recognize that Davis does make some exceptions with his concept of the difference between prima facie duties and actual duties, they do not see how Davis allows for adequate discernment when rules inevitably conflict. When such conflict arises and exceptions must be made, Stassen and Gushee argue that the moral agent should follow another rule or principle taught by Jesus, lessons grounded in basic convictions about the character of God and God's kingdom "characterized by salvation, justice, peace, joy and God's presence" (*KE* 60). This basic conviction or worldview shapes the character of Christians to become Christlike—conformed to the image of Christ, which includes Jesus's entire life and not simply a particular principle such as the law of love (*KE* 70)—and becomes manifest in moral decisions and actions.

Like all evangelical ethics, Stassen and Gushee affirm the authority of the Bible. They agree that the Wesleyan Quadrilateral—scripture, tradition, reason, and experience—all have a role to play in ethical decision-making; however, scripture must occupy the central role (*KE* 87). They also affirm the *sola scriptura* or "scripture alone" position of the Reformation, but only "if that means that Scripture is the only authoritative and fully trustworthy source of authority for Christian ethics. . . . The Bible is the 'sun' around which all other sources of authority are brought into orbit" (*KE* 89). Their fundamental orientation is toward Jesus's teaching and discipleship, based upon that understanding of Jesus's teaching found in the Gospels. They are critical of evangelical ethics that do not draw their views about the role of the Bible from the person and work of Christ and that do not employ the same prophetic hermeneutic that Jesus did (*KE* 97). They approach Jesus's orientation toward the law exemplified in the Hebrew Bible differently than Davis does. They are looking through the lens they suggest that Jesus looked through, namely, the prophetic moral framework exemplified in the eighth-century BCE prophets (Amos, Hosea, Jeremiah, and particularly Isaiah). This lends a stronger social justice framework (what Gushee later refers to as center-left) to their approach to contemporary Christian ethics than one finds in many contemporary evangelical ethical positions that overemphasize personal piety and morality.[13]

Jesus used the Torah in the same way the prophets did, and his hermeneutic had four concrete expressions: he interpreted the Torah as gracious divine covenant rather than as "law"; the "prophetic interpretive grid" (*KE* 97) leads to a greater emphasis on the moral rather than the cultic or ritualistic aspects of the Law; Jesus's view of righteousness was prophetic and not legalistic, righteousness that consisted of love, mercy, and justice, especially to the vulnerable; and his focus was on the inward or heart aspects of character (*KE* 91–94). Thus, Stassen and Gushee's approach to the relationship between ethics and scripture includes three elements:

1) Look first to Jesus—examining his incarnation/death/resurrection and his life/ministry/teachings; 2) Read all other Scriptures through the prophetic interpretive grid that Jesus employed and in light of all that we know of Jesus' witness on this issue; and 3) Then look to other sources of authority for help on the basis of the same interpretive grid, remembering that Jesus is alive and continues to instruct his church through the witness of the Holy Spirit (Jn 15). (*KE* 97)

---

[13] This is Reuschling's critique of most evangelical ethics today, and she suggests revisions along the lines advocated by Stassen and Gushee.

Finally, Stassen and Gushee believe that Christians have an obligation to relate the way of Jesus Christ to the public realm in the context of the struggle for justice. They reject any attempt to suggest that Christ's ethic only applies to the church and thus contributes to the "secularizing dualism" so prevalent today, where Jesus has no relevance to the world and thus our ethical norms must come only from secular sources. At the same time, they question the belief that Christians should impose their ethic on the world, because such authoritarianism builds resentment and leads the secular world to oppose the Christian faith. In their view the "trick is to figure out how and where the way of Jesus can be normative for public ethics by persuasion" (*KE* 61).

NATURAL LAW ETHICS

Natural law ethics has a long history within Christian ethics. Although some Protestants have sought to recover aspects of the natural law (as we saw in our discussion of Davis's evangelical ethics), this has been the primary traditional basis of Roman Catholic ethics and politics. Put simply, natural law theory has argued that all human beings share a common nature that is created by God and can be known by human reason. This common nature pushes all persons to seek certain ends or goods that become the basis for the moral norms that prescribe the actions that do or do not fulfill those ends that enable humans to flourish and to find happiness. On the one hand, human beings share certain ends with other creatures, such as self-preservation, the propagation of the species, and the education of offspring. On the other hand, as uniquely rational creatures, human beings also have a natural inclination to know the truth about God and to live in society. The norms or laws deduced by reason reflecting on nature were understood to be (1) universal—common to all humanity; and (2) immutable—not changing over time or because of differences in culture or society. For example, most, if not all, human societies have laws against unjustified killing of human beings. They call such actions murder. Such laws are natural laws because they preserve human life and do not harm it. Cardinal Joseph Ratzinger (later Pope Benedict XVI) captured well the normative element in this tradition: "*Natural law* expresses the fact that nature itself conveys a moral message. The spiritual content of creation is not merely mathematical and mechanical. That is the dimension which natural science emphasizes in the laws of nature. But there is more spiritual content, more 'laws of nature' in creation. It bears within itself an inner order and even shows it to us."[14]

Over the years natural law theory has met with a variety of criticisms (as we saw in the description of Fletcher's stance). Critics question natural law's deductive method (deriving moral norms from general principles), its

---

[14] Cardinal Joseph Ratzinger, *God and the World: Believing and Living (A Conversation with Peter Seewald)* (San Francisco: Ignatius Press, 2002), 160.

legalism, its Eurocentric and patriarchal biases, its abstract universalism, and its neglect of specific Christian ethical traditions. There are also concerns about its moral realism: drawing moral norms ("ought") from facts about nature ("is"). Even the notion of human nature as a basis for clear and stable norms is problematic because of natural and social scientific evidence suggesting that human nature is not static but evolving and adapting across time and cultures.[15]

Is it possible to recover the natural law tradition in a way that speaks to current scientific understandings of the natural world, including the evolution of human nature, and takes account of the cultural pluralism so prevalent in our global society? Moreover, is it possible to do this in such a way that makes it both a distinctively Christian ethic and the basis for a substantive ethic for persons of other faiths or no faith? A few Christian ethicists recently have sought to recover the natural law tradition in response to global ethical concerns that require some collective action to be addressed in meaningful ways. But advocates believe that these actions can only be successful if they "rest on a solid foundational agreement regarding the goods and values that represent the most profound aspirations of man, both as an individual and as member of a community."[16] They believe that the recovery of a "renewed presentation" of the natural law tradition provides the hope for this needed ethical and political foundation. The "objective and universal" precepts and norms derived from "the very nature of the human subject" can "establish and inspire the collection of moral, juridical and political determinations that govern the life of human beings and societies."[17]

One such Christian ethicist is Jean Porter.[18] Porter is a Catholic theologian who is seeking "a contemporary appropriation of the scholastic concept of natural law" (*NDL* 33). Porter distinguishes her approach from those who postulated what she calls the "new natural law theory." They sought to ground natural law on a "rational" foundation that can be known by all persons, whether Christian or not. This foundation enables them to transcend sectarian differences. For example, Richard McCormick argues, "Christian ethics does not and cannot add to human ethical self-understanding as such any material content that is, in principle, strange or foreign to man as he exists and experiences himself."[19] The problem for Porter is that this means that there

---

[15] See Lisa Sowle Cahill, Hille Haker, and Eloi Messi Metogo, eds., *Human Nature and Natural Law* (London: SCM Press, 2010), 7–8.

[16] International Theological Commission, *In Search of a Universal Ethic: A New Look at the Natural Law* (2009), no. 2.

[17] Ibid., no. 9.

[18] I draw my discussion of Porter's natural law ethics from two texts: *Natural and Divine Law: Reclaiming the Tradition for Christian Ethics* (Grand Rapids, MI: Eerdmans, 1999) (hereafter cited as *NDL*); and *Nature as Reason: A Thomistic Theory of the Natural Law* (Grand Rapids, MI: Eerdmans, 2005) (hereafter cited as *NR*).

[19] Richard A. McCormick, SJ, *Notes on Moral Theology: 1965–1980* (Washington, DC: University Press of America, 1981), 637.

would be no distinctive Christian element in it. Porter, on the other hand, is seeking to follow the scholastics, especially Thomas Aquinas (1225–74), who ground their understanding of the natural law on Christian theological and scriptural grounds. She wants to restore that Christian framework while correcting for some of the mistakes that the scholastic position made. Yet against sectarian approaches (such as some versions of evangelical ethics) that seek the distinctiveness of Christian ethics in revelation and not human reason,[20] Porter suggests that the scholastic natural law tradition does not see the radical break with other human moral perspectives. She writes: "In contrast, the scholastics give priority to . . . the doctrine of creation. . . . Indeed, they would expect on theological grounds that there should be some continuities between Christian morality and the moralities of other societies, since these would be further expressions of God's creative wisdom and goodness" (*NDL* 287).

Porter characterizes her revised theory of natural law, which is "in its essentials that of Aquinas, as developed and extended in a contemporary context" (*NR* 46–47), along the lines of the scholastics:

They turned to Scripture in order to identify this primary sense, and in particular, they turned to Paul's reference to the unwritten law of the Gentiles, as interpreted through generations of patristic commentary. This led them to develop a view according to which the natural law is fundamentally a capacity or power to distinguish between good and evil; it is intrinsic to the character of the human soul as made in the Image of God, and therefore it cannot be altogether obliterated; and it is expressed or developed through moral precepts which are confirmed, as well as being completed and transcended, through the operation of grace. Even though the natural law understood in its primary sense does not consist of specific moral rules, it does find immediate expression in the fundamental precepts of the Golden Rule or the two great commandments of love of God and neighbor; these in turn yield the more specific norms of the Decalogue, which can be further specified as warranted by the circumstances of human life. Hence, the natural law more broadly understood does include specific moral norms as well as a fundamental capacity for moral judgment, although there is considerable room for both legitimate variation and sinful distortion at the level of particular norms. (*NR* 13–14)

As we can see, Porter's understanding of the natural law tradition encompasses all the base points articulated by Gustafson. Because of her interest in reaffirming natural law ethics as a Christian ethic, however, the primary

---

[20] Porter has in mind such Christian ethicists as John Howard Yoder, Stanley Hauerwas, and John Milbank.

base point is the affirmation of basic theological convictions, particularly the doctrine of creation and the image of God (Imago Dei).

For Porter, the doctrine of creation provides a theological basis for advocating a naturalistic or moral realist account of ethics: "We believe that God created the world, and correlatively, that the world is an intelligible and good reflection of God's wisdom and loving will; that each kind of creature, including ourselves, manifests divine wisdom and love in the mode of orderly and purposeful existence proper to it" (*NR* 135). Like the scholastics, Porter believes there is something inherent in human nature that is intelligible. But this intelligibility is present in all nature and is morally significant. There are "continuities between human morality and the behavioral norms which the other animals observe," such as propagating the species and sexual intercourse with like animals (*NR* 70). This does not mean that nature determines all human moral norms. In truth, she suggests that nature underdetermines them. The continuities with nature express general inclinations that human reason and culture must then flesh out to discern the norms that promote human flourishing. However, the behavioral norms of other creatures do place some limits on what human beings can or should do with nature.

Implicit here is the idea of norms of flourishing that are intrinsic to every kind of creature (*NR* 89). For Porter, this is where the teleological element comes into play in natural law—our actions ought to correspond to some ideal end or paradigm for a particular living creature, including humanity (*NR* 49–50). The purpose of these ends is to promote flourishing for each creature, person, or society. This is a different teleological approach than the utilitarian calculus noted in the discussion of situation ethics. The ends are not the greatest good for the greatest number. Rather, the ends Porter has in mind relate to the ideal end for each creature, which she speaks about in terms of well-being, flourishing, and happiness. For example, we must have something in mind when we say that a particular dog or bird or tree is robust and healthy or when we say the opposite. These are non-moral ideas that relate to some conception of what the flourishing of a particular creature would look like. Yet they have moral significance: human actions that impede the flourishing of other creatures (for example, "cattle bred to build up so much muscle mass that they cannot walk") are immoral and ought to be constrained in some way (*NR* 102). Thus, the image of an ideal end provides a framework for differentiating between actions that promote flourishing and those that do not.

Porter says the same is true for humanity: we cannot understand what it means to be human beings "unless we have some idea of what it means to do well as a human being" (*NR* 118). And these ideas or ideals provide some indication of what actions do and do not promote such well-being. "There are constraints on human flourishing, and perhaps more importantly, there are recurring components of human existence which will form the basis for happiness and well-being for almost all persons" (*NR* 102–3). This does not mean there is not a great variety; it is not one size fits all. Porter thinks we can make some moral claims based on factual understandings about ourselves, which she thinks a teleological conception of human nature makes possible. In her view, "human morality in all its culturally diverse forms is an expression of the distinctive inclinations and activities proper to the human animal, especially (but not only) the distinctive forms of human social behavior" (*NR* 125–26).

The second theological conviction Porter affirms is the notion of humans as created in the Imago Dei: "Human beings are images of God in a more distinctive sense, sharing in some way in divine capacities for self-determination and providential care" (*NR* 135). All persons, however marred by human sin, reflect God's image. Porter's contention is that regarding the universality of the natural law, the scholastics' emphasis was on "a God-given capacity for moral judgment" and not about universal moral norms (*NR* 16). All human beings have some capacity to distinguish right from wrong, good from evil. It is not the sole province of those of Christian faith. This capacity opens the door for people who do not share the Christian faith to find common ground with those of faith. For example, most religious and humanistic traditions have some version of the Golden Rule: do to others what you would want done to you (or stated negatively, as many traditions do, do not do to others what you would not want done to you). This undergirds a fundamental moral precept implicit in the natural law: do no harm.

The Imago Dei also affirms the importance of human agency, and the human person "as a free and self-determining agent . . . enjoying certain powers on the basis of his or her capacities for choice and self-direction" (*NR* 359). In the past, criticisms of natural law ethics suggest that it relegates the human agent to one of passive obedience to natural laws. Porter argues, however, that this is not the case. We use our reason to understand the ends toward which nature and humanity are inclined and choose to act in ways that enable the achievement of those ends. This is not a passive enterprise. There are some norms, but these are not hard and fast. Rather, there are common inclinations that get reflected in various forms of laws and societal structures. There is diversity in these, but they are all about achieving the same fundamental inclinations. "A given morality can thus be understood as a culturally and historically specific way of expressing the general social structures natural to us as a species" (*NR* 131). She suggests that the broad areas of convergence across cultures are what provide some consensus about moral questions, particularly about fundamental virtues and vices (such as a need to restrain violence or the undesirability of selfishness) (*NR* 132).

Like Aquinas, Porter differentiates between well-being and happiness. Well-being includes "all the components of a humanly desirable life, including life itself, health, security, and participation in a network of family and social relations" (*NR* 143). Happiness is morally richer because it acts as a qualifier by "specifying the best or most appropriate way in which men and women can attain and enjoy the activities constitutive of well-being" (*NR* 143). The natural form of happiness or end for humanity is perfected by the acquisition of the four cardinal virtues of prudence, courage, temperance, and justice. By acquiring and practicing the virtues, people can achieve within limits their natural end of happiness: "the virtues are themselves perfections of the active powers of the human creature" (*NR* 169). Thus, like Stassen and Gushee, this teleological understanding of natural law brings together all three strains of Christian ethics: laws, ends, and virtues.

Porter maintains the scholastic distinction between nature and grace (the latter understood as the power of God to elevate and perfect nature). The true end of humanity is union with God. This requires the infusion of the theological virtues of faith, hope, and love (charity). These infused virtues affect the acquired virtues and deepen them. "Hence, someone who has charity also possesses distinctive forms of prudence, justice, temperance and fortitude and their associated virtues, each of which orients an intellectual appetitive faculty toward union with God, and each of which is correlatively specifically different from its acquired counterpart" (*NR* 389). She argues that based on this view the relationship of justice to charity or love is reciprocal. "That is, not only do the demands of justice inform charity; charity also gives rise to normative ideals which inform and transform our conception of justice, and correlatively, our sense of the substantive content of the natural law" (*NR* 390). In her view all virtuous acts will be acts of more than one virtue. For example, "the other-regarding acts of charity are also acts of justice" (*NR* 392). Her point is that what the infused virtue of charity does is take the other-regarding view of justice in a new direction. It means "to love the neighbor *for the sake of* God, and also, to the extent possible and appropriate, to love the neighbor *as* God loves the neighbor" (*NR* 392). And this requires some theological reflection on the nature of God and what it means to say God loves us. In this way charity transforms justice. For example, while justice may demand some form of retribution to right the wrongs committed, the forgiveness required by charity might lead us to forgo some forms of that punishment. This also requires that our other-regarding acts become more universal in scope as required by charity. "If this is so, then it implies that we must specify the domain of justice in such a way as to include all persons, and to regard them all as equally valuable in some fundamental respects—judgments we would not otherwise be compelled to make, rationally or on broader natural considerations" (*NR* 393).

The concept of the image of God, which affirms the human person "as a free and self-determining agent, and moreover, as an entity enjoying certain powers on the basis of his or her capacities for choice and self-direction" also grounds Porter's support for a theory of natural rights. She says that although we cannot discern a substantive notion of rights that transcend all cultures and societies and that would be morally significant and upon which all persons would agree, we can "identify certain recurring aspects of moral practices which do seem to cut across cultural and historical lines" (*NR* 363). She refers to them as species-specific patterns of behavior that provide one basis for evaluating moral theories. Her point is that the doctrine of natural rights may be limited in terms of its universality, but the fact that it is a kind of moral language that has great resonance across cultures means it can be "used in a variety of ways to express basic aspects of human nature, in such a way as to respond effectively to recurrent needs" (*NR* 364). It is part of our shared inheritance. Absolute-rights claims generate corresponding absolute prohibitions (*NR* 374). On the international level Porter thinks these are emerging with respect to genocide, ethnic cleansing, rape, and torture.

For Porter, a Christian theory of rights would include three components: "a commitment to the freedom and self-determination of the individual, seen as the fundamental expression of the Image of God within which each person is created; the recognition that the human capacity for self-determination exercises moral and juridical force, which every society is bound to acknowledge; and . . . the further acknowledgment that the relevant claims have force, even over against community and tradition" (*NR* 369). Can Christians try to impose their view of natural rights on others? Porter says no. The challenge is to persuade others in a real form of solidarity and dialogue with those who have different visions of what the good life entails (*NR* 373). She recognizes that the Christian way of life may not represent God's only will for humanity; other moralities may as well. She sees the diversity of moral systems as a good thing: "The diversity of moral traditions reflects a providential way of preserving distinctive forms of human goodness, which could not be captured in any one overarching moral system, however admirable and just" (*NR* 378). God's grace will be continuous with God's creative goodness.

LIBERATIVE ETHICS

According to Miguel De La Torre, "Liberative ethics is a spiritual response to unexamined normative and legitimized social structures responsible for privileging a powerful minority at the expense of the disenfranchised majority."[21] All liberative ethics share the base point of being contextual, but the context is "rooted in the social location of those seeking faith-based responses to their oppressed situations."[22] The methodology is not deductive, drawing from their basic theological premises and principles to apply to specific situations as some traditions do, but inductive, working from the lived realities of those experiencing the injustice of sexism, racism, and classism to challenge and reformulate theological beliefs and ethical norms with an eye toward dismantling the structures that dehumanize and destroy so many lives. Thus, the methodology moves from orthopraxis, right action, to orthodoxy, right beliefs, rather than the reverse; it begins in solidarity with those who have been marginalized by society, whose voices have been muted because of their class, their gender, or their race. "Liberative ethicists envision a new creation

---

[21] Miguel A. De La Torre, *Ethics: A Liberative Approach* (Minneapolis: Fortress Press, 2013), 3.

[22] Ibid.

free of injustices, where human dignity and the freedom to seek one's own destiny reign supreme."[23]

Feminist Ethics

One liberative ethics is feminist ethics.[24] The category of feminist ethics covers a wide range of positions that have evolved significantly, especially over the past several decades. At their core, however, approaches to feminist ethics emerge initially as criticisms of the way ethics has been done because most approaches to Christian ethics have been focused only on men (mainly elite, white men), dealing with male experiences and male behavior, while excluding women, persons of color, and the poor. Ethics has frequently not attended to women's experiences or the private sphere, where much of women's lives and work have focused historically. From these criticisms feminist ethicists have developed strong positions of advocacy for women and other subjugated groups, attending to areas and issues that have been marginalized in ethical constructions. These concerns result in a number of common areas of focus for Christian feminist ethics: (1) intentionally paying attention to women's experiences as a source for moral deliberation; (2) promotion of the equality of all, regardless of gender, with particular advocacy for women because of their marginalization within patriarchal societies; (3) attention to bodies and embodiment as central to moral agency; and (4) recognition of relationships and communities as key sources in moral deliberation rather than an exclusive focus on individual moral deliberation and action. Different feminist approaches diverge in how best to deal with these concerns.

Beverly Wildung Harrison was a pioneer in Christian feminist social ethics. Harrison makes clear that justice for women and others who live on the margins of society should be of central importance for all Christian ethicists. In her groundbreaking essay "The Power of Anger in the Work of Love" Harrison lays out the basis for a "feminist liberative ethic."[25] A feminist ethic must begin, contends Harrison, with women's experiences of marginalization and oppression, with the struggle for liberation. It is from such human struggles, deeply grounded in *this* world rather than abstracted to the "other" world, that we experience the revelation of what is divine.

These experiences of the divine in human struggles provide challenges to the dominant theologies in what Harrison calls "basepoints" of a feminist liberative ethic. The first basepoint is *the priority of activity over passivity as*

---

[23] Ibid., 5.

[24] I wish to express my gratitude to Dr. Dianne Oliver, dean of Arts and Sciences, Nazareth College, who developed the following paragraphs that lay out basic approaches of the feminist and womanist ethics models.

[25] The essay appears in Beverly W. Harrison, *Making the Connections: Essays in Feminist Social Ethics*, ed. Carol S. Robb (Boston: Beacon Press, 1985) (hereafter cited as *MC*).

the mode of love. While passive qualities of contemplation and noninvolvement are often held up as spiritual, and frequently associated with women's roles, Harrison contends that love is never passive but is always active, a "do-ing" (*MC* 11). Women have been involved historically with not only bearing human life, but also with nurturing life for humanity to survive. Such active "do-ing" is love, "the power to act-each-other-into-well-being." This power also harbors its flip side—not only the power for good, but also the power to "thwart life and maim each other" (*MC* 11). We have the choice of setting free God's love in the world, to "build up dignity and self-respect in one another," but we also have the possibility "to tear each other down" (*MC* 12). Harrison's vision offers no place for a trivial understanding of love as only a feeling or something that occurs between two individuals; rather, love is the very power of God in the world that we as human beings have the ability to set free or to stop, a responsibility we often wish we did not have.

How we exercise this power to enable or diminish God's love in the world begins from *our experiences as embodied selves,* the second basepoint. While we often think of there being a mind/body split, Harrison, like most feminist ethicists, argues that no such dualism exists. We are our bodies; we are embedded in the life struggle that we experience in and through our bodies. One cannot transcend the nitty-gritty of everyday life to live in a world of abstract principles from which we can make rational, ethical decisions, as some moral philosophy has suggested. "Our bodies, ourselves" suggests that our knowledge, including moral knowledge, comes from our senses—"our ability to touch, to see, to hear"—and is connected to the world rather than abstracted from it (*MC* 13). While love is not simply a feeling, as embodied selves what we feel is important and central to our moral deliberations. As Harrison describes it, "There are no 'right' and 'wrong' feelings. *Moral quality* is a property of acts, not of feelings, and our feelings arise in action. The moral question is not 'what do I feel?' but rather 'what do I do with what I feel?'" Feeling is "the basic ingredient *in our relational transaction with the world*" (*MC* 49).

Such an embrace of feelings as central to doing ethics contrasts with certain ways of moral deliberation where one tries to rise above one's feelings, or to suppress emotion, especially strong emotion. Harrison is clear that while Christianity has often seen anger as a sin and the opposite of love, nothing could be further from the truth. "Anger is a mode of connectedness to others and it is always a vivid form of caring. . . . Anger is . . . a sign of some resistance in ourselves to the moral quality of the social relations in which we are immersed" (*MC* 14). In other words, anger emerges when we see something wrong in the world, something to which we are morally opposed. Anger provides the energy to act in love to overcome what is amiss. It is not something to be avoided but something to be nurtured for its contribution to moral action. The moral act of love and care depends on the power of anger.

The third basepoint, and the one that Harrison contends is the most important, is *the centrality of relationship.* There are no individuals who exist apart from relationship. As human beings we are always already in relation to others—we never exist as isolated individuals apart from relationship to other people. In those relationships what we desire is a mutual love, "love that has both the quality of a gift received and the quality of a gift given" (*MC* 18). It is in relationship to others that we make ourselves vulnerable to what we receive from another, insists Harrison. Jesus was radical, claims Harrison, not in his suffering on the cross but in his power of mutuality, of mutual love. Jesus's death on the cross was not an act of sacrificial moral virtue but was "the price he paid for refusing to abandon the radical activity of love—of expressing solidarity and reciprocity with the excluded ones in his community." Thus, from an ethical perspective, Harrison argues that we are called to a "radical activity of love, to a way of being in the world that deepens relation, embodies and extends community, [and] passes on the gift of life" (*MC* 18). Jesus stood for radical love all the way to the cross, and it was that stance, rather than the sacrifice itself, which is Jesus's action of "doing justice" that we should emulate. "We are not called to practice the virtue of sacrifice," insists Harrison (*MC* 19). Instead, we are called to deepen our relationships, to transform unjust relationships and structures, and to live out the radical activity of love.

In other essays in *Making the Connections* Harrison offers a clear and consistent method of how one should approach the task of Christian ethics to achieve this vision highlighted above, laying out the key points in approaching any ethical analysis that seeks human liberation as its end. These key points are not about simply finding an intellectually rigorous approach to ethics, though this method is certainly such an approach. For Harrison and other feminist ethicists, "life and death issues *are* at stake in the way we perceive, analyze, and envision the world and therefore in what we say of God and human hope. The critical intellectual task of theology is the serious one of re-appropriating all our social relations, including our relations to God, so that shared action toward genuine human and cosmic fulfillment occurs" (*MC* 245). It matters for Harrison how we approach theological tasks and ethical analysis; we are not just choosing one among a series of options in how we do ethics. Some approaches result in unjust societies, in oppression and suffering, while others are seeking and advocating for liberation from such oppression and suffering. Harrison argues that feminist ethics clearly advocates for the latter in its goal of overcoming the marginalization and subordination of women.

In Harrison's view of feminist ethics, the starting place of all ethical analysis is *conscientization*, that is, raising one's consciousness (*MC* 243). This occurs through sharing the private experiences of injustice with others in order to see that we are not alone; our experiences are shared with others because of the structural, public injustice under which we all suffer. There are times when one is experiencing injustice when it is almost assumed that the current reality is "just the way things are." Conscientization breaks the silence, making people realize ways that injustice is caused by the very systems of which we are part. The history of oppression and subjugation must be named so that the community can begin the work of overcoming the structures of injustice that marginalize and oppress (*MC* 243, 249). Ethics must begin from the situation of oppression and thus must begin by bringing to light the history of how the situation came to be the way that it is. In looking at Gustafson's four categories identified earlier, Harrison's feminist ethics clearly begins from situational analysis, from the concrete and particular. Yet, unlike in situational and contextual ethics, which start from a particular situation to which one seeks to respond ethically, Harrison's view begins from the over-all lived realities of women in a patriarchal society. In situation ethics one asks questions of a particular situation in order to determine the best way to embody the abstract ideal of love in that situation. Feminist ethics begins from particular experiences of those on the margins of society in order to determine what love or justice would even look like. There is no abstract ideal of love or justice; instead, love and justice are determined through the lived realities of those who are oppressed.

The second step, then, in doing ethics comes through "explicit historical and socioethical analysis" (*MC* 249). Harrison is a strong advocate of the need to use social theory and analysis in order to look concretely at the lived realities of those affected by the ethical dilemmas in question. Ethics is not about abstract principles that can simply be applied to particular situations for Harrison. Instead, it is by looking at the history of a society, at the particular struggles of those who have gone before us, that we are enabled to see the past as "the results of collective human agency" (*MC* 249). If the situation we are in now is the result of human agency, then the conclusion is clear: if we have done it, it can be undone. Thus, for Harrison, ethics must clearly explore how things came to be the way they are now, how situations of op-pression and injustice were established, if one is to offer ethical arguments for what ought to be done going forward.

In addition, it is only through looking at the history of how things came to be the way they are that we can identify not only the actions and efforts of the "winners" of history, whose decisions contributed to present injustice, but also the "history of survival and resistance to oppression," the voices of resistance coming from the marginalized in the history of our current society. It is both together, "privilege and resistance to privilege," that bring us to our current situation, and both must be examined in their complexity to help us see the ways forward to move beyond the present injustices (*MC* 249). While there are times when those who are in positions of privilege can justify their privilege as somehow ordained by God, those on the margins in the current society "do not credit God with sanctifying widespread human bondage and oppression" (*MC* 246). Thus, the voices of the oppressed, of women who are subjugated because of a patriarchal society, or of persons of color who are marginalized because of their race must continually be attended to if the current situation is to be transformed.

Analysis as just described helps clarify the current situation and the issues that must be confronted to move forward with ethical decisions. The next step in feminist ethics is to move from such analysis to "clarifying . . . options for action" (*MC* 251). Feminist ethics recognizes both the pragmatic need to move forward with actions that work—that make a difference in situations of oppression—while balancing such pragmatism with the longer-term vision of alternative realities that can be imagined for the future. Harrison argues that many only look at short-term consequences without holding out hope and imagination for real transformations in our world, where unjust structures can be overturned. Focusing too much on only short-term realities prevents action that holds out the possibility of sustained, systemic change.

Part of this engagement with clarifying options requires that one hang on to the ideals of feminist ethics from which Harrison began as *norms* or *principles* that shape ethical decision-making going forward. Strategic options for various actions must be evaluated, considering such norms for bringing out justice and liberation. According to Harrison, this approach is different than traditional ethical approaches that emphasize moral principles as the starting point for doing ethical reflection. Instead, norms of justice and liberation are continually evaluated considering concrete situations of oppression and injustice. Thus, the moral principles or norms themselves emerge from the situation and become part of a more complex ethical conversation. The norms are only *one dimension* of moral decision-making, rather than the key or primary aspect (*MC* 255).

Womanist Ethics

Womanist ethics as a discipline emerged in the late twentieth century as African American women began to give voice to the unique intersection of race, class, and gender that defined the experiences of black women in the United States and the effect of such experiences on doing ethics. For black women, neither feminist ethics (largely white) nor black ethics (largely male) dealt constructively with the unique situation of their experiences of oppression based not only on gender or only on race, but at the intersection of multiple oppressions. Gloria Hull described this unique situation in *All the Women Are White, All the Blacks Are Men, But Some of Us Are Brave.*[26] Black women found some shared experiences with feminist ethicists, yet they also found too much inattention in that movement to issues of race and class. While the huge strides made by black theology and ethics on behalf of liberation of blacks from oppression were significant for all in the African American community,

---

[26] Gloria T. Hull, Patricia B. Scott, and Barbara Smith, eds., *All the Women Are White, All the Blacks Are Men, But Some of Us Are Brave* (New York: Feminist Press at CUNY, 1993).

black women found that gender issues were not a central concern for that movement, and so the perspectives of black women remained marginalized. Thus was born womanist theology and womanist ethics, reflecting those unique experiences of black women and the connection among various forms of oppression that was central to those experiences.

The term *womanist* was coined by Alice Walker, African American novelist and poet. Walker used the term to get at the cultural values embodied in the experience and wisdom of black women. In her now classic book, *In Search of Our Mothers' Gardens*, Walker provides a fourfold definition of a womanist, beginning with the following:

> WOMANIST 1. From *womanism*. (Opp. of "girlish," i.e., frivolous, irresponsible, not serious.) A black feminist or feminist of color. From the black folk expression of mothers to female children, "you acting womanish," i.e., like a woman. Usually referring to outrageous, audacious, courageous or *willful* behavior. Wanting to know more and in greater depth than is considered "good" for one. Interested in grown-up doings. Acting grown up. Being grown up. Interchangeable with another black folk expression: "You trying to be grown." Responsible. In charge. *Serious.*[27]

As described by the editors of an important collection of essays in womanist ethics, in her definition Walker:

1. Validates femaleness that is characterized by an inquisitiveness that seeks to understand that which is essential to know oneself.
2. Sees personhood as defying social constructions. Womanism invites us question perceptions of human sexuality that contradict our sense of unconditional acceptance.
3. Encourages us to celebrate life in its totality. Ultimately, from our ability to love ourselves we develop an appreciation for ways in which we must respond, without pretense, to issues of life and death.
4. Demands a deeper, more intense critique relative to the multiple dimensions of Black women's lives, individually and collectively.[28]

Womanist ethicists and theologians adopted Walker's term as describing their work to stand against the multiple oppressions and to work to change the social structures that created those situations of marginalization, violence, and injustice. As is true for many groups on the margins of society, much of the wisdom and insight of black women had not been codified or even addressed

---

[27] Alice Walker, *In Search of Our Mothers' Gardens* (New York: Harcourt Brace, 1983), xi.

[28] Katie Geneva Cannon, Emilie M. Townes, and Angela D. Sims, eds., *Womanist Theological Ethics: A Reader* (Louisville, KY: Westminster John Knox Press, 2011), xvi.

in academic settings. In addition, the assumptions made in the ethics prevail-ing in the academy and the church focused on the experiences of those who were part of the dominant groups in society—rendering black women and their vision of truth, value, and moral agency invisible. To reclaim the voices of black women, womanist ethicists turn to several sources, including black women's literature and historical accounts of and by black women. Thus, one key source for womanist ethics is found in the tradition of black women's literature—the narratives and stories of the embodied lives of black women, their families, and their communities—that gives voice to the ethical values, norms, and virtues that are reflective of the black community. Another key source for womanist ethics is found in sociohistorical analysis: investigating the historical and contemporary events, persons, and cultural situations of black women and the cultural contexts in which they live in order to mine these situations for the ethical visions they embody.

Emilie Townes is a central voice in the field of womanist ethics. Townes begins clearing space for her vision of womanist ethics by criticizing dominant modes of ethics that argue for certain universals—common values, transcen-dent norms—as if they exist apart from the communities from which they emerge. Townes insists that "rather than argue for universals, womanist ethics begins with particularity."[29] This means that what is claimed as universal is often simply the norm of whatever group is dominant in a society or culture; because it is dominant, it is "seen as the norm and therefore neutral" ("Souls" 37). Thus, what the dominant ethics tradition identifies as a given *norm* to which all ethical decision-making must conform is really a *value* that emerges from the dominant culture itself. Townes argues that "because all discourse is rooted in the social location of those who speak (or are silent or silenced), such discourse is particular and ultimately biased. The task of womanist ethics is to recognize the biases within particularity and work with them to explore the rootedness of social location and the demands for faithful reflection and witness in light of the gospel demands for justice and wholeness" ("Souls" 37). For Townes, this means that a first move for womanist ethics is the criticism of the claimed neutrality of dominant modes of ethics, that is, criticizing the largely white, male ethical standards and principles because they reflect only *one strand* of experiences, norms, and forms of moral agency. The criticisms were not only from the vision of justice in the Christian gospel, but also from the experiences of marginalized communities.

Beginning with the particularities of the black community, and specifically black women's experiences, is thus central for Townes's womanist ethics. This move is not to suggest that only black women have a voice in defining what is ethically good, but to recognize that the moral agency of African American women emerges from their unique experiences, which need to be included at the table of ethical constructions. In addition, those important experiences

---

[29] Emilie M. Townes, "Ethics as an Art of Doing the Work Our Souls Must Have," in *Womanist Theological Ethics: A Reader* (Louisville, KY: Westminster John Knox Press, 2011), 36 (hereafter cited as "Souls").

provide a key source for the *prescriptive* task of ethics, that is, going beyond what *is* to what one *ought* to do. Townes looks to the descriptive experiences of black women to define key concepts and values for ethics in order to prescribe how we ought to act. Descriptive leanings lead to prescriptive visions. Townes suggests that the experience of the black community, women in particular, provides an important resource for helping us to develop such a prescriptive vision.

By looking at the experiences of black women, especially in the slave era in the United States, Townes culls two key concepts that define a womanist ethics that embraces both justice and wholeness: liberation and reconciliation ("Souls" 39). The idea of liberation intends to "restore a sense of self as a free person and as a spiritual being" ("Souls" 39). For Townes, it is the "God-presence" in each of us that provides the strongest sense of self, through which we relate to others. While one "gives through love," Townes is clear that giving of ourselves can *never* be at the expense of ourselves ("Souls" 40). And although concern for others and love of others in relationship is central to recognizing and living through the God-presence in all of us, Townes remains concerned that this love and concern have frequently been used to diminish black women who were called to sacrifice themselves on behalf of others. Wholeness can only be achieved when *both* justice and wholeness are embraced together. Thus, liberation must include both participation in the world for the sake of justice and a strong self-affirmation that claims the right of being for each person ("Souls" 40). One never "achieves" liberation but is always in the process of working for justice and doing so by cultivating wholeness of the self. Ethical action emerges as that which moves forward the process of liberation.

In addition to liberation Townes also argues for the importance of reconciliation in a womanist ethics. "Reconciliation has both an objective realm and a subjective realm. The objective realm is God's activity in our lives in which God creates a new relationship with us. This new relationship is the gift of freedom" ("Souls" 41). God works in and through our lives for freedom, which is an objective reality. While this God-presence in each of us reflects the objective realm of reconciliation, it is "what we do among ourselves" through seeking to restore harmony with others in the world that defines the subjective realm. As Townes describes it: "Through the objective realm, God liberates us for freedom; through the subjective realm, we acknowledge and then accept God's gift to us through faithful and loving relationships with others and the whole of creation" ("Souls" 41). It is God's liberation of us that enables our ethical action in the world to transform unjust societies and structures. The problem confronted by black women is that their "freedom" is greatly diminished in a culture that keeps their lives on the margins. While dominant ethics lauds virtues that promote economic success—"self-reliance, frugality, industry"—and "assumes that the moral agent is free and self-directing" ("Souls" 37), the limits to freedom in the world and the advocacy of virtues that only further support the norms and values of the oppressive culture require a rethinking of moral agency and what counts as virtues for womanist ethics.

While these key concepts of liberation and reconciliation emerge from the experiences of black women, Townes contends that a womanist ethics "cannot be content with a justice that addresses only a particular person's or group's wholeness" ("Souls" 42). The *prescriptive* element of womanist ethics must look beyond only its own community to see ways that others suffer injustice and work to transform all toward justice and wholeness. A womanist ethic must confront injustice in all its forms, exposing the oppressive nature of society and cultivating a community that can partner together to work toward justice—even though such justice is "always within our grasp and just beyond it," calling us toward more than what is ("Souls" 45–46).

Ethical values and norms can *only* emerge from particularity; they do not provide us with universal truths, but they do suggest values and norms to define our ethics. These values and norms are always negotiated in an ongoing way through the specific communities from which they emerge. While this may seem like a form of relativism in which each community then defines its own values to determine what is good or right with no sense of values or norms that transcend these particular communities, this is not a completely accurate description of what womanist ethicists are attempting to do. It is in the *particularity*—the real, lived, specific, concrete stories and experiences of those in the marginalized community of black women—that values and norms rise up to criticize the grand narrative and seemingly universal claims of the dominant culture, which pretends its values are *not* particular when they really are. Womanist ethics thus begins from the particular experiences of black women in order to reclaim both the experiences of oppression as well as acts of resistance that can be found in those particular stories. The stories, then, provide the source for defining norms and values that are attended to in ethical deliberation. How ought we to act? Look at the values that helped the black community resist the horrors of slavery, Jim Crow laws, and ongoing racism, sexism, and classism to see what can take us toward the vision of justice and wholeness that emerges from the Christian gospel. Thus, for womanist ethics, while the beginning base point of doing ethics is the experience of oppression and resistance, the other aspects of Gustafson's ethics emerge out of that initial attention to those experiences. Womanist ethics (1) makes theological claims—about the God-presence in all of us, about justice and wholeness as central to the gospel, and about the call for liberation that emerges from Christian scripture—that connect with the experiences of black women; (2) recognizes that oppressive structures that limit freedom do not remove moral agency; and then (3) develops a set of values and an evolving prescriptive vision that always moves the community forward toward justice.

Hispanic Ethics

Like feminist and womanist ethics, Hispanic Christian ethics draws from the lived religious, cultural, ethnic, and social realities of Hispanics living in the

United States. It engages in an interdisciplinary analysis of that social reality "to expose how present social structures perpetuate racist, sexist, and classist agendas."[30] Because of their own identity as a marginalized minority, they stand in solidarity with and for other disenfranchised groups and reject any ethics that seeks to rationalize domination and exploitation. Their ethics is explicitly Christocentric and praxis-oriented in response to their liberating reading of the Bible and the life and work of Jesus the Christ, who understood his God-given mission to bring justice and liberation to the poor and oppressed (Lk 4:16–30). Justice from this perspective begins with affirming *dignidad* (dignity): because all persons are created in the image of God they are endowed with basic human dignity, and justice requires that essential needs are met so that all persons, especially the poor and oppressed, may live life abundantly.

To discuss Hispanic ethics we draw from the work of Miguel De La Torre, who has written extensively on this tradition. He is critical of the deductive approach of the Eurocentric model of social ethics, which develops abstract beliefs and principles and then seeks to apply them to various moral dilemmas. Instead, he contends that "doing ethics from the margins," including Hispanic ethics, must be inductive, following a five-step hermeneutical circle: observing, reflecting, praying, acting, and reassessing.[31]

The first step, observing, requires some historical and interpretive analysis of how certain groups, including Hispanics, came to experience marginalization and oppression in the first place. Because history is usually written from the perspective of the powerful or dominant group, the voices of the marginalized have been suppressed; they are viewed as "objects" rather than "subjects" of their reality. "Those with the power to define set the discourse, to the detriment of those lacking that power, who should be subjects, but are instead reduced to mere objects" (*LSE* 101). The structures that have emerged in this context privilege the dominant group and subject the marginalized to the injustices of poverty, racism, and sexism. Sadly, the oppressed have too often adopted the worldview of their oppressors, which has undermined their personal and social dignity. In response to their oppression the marginalized have begun to question the dominant worldview and to discern their reality for themselves, observing from below, and articulating their own view of justice—based on biblical texts—and the ways justice for them has been denied. That is why De La Torre writes: "For this reason, ethics done on the margins is and must remain a contextual ethics that seeks to see the liberating work of God through the eyes of those made poor, those victimized, and those

---

[30] Rubén Rosario Rodríguez, "Hispanic Liberative Ethics," in De La Torre, *Ethics: A Liberative Approach*, 99. The remainder of the paragraph draws from pages 96–99.

[31] Miguel De La Torre, *Doing Ethics from the Margins*, 2nd ed. (Maryknoll, NY: Orbis Books, 2014), 56; and idem, *Latina/o Social Ethics* (Waco, TX: Baylor University Press, 2010), 85 (hereafter cited as *DEM* and *LSE,* respectively; these will be the two primary sources for developing this tradition).

made to suffer because they belong to the 'wrong gender, race, orientation, or economic class'" (*DEM* 49–50).

The second step, reflecting, requires a thorough social analysis of the current situation of domination and injustice using the tools of the social sciences. "Society cannot be transformed if it is not first analyzed" (*LSE* 86). Sociological, anthropological, economic, and political analyses can provide the data needed to reveal the underlying problems with social structures that have legitimized racist, sexist, heterosexist, and classist norms. Of course, no social analysis is purely objective. However, given the history of illegitimate oppression of marginalized groups, their understanding of their reality must be given more weight, an "epistemological privilege," because unlike privileged groups, they know what it is like to live under dehumanizing conditions. "Consequently, the primary source for doing ethics is the lived, everyday experience of marginalized people" (*DEM* 50).

Praying, the third step, involves theological and biblical analysis, which must be done to call one's ethics Christian. When talking about prayer, this is not simply the prayer of individuals of faith to God but the prayer of the *comunidad* (community), "where members of a Latino/a faith community accompany each other and stand in solidarity during trials and tribulations" (*LSE* 86). As noted earlier, the community draws inspiration from a liberating reading of the gospel and an understanding of the character of God as exemplified in the teachings of Jesus. God is a God of love, who identifies with the poor and the outcast and challenges the social order that perpetuates their oppression and calls for justice. "Salvation through Christ is at its essence a relationship with God and with one another, a justice-based relationship whose very nature transforms all aspects of humanity so that the abundant life can be lived by all to its fullest" (*DEM* 34–35).

Like some of the other traditions we have discussed thus far, De La Torre rejects any separation of the biblical commandments to love and to do justice, which he finds in some Christian ethical traditions that argue that love is the ideal for interpersonal relationships, but that approximations of justice are all that can be expected in the social order. "Compartmentalizing love and justice into two separate spheres of human experience allows a person to claim to be a Christian (hence full of love) while supporting public policies that perpetuate mechanisms of death for marginalized persons" (*DEM* 41). Instead, he argues that love and justice are inseparable. Justice is "done in obedience to love" and love "is the deed of justice" (*DEM* 9). To bring about a more just social order, it is not enough for privileged people to have a change of heart. "The social structures themselves require transformation and conversion" (*DEM* 35). "The love that liberates can be known and experienced only from within relationships established upon acts of justice" (*DEM* 9). The image of God bestows worth on all and needs to be recognized and restored in the marginalized. Unfortunately, that dignity has been marred and obscured by the dominant ideology that labels some as superior and some as inferior, and by social structures that inhibit the full awareness and development of self-identity as a child of God with inestimable worth. God's identification with the poor and oppressed seeks to restore awareness of their value and challenges the structures that undermine it. Dismantling structures of oppression, not merely changing attitudes, is the only way to restore full humanity to all—oppressed and oppressor (*DEM* 14).

Because he sees God's call for justice for the poor and the marginalized embodied in the life and work of Jesus, his ethic is Christocentric, affirming Jesus as ontologically Hispanic, much as African American ethicists affirm that Jesus was black. Jesus is Hispanic because the character of God portrayed in the Bible and in the life and work of Jesus the Christ is that of one who sides with the poor and oppressed and against those who oppress them. "To commune with a Hispanic Christ is to incarnate the gospel message within the marginalized spaces of the *barrios* so that the actions and words of Jesus can infuse *la comunidad* with the hope of survival and liberation" (*DEM* 81).

The fourth step in De La Torre's hermeneutical circle is acting: the implementation of praxis, behavior, and actions. The first thing to note about this step is that it gives shape to the theological ideas discussed in the third step. For many ethicists, orthodoxy, or right doctrine, takes precedence over action. Based on one's theological beliefs and moral principles, one then decides what to do in each situation. De La Torre turns this formula on its head. For him, orthopraxy, or right practice, takes precedence over and gives shape to right doctrine. Theology is formed as a reflection on praxis, particularly the practice of acting with and for justice for the marginalized. Ethics must arise from the disenfranchised reflecting on their survival praxis—the principles and practices they utilize to challenge the patterns and structures that seek to undermine their dignity (*LSE* 119).

The final step is a reassessment leading to new ethical perspectives. While the praxis of liberation for the marginalized and for the oppressor can bring about a new awareness of the reality of oppression and injustice, such awareness is not enough. The question must be asked whether the actions taken have brought about justice for the oppressed. If yes, then we must ask what additional actions must be taken to further that end. If not, we must ask what other actions we might put in place of those practices to make justice for the oppressed a reality. Such reassessment of the liberative practices gives shape to doctrine, to the understanding of biblical texts, and to the system of ethics that emerges (*DEM* 55–56).

This hermeneutical methodology leads De La Torre to explore Hispanic ethics that have emerged in recent years. It is an ethics *en lo cotidiano*. What this means is that Hispanic ethics is contextualized into the everyday experiences of the dispossessed rather than constructed from some abstract reasoning process. It draws from the stories of those who are marginalized as they speak about their efforts to survive amid oppressive structures. This autobiographical stance gives a sense of what it means to be a self and a moral agent in the context of these relationships. "The trials and tribulations of Hispanics struggling for their humanity and dignity become the starting point for any type of indigenous Latino/a ethical framework" (*LSE* 72).

Hispanic ethics is also a communal ethics for people who experience *la lucha* (the struggle). "To be in *nepantla*, living on the borders between marginality and acceptance, is to struggle for your family's daily bread, to fight for your family's basic human dignity" (*LSE* 74). While not every Hispanic resides at the borders, those who do—the culturally, socially, and economically oppressed—have the preferential position when speaking about Hispanic ethics. It is a collaborative ethic, *en conjunto*, that seeks "to understand faith and vocation as contextualized in the lives and struggles of Latino/as" (*LSE* 76). Persons engaged in Hispanic ethics must stand side by side with the marginalized. It is an incarnational approach to ethics, much like their understanding of the incarnation of God in Jesus, who stood side by side with the poor and marginalized. This struggle for survival not only describes their experience but also influences the worldview that seeks to construct a liberative view of themselves and their moral agency rather than accepting the dehumanizing view placed upon them by the dominant ideology. The goal of Hispanic ethics, however, "is for all humanity, including Latino/as, to experience the fullness of life as willed by the God of life" (*LSE* 75). The practice of Hispanic ethics reaffirms the hermeneutical circle:

> The goal of ethics *en conjunto* is for the marginalized community to (1) analyze the reality of *lo cotidiano*, (2) reflect on what the good news of the biblical text has to say about this reality, (3) implement praxis that can bring about a more just society, and (4) reflect on the results of this praxis to ascertain if new actions are required. (*LSE* 76–77)

De La Torre's assessment of Hispanic ethics leads him to articulate several ways in which this ethic needs to move forward. He contends that Hispanic ethics needs to be a disruptive ethics, an ethics *para joder* (screwing with) and subverting the prevailing social order to disrupt its "stranglehold on the marginalized" (*LSE* 99). Hispanic ethics cannot just follow the rules set by a binary understanding of good vs. evil; instead, it must build upon the relational moral agency of the Hispanic community in more subversive ways to "move beyond how the dominant culture has come to define the good" (*LSE* 101). It is a moral imperative. His ethics employs the cultural symbol of the trickster, or *joderone*, found in myths, stories, and even the Bible. Tricksters live in a liminal state, betwixt and between, where the normal rules of society are called into question and broken, giving them a liberative moral agency. They unmask the oppressive structures and how these become internalized in the Latino/a psyche, raising the consciousness of the oppressed (and even the oppressor) to these injustices. "The trickster, as the ultimate *joderone*, disrupts the norm to force those being tested to seek new options, opportunities previously unrecognized" (*LSE* 105). For De La Torre, Jesus, whose actions and teachings "screwed with" and subverted the legitimacy of the prevailing religious and political authorities of his day, is a premier example of a *holy joderone* (*LSE* 115). This is the Christ, the one who identifies with and seeks to liberate the oppressed to live life to the fullest, upon which a Hispanic Christocentric ethics should be based.

Hispanic ethics also needs to be an ethics of civil initiative, generating practices that support international human rights and laws even when one's nation engages in actions that violate those standards. Civil initiative is different from the civil disobedience prevalent in the civil rights movement spearheaded by Martin Luther King Jr. and others. By breaking what they saw as unjust laws, civil rights activists sought to bring attention to the injustice of those laws. Civil initiatives demonstrate how the country is not embodying the rights and laws of the international society by engaging in alternative practices that do. Some examples include the development of sanctuary churches and cities that welcome refugees and immigrants in the face of inhumane anti-immigrant policies, and the practice of leaving food and water along immigrant trails to ensure their well-being. Each practice requires a "feet on the ground" presence with those who are marginalized (*LSE* 121).

A final element of an ethics *para joder* is that it is pastoral, emerging with and from the marginalized. This is not a disruptive ethics for the sake of disruption; it is done out of a pastoral concern for people to experience the fullness of abundant life that they are unjustly denied at present. Those who employ this ethic "are activists with pastoral concerns, that is, putting the liberation of the disenfranchised first" (*LSE* 122). It requires getting one's hands dirty. It may result in confrontation with authorities, even loss of one's freedom, but this is not sought out because such confrontation often takes the focus away from the unjust treatment of the oppressed and places it on the activist. In fact, this ethics is a "proactive way" of bringing about justice for the marginalized (*LSE* 123).

RESOURCES

Discussion Questions

1. How do Gustafson's base points of accurate situational analysis, basic theological affirmations, moral principles, and a conception of human moral agency play out in the context of each of the Christian ethical traditions discussed above? What differences in their understandings of those base points do you see? Why do they emphasize the importance of some over others?

2. A review of each of the Christian ethical traditions above reveals some discussion about the relationship between the Christian principles of love and justice. How do these ethical traditions understand this relationship? Are love and justice two sides of the same coin? Or is love reserved for interpersonal

relations and justice for social relations? What is your perspective on their relationship?

3. For some Christian ethical traditions, especially liberative ethics, social location plays a significant role in their development along with a rejection of the claim that ethics must be objective and impartial. Why do you think this is the case? Do you agree with their claims? Why or why not?

4. Typical discussions of ethics revolve around debates over three basic approaches: deontological (where duty or law is emphasized over consequences); teleological (where ends or consequences play a role); and virtues oriented (where the development of character and virtues is primary). How do the traditions discussed in this chapter resolve these debates? Which approach does each emphasize most?

5. The issue of methodology is one of the debates among the Christian models discussed in this chapter. Should they follow a deductive methodology, drawing from their basic biblical and theological premises and principles to apply them to specific situations, or should they follow an inductive methodology, working from the lived realities of those experiencing injustice to challenge and reformulate theological beliefs and ethical norms—in other words, moving from orthopraxis, right action, to orthodoxy, right beliefs, rather than the reverse? What is your view? How does that perspective lead you to favor some Christian ethical traditions over others?

Activities

1. Have students define the values of love and justice for themselves. Have them compare their views with two of the Christian ethical traditions discussed above.

2. Gather the moral questions of members of the class or study group. At the beginning of the session ask students to write questions regarding any ethical concerns they have but instruct them not to include their names. Place the questions in a box or bag. Periodically, at the beginning of the class, draw questions that the entire class will attempt to answer together using language and concepts from the text.

3. Divide the class into groups, each representing a different Christian ethical tradition. Have each group analyze its tradition according to Gustafson's base points—accurate situational analysis, basic theological affirmations, moral principles, and a conception of human moral agency—and write down their responses. Lead the class in a discussion of the similarities and/or differences discovered in the analyses.

4. Watch episode 6 of season 2 of *The Good Place*, which highlights the "trolley problem." Review all of the Christian social ethics models in this chapter to see how they might resolve it.

5. Watch one or more films that raise significant moral issues from the list of films below. Do an analysis of the films, discerning the approach the

filmmaker takes on the moral issue in question. Compare and contrast that approach with how one or more of the models in this chapter would approach the issue.

Audiovisuals

Do the Right Thing. 40 Acres and a Mule, Universal Pictures, 1989. Directed by Spike Lee, who also plays the lead role alongside Danny Aiello, this film explores a Brooklyn neighborhood's simmering racial tension, which culminates in violence and a death on a hot summer day. The film forces viewers to think about the difference between damage to property and the death of a black man, questions that continue in the recent protests and riots over the death of George Floyd at the hands of Minneapolis police officers.

Green Book. Universal Pictures, 2018. Directed by Peter Farrelly and starring Mahershala Ali and Viggo Mortensen, this film set in 1962 chronicles the experiences of African American classical pianist Don Shirley and his driver as they toured the Deep South, where racial segregation was still the law of the land. The title comes from the name of a tour book written for African Americans about places to stay and eat that would allow blacks. Critics claimed that the film combines the white savior trope with a white bigot's redemption, but the director suggests the film is about two people from opposite walks of life forming a lifelong friendship.

John Q. New Line Cinema, 2002. Directed by Nick Cassavetes and starring Denzel Washington, this film details the struggles of a working-class family seeking expensive medical treatment for their son who needs a heart transplant. The film draws attention to the problems of employer-sponsored health insurance, the dilemmas faced by hospitals in providing care for indigent patients, and the debate over the right to health care vs. the ability to pay.

Parasite. C.J. Entertainment, 2019. Directed by Bong Joon-ho and starring Song Kang-ho and Lee Sun-kyun, this South Korean film follows the members of a poor family who scheme to become employed by a wealthy family by infiltrating the household and posing as unrelated, highly qualified individuals. The film highlights the economic and social disparities between the rich and poor.

Philadelphia. TriStar Pictures, 1993. Directed by Jonathan Demme and starring Tom Hanks and Denzel Washington, this film chronicles the legal battle over the discrimination against a lawyer who was fired because of his homosexuality and his AIDS. The film also draws the relationship between the plaintiff, Tom Hanks, and his lawyer, Denzel Washington, and how the friendship that develops between them helps Washington's character overcome his homophobia and fear of AIDS.

Spotlight. Open Road Films, 2015. Directed by Tom McCarthy and starring Mark Ruffalo and Rachel McAdams, this film recounts the efforts by Spotlight, the investigative unit of the *Boston Globe*, to find and report evidence of the Catholic Church's cover-up of sexual abuse by priests and the role that the courts and the police played in keeping the scandal quiet.

2

Sexuality and Marriage

CASE STUDY:
MARRIAGE BETWEEN PERSONS OF THE SAME SEX
IN THE UNITED STATES

While there is a long and documented history of same-sex relationships and the legal as well as religious formalization of such,[1] the case of legal support for marriages between couples of the same sex garnered significant national attention in the United States in the latter part of the twentieth and early part of the twenty-first centuries. The federal legislative action known as the Defense of Marriage Act (DOMA) defined marriage as occurring between one man and one woman and gave states the right not to recognize same-sex marriage or marriage-like relationships affirmed by other states.[2] DOMA passed both houses of Congress and was signed into law by President Bill Clinton in 1996, even though he felt it was divisive and unnecessary. DOMA provided the first federal definition of marriage, while still leaving room for states to make their own laws regarding same-sex marriage or other formal relationships of persons of the same sex, such as civil unions or domestic partnerships.

On the heels of DOMA the issue of same-sex marriage emerged most significantly in the national spotlight following judicial action that overturned existing state laws concerning the sex of couples to be married. While there had been previous questioning of the constitutionality of state bans on legal

---

[1] For examples, see John Boswell, *Christianity, Social Tolerance, and Homosexuality* (Chicago: University of Chicago Press, 1980); John Boswell, *Same-Sex Unions in Premodern Europe* (New York: Villard Books, 1994); and Bernadette J. Brooten, *Love between Women* (Chicago: University of Chicago Press, 1998).

[2] The Hawaii Supreme Court, in *Baehr v. Lewin* (later *Baehr v. Miike*), ruled that a statute in the state that banned same-sex marriages violated the equal protection clause of Hawaii's constitution. The response to that ruling was to add an amendment to Hawaii's constitution that banned same-sex marriage.

marriage between persons of the same sex, a 2003 decision by the Massachusetts Supreme Judicial Court in the *Goodridge v. Department of Public Health* case declaring the ban on same-sex marriages unconstitutional set the stage for Massachusetts to become the first state to recognize legally marriages between two persons of the same sex. A stay was issued on the decision in the *Goodridge* case to allow the state legislature time to enact legislation on the issue. Initial responses to the judicial ruling by Governor Mitt Romney and the state legislature attempted to offer legislation allowing civil unions for persons of the same sex, which had all the rights and benefits of marriage, in hopes that this would satisfy the constitutionality issue in *Goodridge*. The Supreme Judicial Court responded that this essentially gave same-sex couples "second-class status" and therefore remained unconstitutional. Ultimately, the judicial ruling was upheld when no legislative action that was acceptable to the Supreme Judicial Court was put in place, and Massachusetts began issuing marriage licenses to same-sex couples in May 2004. Several states joined Massachusetts through the next decade, either through legislative action, judicial decisions, or popular vote.

Because the federal government passed DOMA in 1996, there was no legal standing granted by the federal government for same-sex marriages, even if they were legal at the state level. The Obama administration, although it thought the law was unconstitutional and would no longer defend DOMA in the courts, continued to enforce the law out of deference to the Congress and administration that passed it. In 2013, the *United States v. Windsor* case came before the US Supreme Court. In this case Edith Windsor, a resident of New York, was legally married in that state to Thea Spyer. When Spyer died, she left her estate to Windsor. Windsor was forced by the IRS to pay estate taxes on the estate since her spouse was of the same sex and thus did not meet the IRS's definition of spouse. Windsor argued that DOMA violated her rights under the due process clause of the Fourteenth Amendment because of its definition that "spouse" did not apply in her situation. The Supreme Court's 5–4 decision in favor of Windsor opened the door for federal agencies to recognize legally the marriages of persons of the same sex. Thus, immigration laws, tax regulations, and a variety of other federal laws and statutes were interpreted to allow for the recognition of same-sex marriages if such marriages were performed in states that legally recognized them. This shift in federal policy resulted in something of a watershed in relation to the number of states that followed suit.

In 2015, the *Obergefell v. Hodges* case came before the US Supreme Court. In this case, James Obergefell and John Arthur, who were married in Maryland, sought legal recognition of their marriage in Ohio, which banned same-sex marriage. John Arthur was terminally ill, and the couple sought recognition of James Obergefell as the surviving spouse on the death certificate. The Supreme Court combined this case with several others that challenged state bans on same-sex marriage and, in a 5–4 decision, ruled that both the due process and equal protection clauses of the Fourteenth Amendment guaranteed a fundamental right to marry for same-sex couples and required all fifty states and the District of Columbia to perform and recognize the same rights and privileges as opposite-sex couples.

ISSUES AND CONCERNS

While proponents of same-sex marriage applauded the decision that made same-sex marriage a legal right throughout the nation with all the privileges that opposite-sex couples enjoy, others were concerned about the legal implications of the ruling on the possibility for plural marriages and on the democratic process and religious liberty. These concerns were raised by the justices who dissented from the ruling. Chief Justice John Roberts noted that changing the historical and traditional core definition of marriage from "between a man and a woman" could open the door to recognition of plural marriages that would include more than two persons. He writes:

> It offers no reason at all why the two-person element of the core definition of marriage may be preserved while the man-woman element may not. Indeed, from the standpoint of history and tradition, a leap from opposite-sex marriage to same-sex marriage is much greater than one from a two-person union to plural unions, which have deep roots in some cultures around the world. If the majority is willing to take the big leap, it is hard to see how it can say no to the shorter one.[3]

The majority did not see this as a concern, even though there were some court cases where this issue had been considered (*Brown v. Buhman*, for example). Others would suggest that the focus should be on supporting the stability of marriages rather than worrying about the form.

Justices Roberts and Scalia also contend that, in their rush to declare a right to marry for same-sex couples, the majority undermined our representative democracy. It is not the place of the five Supreme Court justices to use their judgment to declare what marriage is, they claim; it is the responsibility of the people working through the democratic process. Scalia writes: "Until the courts put a stop to it, public debate over same-sex marriage displayed American democracy at its best. Individuals on both sides of the issue passionately, but respectfully, attempted to persuade their fellow citizens to accept their views" (*OH* 2). Roberts suggests that, while winning the right to marry, proponents of same-sex marriage have lost "the opportunity to win the true acceptance that comes from persuading their fellow citizens of the justice of their cause. And they lose this just when the winds of change were freshening at their backs" (*OH* 27). While Justice Kennedy, writing for the majority, agrees with the importance of the democratic process, he highlights its limits when fundamental rights are at stake: "Of course, the Constitution

---

[3] *Obergefell v. Hodges,* 576 U. S. 20 (2015) (hereafter cited as *OH*).

contemplates that democracy is the appropriate process for change, so long as that process does not abridge fundamental rights. . . . An individual can invoke a right to constitutional protection when he or she is harmed, even if the broader public disagrees and even if the legislature refuses to act" (*OH* 24).

On the issue of religious liberty, the majority affirmed that the First Amendment's free exercise of religion clause protects those with sincerely held religious beliefs that same-sex marriages should not be condoned and stated that they can continue their practices within the confines of their religious organizations, such as refusing to allow same-sex wedding ceremonies to be held at their places of worship (*OH* 27). What the state cannot do is bar same-sex couples from participation in the practices of civil marriage for religious reasons. Justice Thomas notes, however, that marriage is both a governmental and a religious institution and that it is "inevitable that the two will come into conflict, particularly as individuals and churches are confronted with demands to participate in and endorse civil marriages between same-sex couples" (*OH* 15). Roberts agrees and highlights some possible conflicts, such as a religious college providing married student housing only to opposite-sex couples or religious adoption agencies refusing to place children in same-sex homes. "There is little doubt that these and similar questions will soon be before this Court" (*OH* 28).[4]

While these issues regarding the institution of marriage may have some legal implications, they also help us see the underlying ethical debate about the nature of marriage and differing views of human sexuality. What is the purpose or function of marriage? Both the majority and the minority of the Supreme Court, as well as supporters for both sides in this case, agree that marriage is important because it provides certain benefits to the married partners, to their families, and to society. These benefits include love and intimacy for the partners and a stable environment for having and raising children to be moral and productive citizens. Michael Wald writes: "In marriage people learn to define themselves as caring rather than egoistic beings, as connected to, rather than alienated from, the concerns and well-being of others. As a result, they are more likely to give to society."[5] Where traditionalists and same-sex marriage advocates disagree is on the appropriate form these marriages should take. Those traditionalists who support heterosexual marriage to the exclusion of other forms declare that this has been the form most societies have supported for millennia. While there has been some evolution from marriages based on familial arrangements to marriages based on romantic love, they have continued to be heterosexual. Some religious folks go further to suggest that it is part of the divinely created order: "Therefore a man leaves his father and his mother

---

[4] His comment anticipated a number of cases before the court in relation to persons denying wedding services, such as making a cake or providing flowers, to same-sex couples because of the service provider's personal religious objections to same-sex marriage.

[5] Michael Wald, "Same-Sex Couples: Marriage, Families, and Children," Stanford Law School, Public Law, and Legal Theory Working Paper No. 6 (December 1999).

and clings to his wife, and they become one flesh" (Gen 2:24). Advocates of same-sex marriage counter this argument by suggesting that the Genesis account is reflective of a patriarchal society's view of the form of marriage and not the design of the Creator. Moreover, given that the heterosexual form of marriage has evolved over time, they see no reason why that evolution cannot include same-sex marriages, which would enable couples to experience the relational unity that is at the heart of the biblical text.

The issue of the form of marriage also raises the question of the justice of heterosexual monogamous marriage. While the majority of the Supreme Court addressed the issue of same-sex marriage in terms of rights, others took issue with the social injustice that current forms of marriage have taken. Some critics of same-sex marriage within the LGBTQ community contend that granting same-sex couples the right to marry and gain the privileges attendant to that institution does nothing to address the flaws in the institution of marriage. By couching it in the language of rights, nothing is done to look at the various ways in which injustice is present in the patriarchal, heterosexist, monogamous form of marriage. Moreover, not all those who identify as gay or lesbian necessarily support marriage as an appropriate institution for them because, they argue, marriage is not a gay-friendly institution. They state that extending the right to marry to same-sex couples will only reinforce the cultural obsession with policing sexual activity among gays and non-gays. Others who highlight the question of justice in marriage raise other possibilities, however. Same-sex marriage, they suggest, may lead to more egalitarian models for relationship patterns for all forms of marriage. Moreover, instead of reviewing the issue through the lens of negative rights—in this case, freedom from interference—society should focus its energies on positive rights or entitlements. The question should not be whether same-sex couples should be granted the same rights, privileges, and responsibilities as opposite-sex couples. Rather, we should be asking how we can promote the social conditions in which all marital and familial arrangements can flourish. This moves the question away from rights to privacy and toward the societal obligation to promote the common good.[6]

A further ethical issue regarding marriage surrounds the functions of marriage. What purposes does marriage serve? Most people would agree that because marriage provides stability for the partners, the family, and society, we should provide certain privileges in our laws and our entitlements to married couples in support of this institution. Advocates of same-sex marriage contend that these same functions can and do take place not only in opposite-sex marriages but also in same-sex arrangements. Moreover, with the divorce rate as high as it is, it is not clear that opposite-sex marriages are fulfilling these functions adequately. Marriages also provide venues for moral expression of sexual desire that sustain a network of social relationships. But

---

[6] See Marvin Ellison, *Same-Sex Marriage? A Christian Ethical Analysis* (Cleveland: The Pilgrim Press, 2004), 85.

it is not the form of marriage—opposite-sex—that enables marriage to serve these functions. Same-sex couples can also embody these same norms and functions, and supporting them in this is a matter of justice.

One cannot discuss the issue of marriage without some discussion of the family, which many contend is the basic institution of society. Families have evolved over time, from extended to nuclear to blended, and there is no one arrangement anymore, although the two-parent-with-children model continues to be held up as the ideal. This is because it is considered to provide a safe and stable environment for the propagation and education of offspring for moral citizenship. But advocates of same-sex marriage contend that these same functions of families can and do operate within a same-sex family structure. They point to evidence that children raised in these homes are as stable and well-adjusted as children raised in opposite-sex homes. Some would contend that you need both a mother and a father to raise children fully and properly. But this is coming into question as more children are raised in stable, same-sex family structures and demonstrate solid psychological and moral development.

In addition to the form and function of marriage, a crucial ethical issue underlying the case of same-sex marriage revolves around the nature and purpose of sexuality. Those who argue that sexual orientation is an inherent quality of a person, determined by genetics (nature), often conclude that persons with such genes should not be punished for their sexual orientation any more than we would punish someone for having brown eyes or pale skin or being left-handed. In this view one person being attracted to another of the same biological sex is a fact of nature, thus essentially removing any ethical issue about one's orientation as there is no choice involved. The distinction between sexual orientation and sexual behavior, however, adds another complicating factor. The American Psychological Association (APA) describes the results of research that suggests that sexual orientation, defined as referring to "an enduring pattern of emotional, romantic, and/or sexual attractions to men, women, or both sexes," is a characteristic that "ranges along a continuum, from exclusive attraction to the other sex to exclusive attraction to the same sex."[7] Some argue that since sexual orientation is focused on attraction to others, as outlined in the APA's definition, one's orientation can be evaluated distinctly from one's sexual behaviors. In this view, how one acts on sexual attraction is the morally relevant question, and while they would not condemn individuals for their sexual orientation, some would condemn same-sex sexual activity as morally wrong. Thus, having the attraction to someone of the same sex is not seen as morally wrong, but engaging in same-sex sexual activity is, since such action is chosen by the individual and goes against a set of norms, often derived from religious tenets. Some Christian ethicists refer to this perspective as welcoming but not affirming.[8]

---

[7] American Psychological Association, "Sexual Orientation and Homosexuality" (Washington, DC: APA, 2008), 1.

[8] See Stanley Grenz, *Welcoming but Not Affirming: An Evangelical Response to Homosexuality* (Louisville, KY: Westminster John Knox Press, 1998). See also the

The biblical view of human sexuality in Genesis as a good aspect of human nature—"they become one flesh" and "be fruitful and multiply"—gave way early among church fathers "to despair over sex in all its disastrous fallenness or a grudging toleration of sex as the means of procreation."[9] Augustine argues that holding lustful tendencies in check is a prime reason for people to get married, so that sexual libido can serve the purposes of procreation. Eventually, the Protestant tradition grudgingly affirmed a positive purpose for sexuality: providing love and unity between the partners, often referred to as the unitive function of sexuality. The Catholic tradition has recently placed the unitive purpose of sexuality on a par with the procreative function but argues that any sexual act should be open to the possibility of procreation. Protestants also believe that couples should be open to offspring in their lovemaking but that the primary purpose is the unity between the partners. This is part of the reason that Protestants historically have been open to the use of artificial means of contraception, allowing the partners to decide when or even if to have children. But in both traditions the fundamental place for moral sexual expression is within the sacrament or covenant of marriage.

Other ethical questions surround the norms for appropriate sexual expression. Many traditionalists contend that heterosexuality is the norm because it fulfills our nature as relational and social creatures and takes responsibility for the generation and flourishing of human life.[10] Advocates of same-sex marriage counter that claim by suggesting it is not the *form* (heterosexual or homosexual) of those relationships that matter, but rather the *function*— whether they promote mutuality and faithfulness among the partners and promote equity and justice for them and their families. Such relationships can also be generative, not necessarily in the biophysical way advocated by traditionalists (although reproductive technologies do offer this possibility), but in ways that enable the participants in the relationship to flourish and grow, whether they are the partners or the children.[11]

EVANGELICAL ETHICS

Recall from Chapter 1 that both evangelical traditions affirm the Bible as the central authority. For conservative evangelicals, John Jefferson Davis says the basic conviction is that the Bible, the "very Word of God" and "the only infallible and inerrant rule of faith and practice," is the "final court of appeals

---

Congregation for the Doctrine of the Faith's "Letter to the Bishops of the Catholic Church on the Pastoral Care of Homosexual Persons."

[9] David Gushee and Glen Stassen, *Kingdom Ethics*, 2nd ed. (Grand Rapids, MI: Eerdmans, 2016), 152 (hereafter cited as *KE2*).

[10] See, for example, Max Stackhouse, *Covenants and Commitments: Faith, Family, and Economic Life* (Louisville, KY: Westminster John Knox Press, 1997).

[11] See Fred Glennon, "Must a Covenantal Sexual Ethic Be Heterocentric? Insights from Congregations," *Perspectives in Religious Studies* 28/3 (Fall 2001): 215–33.

for ethics." Reason, tradition, and science may be used in ethical reasoning, "but divine revelation, found in the canonical Scriptures of the Old and New Testaments, constitutes the 'bottom line' of the decision-making process" (*EE4* 13).[12] Davis argues that the biblical tradition affirms the historical form of marriage: "the divine ideal of lifelong heterosexual, monogamous marriage" (*EE4* 102). The reason for this, he contends, is the Bible's understanding of the function of marriage as both an affirmation of the covenantal relationship between the partners and for "the benefit of a godly offspring" (*EE4* 95). For him, this is divine revelation and part of what he calls the "creation norms" found in Genesis 1—2: "Sexual differentiation is the basis of human marriage, procreation, and family life, which is the primal form of human community" (*EE4* 115). Any variation (or deviation) of the form and function of marriage from these creation norms runs counter to the "very Word of God." Even divorce, which is commonplace in the United States today, runs counter to the biblical mandate that, he argues, indicates God hates divorce (*EE4* 101). He does make some allowance for the dissolution of the marriage covenant because of sexual infidelity or desertion by an unbelieving spouse. But for Christians, these should be rare.

Progressive evangelicals Glen Stassen and David Gushee also affirm the "authority of Scripture," but they view it through the lens of Jesus's life and teaching as seen in the Sermon on the Mount. Their views on biblical authority are important for understanding both the similarities and differences in their views on marriage and sexuality. Stassen and Gushee, writing in 2003, also affirm the historical form of marriage. They write, drawing from the creation stories in the book of Genesis: "Marriage is a male-female covenant partnership established by God for God's purposes" (*KE* 275).[13] These purposes include procreation and childrearing, stewardship over creation, and the relational intimacy and sexual union that promote God's desire for bonding and community. This one-flesh union embodied in the marriage covenant is one of "God's gracious gifts to human beings" (*KE* 276). Like Davis, they agree that the marriage covenant is intended to include fidelity and permanence. Such qualities enable the purposes of God in marriage and "contribute to human well-being far better than the alternatives" (*KE* 276). The problem with divorce, as they look at Jesus's teaching on marriage and adultery in the Gospels, is that the freedom to dissolve a marriage tempts one toward infidelity, weakens future marriage bonds, and has potential negative effects on the children—all of which undermine God's purposes in the institution of marriage. If marital problems emerge, the primary focus should be on reconciliation, with divorce only as a last resort (*KE* 289).

This understanding of marriage has implications for all forms of appropriate sexual expression. Stassen and Gushee have a positive assessment

---

[12] John Jefferson Davis, *Evangelical Ethics*, 3rd and 4th eds. (Philipsburg, NJ: P&R Publishing, 2004, 2015) (hereafter cited as *EE3* and *EE4*).

[13] Glen Stassen and David Gushee, *Kingdom Ethics: Following Jesus in Contemporary Context* (Downers Grove, IL: InterVarsity Press, 2003) (hereafter cited as *KE*).

of human sexuality. They call it a "powerful and mysterious dimension of personhood" (*KE* 290) and a "God-given good for humans to enjoy rather than merely a means to other ends" (*KE* 306). The purpose of sexuality is to generate intimacy and relational bonding between the partners but also for God's purposes in creation, which may or may not include procreation. Although not as explicit in his discussion of sexuality, Davis would agree with this view. This is part of the reason why a biblical and Christian sexual ethic requires strong ethical norms, which for Davis is critical, given his commitment to "contextual absolutism" (*EE4* 15). However, Stassen and Gushee are less concerned with moral norms than they are with moral virtue: "Sexual ethics has to do with sexual integrity, with sexual character—with the total reclaiming of human sexuality for the covenant purposes for which God created it" (*KE* 292). In this context the virtues of "faithfulness, forgivingness, and mutually respective justice and enduring loyalty" are critical for shaping a good sexual character (*KE* 292). Sexual expression is meant to bring about the one-flesh union between a male and a female in the context of a committed covenant relationship. Any sexual expression that occurs outside of a heterosexual marital covenant runs counter to God's purposes (or God's law). Such expressions include casual or promiscuous premarital sex among heterosexuals as well as homosexual sexual activity.

Given that this case study addresses the issue of same-sex marriage, the question of the evangelical position on homosexuality comes to the fore. Stassen and Gushee state the question this way: "What shall we say to, and about, men and women who (a) experience their sexual desire as being insistently directed to members of the same sex; and (b) desire to bond with a member of the same sex in the same kind of permanent faithful monogamy that some heterosexuals enjoy?" (*KE* 310). The initial answer to these questions from both evangelical ethical stances is reflected in the position stated by Stassen and Gushee: "Homosexual conduct is one form of sexual expression that falls outside the will of God, one manifestation of . . . the disordered human condition under the impact of sin" (*KE* 311). Davis agrees that the fallen nature of humanity has had a negative impact on all expressions of human sexuality: "Homosexuality is simply one expression among many of the basic disordering of human life; all lust, whether heterosexual or homosexual, violates the divine law and reflects man's fallen nature. The Bible looks not to the social environment for the source of the human dilemma, but to the heart of man himself" (*EE4* 115). Likewise, Stassen and Gushee agree that every aspect of the human person is both created good and also corrupted by sin, and that is why they place sexuality in the context of God's purposes in salvation: "Redeemed sexuality is part of the reign of God and depraved sexuality marks a setback for that reign wherever it appears" (*KE* 311).

Each of these evangelical ethics traditions highlights the biological, cultural, and biblical questions surrounding homosexual practices. Davis contends that they are a deviation from the perspective of the creation of society. "From a purely biological perspective, it is clear that any human society that did not encourage heterosexual marriage and childbearing over homosexual activity would, in the course of time, fail to reproduce itself" (*EE4* 108). Moreover, he points to cross-cultural studies that illustrate that heterosexual, monogamous expressions of sexuality are what has allowed cultures to flourish. Any other form would be counterproductive to the well-being of society (*EE4* 109). Davis also addresses the issue of what causes homosexual orientation. Based on his review of several studies on sexual attraction, he concludes that the "implication of such results is that sexual attraction can, to a significant degree, be a socially learned response, rather than an orientation fixed from the outset by genetic or hormonal factors alone" (*EE4* 111). He highlights other studies that have suggested that "sexual orientation can, at least in some cases, be reversed" (*EE4* 126). He rejects the argument that the Bible does not address the issue of "constitutional homosexuality," which is intrinsic to the personality of homosexual persons and thus not morally blameworthy (*EE4* 123). Instead, he argues that one's actions come from the heart and that the Bible condemns the lust that is part of homosexual practices. "In the biblical outlook, a recognition of the fallen nature is not intended to provide man with an excuse for unlawful behavior, but to bring him to a recognition of his need for the redemptive grace of God, which can liberate him from moral and spiritual bondage" (*EE4* 124). Citing the "creation norms" of the original male-female distinction in Genesis, he argues that the norms apply to all humanity through general revelation, whether they are believers or not. Thus, he finds uniformity in the biblical and cultural rejection of homosexuality as contrary to the divine will. Regarding behavior toward homosexuals within their midst, he writes: "It would seem that a properly balanced response on the part of the church would require at least two key elements: firm biblical teaching and meaningful personal support for the homosexual who seeks to overcome such an orientation, or to remain celibate if the hoped-for change has not occurred" (*EE4* 125). At the same time, the Church should also recognize that homosexuality is not an unforgiveable sin.

What does this mean for Christians in the public sphere regarding the rights of homosexuals not to be discriminated against? In the 2004 edition of his book, Davis states: "Christians cannot consistently support making a civil *right* of that which the Scriptures teach to be morally *wrong*. . . . A moral *wrong* can never become the basis of a civil *right*" (*EE3* 135). Rights are based on the dignity of the human person as made in the image of God. Homosexuality is not a human good "but a sinful disordering of human nature as originally intended by God" (*EE3* 135). At that time he would affirm some civil rights but not a civil right that enshrines their sinful behavior in an institution as significant as marriage. Instead, he claimed that it would be appropriate for Christians to seek public legislation that would forbid homosexuality as a way of life (*EE3* 25).

In 2015, however, in the next edition of his book, Davis exhibits a change of heart as to where he thinks Christians should expend their energy in the public square. He sees the legalization of same-sex marriage in the United States by the Supreme Court as an "egregious break" with traditional understandings of the nature of marriage (*EE4* 128), and as part of the "end of Christendom" that is one outcome of the long process of secularization that has occurred in this country. In response, he writes that "evangelical Christians can and should continue to hold to the historic biblical teachings on human sexuality . . . recognizing that the legal norms of a secular, pluralistic state differ from the standards for believers in the church" (*EE4* 129). In this post-Christian cultural context Davis suggests that instead of public opposition to same-sex marriage, "Christians would perhaps be wiser to concentrate their time and energy on making their own marriages and sexual behaviors more congruent with the high standards of Scripture and the gospel" (*EE4* 129).

Stassen and Gushee also review the biological, cultural, and biblical issues and express more sympathy for those who seek the ethical legitimacy of homosexual practices. While they agree that biblical references do condemn certain homosexual acts, they claim that the Bible does not address the issue of sexual orientation and that Jesus says nothing at all about homosexuality. They also doubt that God will change a person's sexual orientation with proper prayerful effort on the believer's part. In fact, they suggest that the Christian church has spent an inordinate amount of time and energy on this issue, often in overly judgmental ways, while neglecting other actions to live out the reign of God in their midst. "Spending one's life crusading against homosexuals, as some Christians do, hardly fits with the virtues of love, kindness, humility, peace and patience that are to characterize the followers of Christ" (*KE* 311). They applaud efforts to bring homosexual relationships in line with the norms of mutuality and fidelity reflective of monogamous marriage even though they initially do not support same-sex marriage. However, they reject any effort on the part of Christians or others to deny the rights of gays and lesbians to safety, jobs, housing, government, or other means to participate fully in American society. "We must love homosexual persons while remaining clear in our convictions about God's intentions for human sexuality—and equally clear that all of us stand guilty and in need of redemption" (*KE* 311).

In the second edition of *Kingdom Ethics*, published in 2017, Gushee and Stassen rethink their stance on the issue of homosexuality and same-sex marriage. Part of the reason is because they see that in the American context to demand equal dignity in society and equal protection before the law, as the Supreme Court decision sought to do, is the direction we are moving "no matter how uncomfortable some Christians are about these developments" (*KE2* 153). More important, however, they claim that their change in perspective is in response to numerous "transformative" encounters with God, "and with the humanity and suffering and dignity of those made in God's image, especially those previously marginalized or rejected, more especially those so mistreated by God's own people" (*KE2* 152). Gushee rejects two sexual ethics that some Christians, gay and straight, have developed: the *mutual consent ethic*, which affirms sexual expression as long as it is consensual and no one is harmed; and the *loving relationship ethic*, where couples in love restrict their sexual activity to one another as long as the relationship lasts.[14] Instead, he adopts what he calls a revisionist evangelical position, where it is morally permissible in God's sight for gay and lesbian people to enter marital covenantal same-sex relationships. "We believe that the Bible makes room for both celibate singleness and faithful monogamy as equally legitimate expressions of human sexuality for those who would follow Jesus" (*KE2* 152). Gushee rejects conservative claims that challenging the sexual complementarity of divine intent in creation goes against the biblical teaching in favor of what Davis calls "shifting currents of human opinion and fashion" (*EE4* 127). Rather, Gushee concludes, "if what we are talking about is carving out space for serious committed Christians who happen to be gay or lesbian to participate in society as equals and in church as kin, I now think that has nothing to do with cultural, ecclesial, and moral decline, and everything to do with treating people the way Christ did" (*KE2* 154).

FEMINIST LIBERATIVE ETHICS

As noted in Chapter 1, feminist Christian ethicist Beverly Harrison makes clear that justice for women and others who live on the margins of society should be of central importance for all Christian ethicists. So, when assessing the question of the morality of same-sex marriage, not only would she review the form and function of marriage and the nature and purpose of sexuality, she would also explore the justice implications of both. Is marriage, whether opposite-sex or same-sex, an institution where justice prevails? If not, what qualities of relationship would be required to change the institution so that she might advocate for it?

Many gays and lesbians are wary of affirming same-sex marriage because they find that the current structure of marriage in the United States does not lend itself to just relationships. Harrison has some of those same concerns. When viewing any case from the perspective of feminist ethics, but especially this case, it is important to remember that the starting point is to pay attention to the concrete well-being of people, especially those who have experienced oppression and marginalization. Harrison writes in her essay "The Power of Anger in the Work of Love" that "A genuine liberation perspective is account-able to a praxis that gives priority to the concrete well-being of people, and so its starting point also must be concrete" (*MC* 243).[15] The focus must be on securing justice for the marginalized and their full participation in institutions

---

[14] David Gushee, *Changing Our Mind*, 3rd ed. (Canton, MI: Read the Spirit Books, 2017), 101.

[15] To develop Harrison's views we draw on her *Making the Connections: Essays in Feminist Social Ethics*, ed. Carol S. Robb (Boston: Beacon Press, 1985) (hereafter cited as *MC*); and *Justice in the Making: Feminist Social Ethics*, ed. Elizabeth M. Bounds et al. (Louisville, KY: Westminster John Knox Press, 2004) (hereafter cited as *JM*).

and society. God's justice, in her view, means right relationship that enables a genuine abundance of life that "comes from embodying a solidarity with one another that is deeply mutual" (*JM* 65). In the case of marriage in the United States, the groups most marginalized have been women, gays, and lesbians. We should not romanticize marriage and family, as many Christian ethicists have done, because these are not always places where love, mutuality, and justice prevail, but rather where a great deal of violence and abuse often occurs (*JM* 61). The heteronormative, patriarchal structure of marriage and traditional gender socialization have led to the dominance of heterosexual men and the undermining of the moral agency of others. Instead, Harrison claims that a Christian sexual ethic, if it is going to be adequate, must make the connection between the private and social realms of our experience. "All distortions of power in society reveal themselves in the inequity of power dynamics in interpersonal life" (*MC* 90). Thus, our capacity for love and intimacy and our efforts for justice go together (*MC* 83). Of course, the impetus for change in these institutions must come from the experiences of those who have been marginalized by them: "Women are invited to revision our own being as self-directed, sensuous body-selves, as those who can and must direct our self-expression as sexual beings who are responsible *agents*" (*JM* 57–58). She goes further to claim: "Our society's fears regarding human sexuality and the widespread, confused, and phobic anxieties about same-sex eroticism, together with the disordered relations between men and women generated by deep inequalities of power and respect, are a major source of our inability to tolerate diversity and difference in this world" (*MC* 144).

A key reason for this sex negativity and deep inequalities, Harrison contends, is the dualism that has been part of the historical Christian understanding of human sexuality. Where does this pervasive sex negativity and fear of the power of sexuality come from? She credits James Nelson's *Embodiment: An Approach to Sexuality and Christian Theology* with highlighting two dualisms that have embedded themselves in Christian views of sexuality.[16] One is the spiritualistic dualism where persons are body and spirit (or body and mind) not as an integral unity but rather as an uneasy amalgam. This dualism prizes the spirit or mind as superior and sees anything associated with the body as inferior and the source of temptation and evil. Because of this inferiority, the church fathers could only justify sex for the purposes of procreation. At the same time, the other dualism, gender dualism, holds males as superior to females because of women's association with the less significant aspects of our persons: our sexuality, our bodies, and our closeness with nature. As a result, women were viewed as less capable, less intelligent, and in need of male guidance and control. Good women could either be pious ascetics, which enabled them to overcome their temptress nature, or faithful mothers. Male reality became normatively human, thus guaranteeing male gender

---

[16] James Nelson, *Embodiment: An Approach to Sexuality and Christian Theology* (Minneapolis: Augsburg Press, 1979).

superiority. Protestant Christians believed they had overcome these dualisms because they rejected sexual asceticism by embracing marriage almost as a duty. But their approach did not overcome the negative view of sexuality or of the inferiority of women. With the addition of the unitive function, the role of sexuality was more than procreation, but this was because the marital relationship became "the central, sacralizing institution" in their faith tradition. Yet many Protestants continued to relegate women in the church and in society to an inferior position and highlighted masculine heterosexuality as normative (*JM* 56–59).

Harrison argues that because of these dualistic developments, Christian churches have not adequately developed an appropriate sexual ethic. Instead, she says, "a holistic approach to sexuality, free of the body/mind dualism that sustains patriarchy, will yield a rather simple ethic, one foundationally grounded in mutual respect" (*MC* 149). What does it mean to be an embodied sexual being? Our sexuality is a basic dimension of our personhood, our self-understanding, and our way of being in the world. It is "our embodied, sensuous capacity for relationship" (*MC* 63) and "our connection to all things as female or as male" (*JM* 58). Like Stassen and Gushee, Harrison agrees that sexuality is a gift from God, but we can only recognize this gift when we explore more fully our sexual intimacy grounded in our bodies—sexuality that involves pleasure and erotic intensity as well as "expresses playfulness, tenderness, and a generalized sense of well-being," no matter if one is heterosexual or homosexual (*MC* 114). The theological and ethical principles espoused by feminist and gay ethicists, which include the goodness of sexuality as embodiment, respect for bodily integrity, and self-direction in expressing sexuality, are not just good for women, gays, and lesbians but "are constitutive of everyone's human dignity" (*MC* 88). Thus, she argues against normative heterosexuality as a Christian sexual ethic. Rather, "we must find our way to valuing, celebrating and making normative all deep, respectful, sensuous, empowering relationships, which, wherever they exist, ground our well-being and the bonds of mutual respect" (*MC* 62–63).

Harrison also rejects the idea perpetrated by some Christian traditions that the only fully moral sexual experiences are those that are open to procreation. "The feminist insight is that sexuality is mutual pleasuring in the context of genuine openness and intimacy. That such communication is of 'ultimate value' only when it is shared by procreative potential or procreative intent . . . is simply lingering male supremacist doctrine that reinforces male control of women's self-definition" (*MC* 87). Such control has been a negative experience for women, losing sight of their own moral agency for the sake of some notion of what it means to be a "good" woman. Instead, women, gays, and lesbians need the freedom to understand and direct their own sexuality and to enable their power "as self-regulating moral agents" (*MC* 87). It is this freedom to explore one's sexuality in mutually intimate encounters that promotes the well-being of persons in relationship, where each has the power to affect and be affected by the other. "When we encounter these others as willing our good and we respond by willing their well-being, the 'realm of God'—the power of relation—is released, and mutual well-being enhanced" (*JM* 61).

Harrison also questions the view, advocated by both conservative and progressive evangelicals, that the only appropriate place to engage in sexual activity is within a marital covenant relationship. She writes: "Honoring the decisions regarding sexual expression between consenting adults is not a negative moral norm but a positive value. We ought to possess the conditions for unconstrained expressions of intimacy" (*MC* 113). Such repression undermines our sexual integrity and generates a host of other problems. In the same way that unavailability of marriage penalized same-sex couples, "so our all-or-nothing approach to marriage works to discourage mature, step-by-step relational commitments" (*MC* 109). Thus, while she would agree with Gushee's revisionist evangelical position that affirms same-sex marriage, she would take issue with his rejection of mutual consent and loving relationship ethics. Whether heterosexual or homosexual, Harrison writes, "I do not believe that a sexual ethic can any longer give direct, or even indirect, support to the notion that living one's life in the heterosexual, lifelong family unit places one in a status of special moral merit or that this lifestyle warrants superior theological legitimation" (*MC* 108). She is supportive of long-term committed relationships because they can provide a good environment for personal growth for the partners as well as the children. So, those who choose the possibility of a longer-term same-sex marital arrangement "should be encouraged as positive and ethically appropriate" (*MC* 109). Social policy should be supportive of these unions, as the Supreme Court has been in its ruling legalizing same-sex marriage throughout the United States. But she rejects the idea that the marital covenantal structure of marriage and family should be held up as a normative ideal. "We need to recognize that marriage is not for everyone. At the same time, we can and should affirm, celebrate, and support all covenantal relationships that deepen our capacity for intimacy, creative work, and joyful community, whether or not they accord with the current legally permissible definitions of marriage" (*MC* 110). The choice of the structure of those other living arrangements and covenant commitments should be left to the partners involved.

While many raise concerns about the appropriateness of same-sex families as places for rearing children, Harrison wonders why opposite-sex families do not come under the same scrutiny, especially since many of these marriages are loveless and unstable. The question regarding parenting for Harrison is not one of form but of function; that is, any judgments about the competence of parenting should be made based on actual performance rather than on stereotypes or homophobia (*MC* 107). In that regard, she notes, same-sex married couples are performing as well if not better because of the struggles they have endured and their conscious self-awareness of the need to be good parents.

Finally, while acknowledging with the evangelical ethics tradition that government has a positive role to play in enabling the stability and growth of covenantal relationships, Harrison contends that government should play no role in determining appropriate expressions of sexuality as it has historically done in deeming certain sexual acts between consenting adults as immoral and/or illegal. Rather, Harrison is advocating for sexual freedom in this regard. When it comes to the question of what to do with those marital arrangements that fail, as can often happen in both opposite- and same-sex marriages, she applauds those states that allow no-fault divorce laws because they are both less costly and move away from efforts to lay blame on one partner or the other for a failed marriage. Sometimes marriages just fail, and removing as much animosity and government intrusion in matters related to intimacy to support the dignity and well-being of the persons involved is best for all concerned (*MC* 110).

RESOURCES

Discussion Questions

1. How should Christians attempt to influence public policies and laws in the context of a pluralistic society and the separation of church and state? Should, for example, Christians make a distinction between definitions of marriage for Christians in the church and the legal definition of marriage for a secular state?

2. When addressing the case of same-sex marriage, Beverly Harrison wants to begin with the issue of injustice in the dominant form of hetero-sexual marriage. Why is this the case? What notion of justice is implicit in her view? How does this differ from the perspective of the evangelical ethics traditions discussed?

3. Stassen and Gushee and Harrison affirm the importance of the "reign" and "realm" of God in their assessment of the morality of same-sex marriage. What do they mean by this? How are their views similar? How are they different?

4. Evangelical Christians are judgmental of today's "hookup" culture and the notion that sexual activity between consenting adults without any commitment is ethical if sex is mutual and does no harm to either partner. What are the reasons for their condemnation? Do you agree? Why or why not? What norms do you think are appropriate for sexual activity? What would Harrison say?

5. While many gays and lesbians celebrate the legalization of same-sex marriage in the United States, not all members of the LGBTQ community are advocates for same-sex marriage. What are their objections to marriage? Do you agree with their perspectives?

Activities

1. Do an analysis of the Supreme Court decision in *Obergefell v. Hodges*. Compare and contrast the positions of the majority versus the minority. Where do they agree? Where do they disagree? With which position do you identify? Why?

2. Research how two of the books in the reading list (or books of your own choosing) understand the form and functions of marriage. Compare their views with those of the evangelical and feminist ethics models. Create a presentation to share with your class. Be sure to highlight which model or models you think create the stronger argument.

3. Read through the biblical texts that some Christians suggest make homosexuality unethical (Gen 19:1–11; Lev 18:22; Lev 20:13; Judg 19; Rom 1:26–27; 1 Cor 6:9; and 1 Tim 1:10). Write an analysis of what you think the texts say. Read one or more commentaries on the texts to see what they claim the texts are about. Report your findings to your classmates.

4. Have a debate on the following claim: The only appropriate Christian sexual ethic, whether gay or straight, is one that takes place in the context of a marital covenantal relationship. Draw from both the evangelical ethics and the feminist ethics discussed above. Make sure that participants outline clearly the arguments for and against this stance.

5. Watch one or more of the films listed below. Analyze the films to discern the approach the filmmaker takes on the moral issue in question. How are the ethical issues illustrated? Where do the films fall short in raising the ethical concerns? How would evangelical and feminist ethics analyze the film?

Readings

Boswell, John. *Same-Sex Unions in Premodern Europe*. New York: Villard Books, 1994. This controversial book produces dramatic evidence that at one time the Catholic and Eastern Orthodox churches not only sanctioned unions between partners of the same sex but sanctified them—in ceremonies strikingly similar to heterosexual marriage ceremonies.

Douglas, Kelly Brown. *Sexuality and the Black Church: A Womanist Perspective*. Maryknoll, NY: Orbis Books, 1999. This book tackles the subject of sexuality, which has long been avoided by the Black Church and community. The author argues that this view of black sexuality has interfered with constructive responses to the AIDS crisis and teenage pregnancies, fostered intolerance of sexual diversity, frustrated healthy male/female relationships, and rendered black and womanist theologians silent on sexual issues.

Ellison, Marvin M. *Same-Sex Marriage? A Christian Ethical Analysis*. Cleveland: Pilgrim Press, 2004. A gay man and progressive Christian ethicist who places justice-making at the heart of contemporary spirituality examines the strengths and weaknesses of how marriage traditionalists, advocates of same-sex marriage, and LGBT critics of marriage analyze the issues and frame their arguments.

Farley, Margaret A. *Just Love: A Framework for Christian Sexual Ethics*. New York: Continuum, 2006. Farley, a Roman Catholic ethicist and Sister of Mercy, proposes a framework for sexual ethics whereby justice is the criterion for all loving, including love that is related to sexual activity and relationships. The Vatican Congregation on the Doctrine of the Faith said in 2010 that her theological rationale for same-sex relationships, masturbation, and remarriage after divorce are not in keeping with official church teaching.

Nelson, James. *Embodiment: An Approach to Sexuality and Christian Theology*. Minneapolis: Augsburg Press, 1979. Nelson challenges the historical Christian dualistic view of sexuality and explores what it means to emphasize the embodied nature of our sexuality for our understandings of Christian sexual ethics.

Audiovisuals

Boy Erased. Focus Features, 2018. Written and directed by Joel Edgerton and starring Nicole Kidman, this film explores the story of the son of a Baptist preacher who is forced to participate in a church-supported, gay conversion program after being forcibly outed to his parents.

Loving. Raindog Films, 2016. This film, directed by Jeff Nichols and starring Ruth Negga and Joel Edgerton, tells the story of Richard and Mildred Loving, whose arrest for interracial marriage in the 1960s in Virginia began a legal battle that would end with the Supreme Court's historic 1967 decision *Loving v. Virginia*, which invalidated state laws prohibiting interracial marriage.

The Case Against 8. HBO Films, 2014. This documentary, directed by Ben Cotner and Ryan White, chronicles the efforts to overturn the California ballot initiative known as Proposition 8, which outlawed same-sex marriage. Shot over five years, the film follows the unlikely team of lawyers, Ted Olson and David Boies, who took the first federal marriage-equality lawsuit to the US Supreme Court.

The Kids Are All Right. Focus Features, 2010. Directed by Lisa Cholodenko and starring Annette Bening and Julianne Moore as a same-sex couple raising two teenagers conceived by artificial insemination, this film won the 2011 Golden Globe Award for Best Picture in Musical or Comedy and was nominated for Best Picture at the 2011 Academy Awards.

We Do. CT Media Distribution, 2015. This documentary, directed by Rebecca Rice, details the stories of three LGBTQ couples, their journeys for legal recognition of their relationships, and the impact that the pursuit of marriage equality has had on their lives before and after the Supreme Court ruling in 2015.

3

Corporate Responsibility

CASE STUDY:
NIKE AND SWEATSHOP LABOR

The Nike Company, whose headquarters are in Beaverton, Oregon, is a very successful brand whose website claims that it is "the world's leading innovator in athletic footwear, apparel, equipment and accessories." In 2019, the company boasted of revenues in excess of $39 billion. The company was cofounded as Blue Ribbon Sports by Phil Knight and his former University of Oregon track coach, Bill Bowerman, as an importer and distributor of Japanese track shoes made by Onitsuka Company, Ltd., of Kobe, Japan. In 1971 they changed the name to Nike and adopted the world-recognized Swoosh logo designed by Carolyn Davidson. "She designed the simple logo in 1971, while she was still a graphic design student at Portland State University.... She was paid $2/hour for her work, for a grand total of only *$35*."[1] In 1985, Nike created the athletic shoe Air Jordan, named after then-NBA-rookie Michael Jordan, which has become the best-selling shoe of all time. With the signing of Tiger Woods in 1996 to sponsor Nike Golf, the rest, as they say, is history.

From the beginning Nike used subcontractors to produce its shoes, apparel, and equipment, beginning in Taiwan and Korea and then moving to such Asian countries as China, Indonesia, and Vietnam, where unemployment and under-employment were high and wages were low compared to US standards (less than $1 per hour). As one might expect, the host countries were eager to attract the economic benefits such foreign investment would bring, such as helping to provide jobs to their workers and raising living standards. The problem was that not only were wages extremely low (although better than what might be earned through farming), but the workers, including children, often labored in unhealthy and unsafe working environments (for example,

---

[1] Matt Cannon, "Creative Titans: Carolyn Davidson and the Nike Swoosh," Branding Times/Works Design Group blog, February 5, 2014.

using toxic glues and chemicals without proper masks or gloves). Workers' rights, such as the right to organize and bargain collectively, were nonexistent, not supported, or actively repressed.[2]

In the 1990s Nike came under fire because it did not manufacture its products in the United States, because it paid such low wages overseas, and because it turned a blind eye to the working conditions in these host countries.[3] At first, Nike defended its actions. It did have two factories in the United States from 1977 to 1984 but closed them when they became unprofitable because of worker competition. Moreover, Phil Knight contends that Nike's experiences led it to believe in the benefits of international trade: not only did it uplift impoverished people, but it also produced better values for consumers in industrialized nations and increased understandings between peoples of different cultures.[4] Given that the factories in Asia employed over a half million people, there were bound to be incidents, but Knight believed that these were minimal; Nike implemented a code of conduct for its factories that would be monitored by a reputable accounting firm.

However, continued reporting of child-labor abuses and poor working conditions in Nike factories by the media caught the attention of human rights groups and consumers around the globe.[5] The question of corporate social responsibility for the welfare of workers versus profitability and economic responsibility to shareholders was raised. In 1997, Nike was given reports outlining the human rights and labor violations being committed in its factories with recommendations on how to stop them.[6] At that point, it became clear that in order to protect the Nike image, which was central to its ability to sell its products, it would have to make changes to remedy the problems.[7] In response, the corporation stopped the use of toxic chemicals that were causing harm to workers. It instituted minimum age requirements to end or minimize the use of child labor. It expanded educational programs available to all workers. And it increased its support to micro-lending programs that

---

[2] See George H. Sage, "Justice Do It! The Nike Transnational Advocacy Network: Organization, Collective Actions, and Outcomes," *Sociology of Sport Journal* 16/3 (1999): 206–35.

[3] Max Nisen, "How Nike Solved Its Sweatshop Problem," *Business Insider* (May 9, 2013).

[4] Phil Knight, speech, May 12, 1998, excerpted in Matt Wilsey and Scott Lichtig, "The Nike Controversy," September 12, 2012.

[5] One such consumer group is United Students against Sweatshops, which since its beginning in 1997 has tried to hold multinational companies like Nike accountable for working conditions where most college apparel is produced.

[6] Keith Hammond, "Leaked Audit: Nike Factory Violated Worker Laws," *Mother Jones* (November 7, 1997). See also César Rodríguez-Garavito, "Global Governance and Labor Rights: Codes of Conduct and Anti-Sweatshop Struggles in Global Apparel Factories in Mexico and Guatemala," *Politics and Society* 33/2 (2005): 203–23.

[7] Many human rights groups challenged Nike's tagline, "Just do it!" with one of their own, "Just don't do it!" (Sage, "Justice Do It").

provided loans to women in these countries to start small businesses that would improve the economic well-being of their families and communities.[8]

While these changes were praised by some human rights groups as steps in the right direction, others were concerned that they did not address two central issues for workers: living wages that allowed workers to meet their basic needs, and the ability to organize and bargain collectively. Nike promised to pay minimum or prevailing wage rates in the host countries. However, these were often set too low by those countries in order to attract foreign investment. In many of the host countries the right to form independent unions did not exist, and workers who tried were often jailed. Without concerted effort by Nike and other international corporations, these conditions would not change, and many believe that corporations have little incentive to change them because they would jeopardize their cheap labor force and their profitability.

Concerns about sweatshop labor continue to plague the garment industry, as demonstrated by the April 2013 collapse of the Rana Plaza garment factory in Bangladesh, which killed over one thousand workers.[9] They also exist for the technology industry; for example, poor working conditions in the Foxconn factory in China that manufactures such products as the iPhone and the iPad have brought Apple under scrutiny.[10] These examples reveal the tension between consumer demand for lower prices and ever newer products, shareholder requirements for healthy returns on their investments, and corporate responsibility for the welfare of workers. The Nike case illustrates that the combination of awareness of problems, external pressure of human rights and consumer organizations for change, and a willingness to modify corporate policies can have some positive, although perhaps limited, impact on worker conditions in overseas factories.

ISSUES AND CONCERNS

Sweatshop labor cases raise several important issues for our global economy. First, what is the social responsibility of corporations? For advocates of capitalism and free market enterprise, as Nobel laureate Milton Friedman stated in 1962, "there is one and only one social responsibility of business— to use its resources and engage in activities designed to increase its profits. . . . Few trends could so thoroughly undermine the very foundations of our free society as the acceptance by corporate officials of a social responsibility

---

[8] See Dietlind Stolle and Michele Micheleti, *Political Consumerism: Global Responsibility in Action* (Cambridge, UK: Cambridge University Press, 2013), chap. 6.

[9] For more on this, see International Labour Organization, "The Rana Plaza Accident and Its Aftermath," ilo.org.

[10] See Charles Duhigg and David Barboza, "In China, Human Costs Are Built into an iPad," *New York Times,* January 22, 2012.

other than to make as much money for their stockholders as possible."[11] To maximize profits requires doing so in the most cost-efficient manner possible. In the Nike case, the company made decisions designed to find the most flexible labor environments for manufacturing their products. If it abided by the local laws and did not intentionally harm its workers, it believed it was doing nothing wrong. It resisted any efforts to expand its role to include other things it considered extraneous to its mission. Others disagreed. They believed that given the power of multinational corporations in the global economy, they have the responsibility to press the locations in which they operate to provide better, safer working conditions for their employees. While Nike did develop a code of conduct by which it expected each subcontractor to abide, many questioned the auditing practices that were supposed to enforce the code and to hold those factories accountable when violations occurred.

The case also illustrates the disparity in the power between capital and labor. Nike was able to move its financial capital to production facilities overseas where labor conditions, in terms of wages and safety regulations, were more favorable to its bottom line. Labor is less mobile, especially in the global marketplace. Closing a factory in the United States means a loss of jobs for the workers and the community. Loose labor markets, where there are too many workers for too few jobs, are also subject to coercive practices. Many of the locations wanted Nike's business for economic development. They were willing to restrict wages and various worker safety regulations in order to attract the economic benefits. While the jobs generally paid better than other work available to the local population, it was difficult to demand better wages and working conditions because workers could easily be fired and replaced. In some instances they were even beaten and jailed.[12]

The issue of wages highlights the different views on who should set wage rates and the fairness of those wages. Many economists and corporations believe that the market should set wage levels. This often means that there should be no minimum wage. If a worker accepts a contract at a particular wage, then the wage is fair and just. Opponents question the fairness of such arrangements, especially in a context where the power of capital over labor is strong and where wages are insufficient to meet worker needs. Minimum wage laws are established by states to provide some equivalence of power between capital and labor and to ensure some basic minimum to meet workers' needs. Labor unions and collective bargaining are also mechanisms to do the same.

The case also raises issues about worker safety. In the United States there are worker safety laws to protect workers from unsafe working conditions, many emerging as a result of significant disasters such as the 1911 Triangle Shirtwaist Factory fire in Manhattan, in which 146 garment workers died

---

[11] Milton Friedman, *Capitalism and Freedom* (Chicago: University of Chicago Press, 1962), 133.

[12] See "Nike Workers 'Kicked, Slapped, and Verbally Abused' at Factories Making Converse," *Daily Mail,* July 13, 2011. This article is about working conditions at a Nike factory in Indonesia.

because the owners had ordered the doors to stairwells and exits locked to keep workers from taking unauthorized breaks. These laws are not always followed, as the Massey Mine disaster in West Virginia and the Deepwater Horizon platform explosion, both in April 2010, make clear. But in developing countries desperate for economic development, such laws may not be in place or, if they are, they may be ignored. The Bangladesh garment factory disasters in 2012 and 2013 are illustrative of this reality.

The case also raises the question of the nature and purpose of work.[13] Work is important for the personhood of each human being. At the most basic level, work is the way that people fulfill their material needs. Harnessing nature for food, clothing, and shelter is work. However, the good of work for each person means more. To be a person means that one is purposive, creative, and self-transcendent. The activities through which the individual expresses and realizes these aspects of his or her personhood are properly called work. Work is also a means to express one's social nature. It is a fundamental activity through which individuals relate to one another. A lack of work severs an important linkage with others in the life of society, a reality that the 2020 coronavirus pandemic and the need for physical and social distancing made abundantly clear. Finally, work is a means by which to enhance the community. Through one's work, one creates the material and social conditions needed not only for one's own well-being but also for the well-being of the communities of which one is a member, such as family, neighborhood, nation, and even the whole human community. Lack of work restricts meaningful participation in important areas of society, denies opportunities to develop one's creative and moral potential, and leads one to question one's usefulness and worth.

Such a broad view of work includes many activities that are currently unpaid in the labor market, such as voluntary work and housework, as well as many forms of leisure. Thus, work is not equivalent to paid employment. There are also some forms of paid activity that are so dehumanizing or destructive of community that they cannot be considered work; they should either be humanized or not done. On the individual level, paid employment is a curse for some because it does not provide for their material needs (for example, low-wage employment) or does not provide the opportunity to develop (for example, "make work"). On the level of community some paid work, such as selling drugs, harms individuals and destroys whole communities. The paid work in this ethical case demonstrates both the possibilities and pitfalls of work in the global economy.

In this case we also see the valuable—some would say questionable—role that human rights and consumer watchdog groups play in efforts to generate a fairer global economy.[14] The extensive use, even abuse, of child labor in the factories making Nike products was brought to light through these

---

[13] This discussion of work draws from my essay "Desperate Exchanges: Secondary Work, Justice, and Public Policy," *The Annual of the Society of Christian Ethics* 12 (1992): 225–44.

[14] See, for example, the Worker Rights Consortium website.

groups' efforts. Most Americans believe that children should be able to attend school and should not be coerced into working long hours in often dangerous conditions. They believe that companies selling products in the United States should make sure that the production of those products should limit such abuse as much as possible. Nike's first response was that it was simply abiding by child labor laws in those countries. However, pressure by human rights and consumer groups threatened Nike's image, especially since so much of its footwear and apparel is marketed to children and adolescents in the United States. Eventually, Nike established minimum age requirements in its factories, which sometimes were greater than those established by the country. Opponents of this move suggest that the result was a loss of income for families who depended on the labor of their children.

Finally, this case illustrates the potential problems of a global economy based on consumption, the prevalence of consumerism, and the disparity in consumption of resources. *Consumerism* refers to the desire for more, newer, and better goods, often driven by seductive marketing and advertising. People desire the newest Air Jordans, the newest iPhone, or the latest fashions. The negative effects of consumerism are multiple. It can lead to greater debt on the part of consumers, especially those of limited means, whose "needs" are shaped by cultural norms even if the result is forgoing some other necessities. Consumerism can result in overconsumption of valuable resources, as when people discard fully functional and usable goods in favor of their newest counterparts, contributing to growing stockpiles of waste products, while others struggle to meet basic needs. Because of the desire to have these goods as cheaply as possible, such consumerism can drive down wages and create the kinds of working conditions highlighted by this case.

PROGRESSIVE EVANGELICAL ETHICS

Recall that evangelicals, whether conservative or progressive, rely on biblical texts to develop their ethical principles in all social areas. Likewise, progressive evangelicals Glen Stassen and David Gushee explore what the Bible says about economic relationships, economic ethics, and economic justice; however, as noted in Chapter 1, they do so through the lens of Jesus's life and teaching found in the Gospels in general and in the Sermon on the Mount in particular. So, what does Jesus say about economic life? What principles can we glean from what the Gospels say about him? Stassen and Gushee contend that Jesus's focus is twofold: the economic behavior of people, especially those who claim the name Christian; and economic and distributive justice of communities, principles Jesus gleans from the perspective of the prophetic tradition in the Old Testament.

Stassen and Gushee highlight Jesus's teaching in the Sermon on the Mount to develop a basic orientation toward wealth and possessions. Where many Christians see some of the teachings in the sermon as hard teachings or ideals unattainable in this world, focused on attitudes but not necessarily on actions, Stassen and Gushee suggest that such Christians fail to see the true intent of the sermon. Instead of a twofold antithesis between a particular issue or problem that keeps people from obeying God's will and an impossible ideal to uphold, they see a threefold pattern that highlights some transforming initiatives that can help Jesus's followers to break free from the behavior that keeps them in sin and bondage. For example, in the case of one's basic orientation toward wealth and possessions, Jesus counsels: "Do not store up for yourselves treasures on earth," which Stassen and Gushee suggest refers to hoarding, greed, and stinginess. The reason is because such actions are folly in the long run: "where moth and rust consume and where thieves break in and steal" (Mt 6:19). Greed and hoarding generate a love for money and material possessions that undermines one's commitment to God's reign and to acting generously toward one's neighbor.[15] Stassen and Gushee are critical of the consumerism that they suggest "constitutes our national religion" (*KE* 426).[16] It is part of the bondage that many people experience. They speak of how in the American context people are bombarded with sophisticated and seductive inducements to think of their desire for the latest gadgets and products not as wants but as needs that must be fulfilled as quickly as possible, even if it means going into tremendous debt or if the competition to produce those goods means ignoring the justice owed to workers in terms of wages and safe working conditions. "If Christian ethics is following Jesus," they argue, "it must involve a clear-eyed analysis and finally repudiation of an economic ethos that ratifies the 'deceitfulness of wealth' and makes Mammon the national idol" (*KE* 426). In other words, one cannot serve both God and money.

As a remedy for this bondage Jesus suggests that we "store up for yourselves treasures in heaven" (Mt 6:20). On the face of it, it seems that Jesus is drawing a contrast between this life and the life to come, and even encouraging a rejection of material possessions. But Stassen and Gushee say this is not the case. Rather, the contrast is between attitudes and behavior toward wealth and possessions that lead to misery and injustice, and attitudes and behavior characterized by God's reign of joy, justice, and peace. Like Jesus, Stassen and Gushee are concerned about greed, which they believe is a spiritual and moral disorder (*KE* 415). They believe that greed "leads to sins against one's neighbor" (*KE* 416). It leads to hoarding and a lack of generosity and blinds Christians to their moral responsibility to their neighbors. They are particularly troubled by the deceitful allure of wealth, which can lead people to misrepresent reality, "concealing or distorting the truth about something

---

[15] The images of senior citizens going to the supermarket to buy food or toilet paper during the 2020 coronavirus pandemic only to find the shelves empty because others chose to hoard them for themselves is a good illustration of the problem.

[16] Glen Stassen and David Gushee, *Kingdom Ethics: Following Jesus in Contemporary Context* (Downers Grove, IL: InterVarsity Press, 2003) (hereafter cited as *KE*). Note that a second edition was published in 2016.

for the purpose of misleading others" (*KE* 418). Some might ask whether this is what was going on with Nike in developing a blind eye to the problems that emerged. They suggest that Jesus's teaching is realistic: "Invest your possessions generously in God's reign of justice and mercy, and you will find your heart is invested there as well" (*KE* 411). The point is that becoming a disciple of Jesus reorients all of one's life toward God's reign of justice, including one's economic life. Storing one's treasures in heaven, the place of God's rule, provides the freedom and desire to bring about God's rule on this earth through one's attitudes and actions. Jesus identifies the problems of bondage that many experience in relation to wealth, but he also offers a realistic and transforming initiative that can help people break free from the cycle of bondage in which they are trapped. "The transforming initiative is to invest one's treasures in God's reign of justice and love through the practices of economic generosity and justice-making" (*KE* 411).

The teaching of Jesus not to worry about material possessions (Mt 6:25–33) is not to suggest that people who live in material comfort should simply learn to be satisfied with the possessions they have. Rather, given the economic exploitation present in Jesus's day (and, by extension, in our own), Jesus's focus was on "the kind of compassionate and merciful justice that delivers the poor from poverty and restores them into community" (*KE* 413). It is a call for disciples to become engaged in justice initiatives that address the poverty and oppression of the most economically and socially vulnerable. In other words, we should not worry about possessions, but we should use our possessions in a way that promotes economic justice for all. Thus, they summarize Jesus's teaching for Christians in the Sermon on the Mount this way: "Living simply, not hoarding wealth for ourselves and trusting God to meet our basic material needs are practices that free us to offer generosity to and seek justice for and with the poor and hungry" (*KE* 414).

Stassen and Gushee move from Christian attitudes and behavior toward wealth and possessions to more economic principles, such as distributive justice, private property, ownership, work, and economic systems. Gushee argues that Jesus, in line with the prophets of the Old Testament, "offered stark prophetic indictments of economic injustice, hurling his charges against the very centers of religious and political power of his time."[17] Gushee contends that Jesus's challenge to the temple system is critical to understanding this indictment. The religio-political aristocracy oversaw the temple system. These aristocrats generated little wealth, but they siphoned off products produced by the poor, the farmers, and the craftsmen to support their way of life. They were in collusion with the wealthy and with the Roman Empire to maintain these inequities. He notes thirty-nine times in the Gospels where

---

[17] David Gushee, "The Economic Ethics of Jesus," in *Faithful Economics: The Moral Worlds of a Neutral Science*, ed. James Henderson and John Pisciotta (Waco, TX: Baylor University Press, 2006), 119. This essay complements the progressive evangelical position he develops with Stassen in *Kingdom Ethics*.

Jesus confronts the powers and authorities of his day on the injustice of greed, domination, violence, and exclusion from community.

The fundamental economic principle Gushee draws from these biblical condemnations of injustice is just economic distribution, a key aspect of God's reign. "That is one absolutely essential contribution of justice in a sinful world where concentration of power needs restraint, checks and balances, and limits on greed. God's will for people cannot be fulfilled without justice."[18] In Stassen and Gushee's view a just economic distribution would mean that every person or family has access to enough productive resources to provide for material needs and to participate meaningfully in the life of the community (*KE* 421), which is in keeping with the prophetic tradition of the Old Testament. "The fight for distributive economic justice amidst varying levels of injustice is (sadly) a perennial aspect of human responsibility and a key dimension of the Christian ethical task" (*KE* 420).

Work is the fundamental means through which people contribute to their own development, to the well-being of their families, and to the common good. Private property provides incentive to work and, if we continue to meet our public ethical responsibilities, is legitimate in terms of justice. This does not mean that there should be equality of outcome, where everyone enjoys comparable economic well-being. Rather, the primary responsibility of a just economy in wealth creation "is not extravagant bounty for the few but access to economic opportunity and participation in economic community for the many" (*KE* 421). While the Nike business models and factories did provide some opportunities, the way they were structured did not allow for this to happen for all people.

When it comes to assessing economic systems, Stassen and Gushee realize that no economic system is perfect. There are benefits to liberal capitalism that cannot be ignored, including wealth creation, job opportunities, and the like. But they are critical of conservative evangelicals who have downplayed the systemic problems with this economic structure. In their view, the levels of wealth inequality within and between nations, exploitation of the poor by the rich and powerful, and the ever-growing rise of acquisitiveness and consumerism generated by liberal capitalism have negative cultural and moral ramifications that must be recognized and confronted (*KE* 424). This is especially true because their vision of God's reign is a reign of justice, especially for the poor and the vulnerable. They suggest: "The real debate in Christian economic ethics . . . is essentially over an analysis of the sources and extent of existing economic injustice and the right mix of strategies for addressing such injustice" (*KE* 424). They would favor a balanced capitalist system that includes (1) more aggressive government actions to bolster the economic empowerment of the poor and marginalized; and (2) revised international economic policies on the part of wealthy nations that reduce

---

[18] Ibid., 117.

their exploitative practices that consume excess amounts of resources and generate damage to communities and the environment.

So, what do Stassen and Gushee's perspective and principles suggest about the ethical issues of the Nike case? First, drawing on their point about the way the desire for wealth can contribute to self-deception, we can see a great deal of self-deception operative here. Nike executives said that they were unaware of the problems that were going on. They felt that by following the laws and norms of the countries where their products were manufactured, they were blameless. In addition, they felt that if companies followed their code of conduct, the problems would be lessened. However, as human rights groups illustrated, they ignored the injustices that were being perpetrated. Even the accounting practices designed to ensure proper following of the code of conduct were suspect. Instead of dealing with the issues as soon as they emerged and changing their business practices, they fought them until it was clear that the workplace problems would tarnish the image Nike was seeking to project and protect.

In addition, the case reflects the way in which unfettered market capitalism can lead to huge disparities in income and equality. As noted above, Stassen and Gushee are not seeking equality of outcome. However, their conception of distributive justice does require that work should produce enough remuneration to enable families to live in reasonable comfort. Their economic ethics also raises questions as to how wages are set. Liberal capitalism assumes that the market sets wage rates that are fair. But in a context where the money and power of the few can work against the interests of many, primarily workers, it is not clear that this is true. The wages in Nike factories may have been better than what families could get on subsistence farming, but they did not provide adequately for the workers and their families. Allowing the markets to set the wage rates, especially in contexts of political repression, would be deemed irresponsible. They would applaud the efforts on the part of Nike to establish minimum wage rates above what was the norm in these countries but would note that its commitment to its own wealth and well-being led it to act slowly and grudgingly.

In addition, if one is committed to distributive justice, Stassen and Gushee recognize that in our current climate and the reality of human sin, this only comes with a balance of power. One way to balance power is to allow workers to bargain collectively for wages and working conditions. Stassen and Gushee also endorse other governmental efforts to ensure the fairness and justice of the economic exchange and distribution. These efforts would include laws to make the workplace safe so that workers can develop their skills and provide for their families in reasonable safety. They would also endorse efforts by various activist initiatives and labor groups to challenge such practices and demand better wages and working conditions for all workers.

Because work is not simply for income but also for self-development, any situation where work is dangerous and undermines the capacities of workers is considered unjust. This is certainly the case for Nike workers and other workers in the garment industry, as the problems in Bangladesh make evident. Unsafe working conditions, excessive hours, and wage theft (such as requiring employees to work overtime but not paying them for that overtime, or charging excessive amounts of money for equipment and clothing) violate the kind of basic dignity of labor that the biblical account seeks. This is also true for child labor. Stassen and Gushee indicate that they favor governmental interventions in the operation of liberal market capitalism because they realize that this is the only way to produce the kind of justice that is part of God's reign. These would include minimum wage laws, worker safety laws, and child labor laws. They would not see this as an infringement on the free market but as frank recognition that market capitalism can and does generate unintended and unjust conditions.

They also would have an issue with the whole effort of marketing products to promote acquisitiveness and inordinate consumerism. For example, Nike shoes, such as the ones with an athletic celebrity's name attached, appeal to young people in low-income neighborhoods. The costs of Nike shoes and clothing are often beyond the scope of some of the families of these communities, and yet they are left to feel they need them to live a rewarding life relative to their peer groups and the culture at large. The insidious way in which advertisement and peer pressure works on the psyche of people is a problem for them. The result is often a conflict between what people need and what they can afford, with some choosing the shoes over basic necessities. Thus, while Stassen and Gushee would support Nike's right to exist and to develop, they would contend that it needs to demonstrate corporate responsibility to the world around it, especially to the people who produce and consume their products, rather than simply focusing on shareholders and profits.

HISPANIC LIBERATIVE ETHICS

Because Hispanic ethics is Christocentric, there is a great deal of overlap between this perspective and that of progressive evangelicals; for example, how each emphasizes the role of Jesus's teaching on ethical issues. However, based on the contextual aspect of Hispanic ethics, this tradition explores business ethics through the lens of those who have experienced marginalization at the hands of global economic forces and corporate actions. This means that the discussion of moral rights or what is owed to persons will be on the disenfranchised, which in this case are the workers, not the corporate leaders or the shareholders. As Miguel De La Torre notes, for those doing Christian ethics from the margins the focus "must be contextualized in *lo cotidiano*, the everyday experience of marginalized people, the subject and source for all ethical reflection."[19] So, when looking at the Nike case, the questions

---

[19] This discussion is drawn primarily from Miguel De La Torre, *Doing Ethics from the Margins*, 2nd ed. (Maryknoll, NY: Orbis Books, 2014) (hereafter cited as *DEM*).

become: What is happening to the workers who are suffering deprivations in wages, in workplace safety, and in other ways? What are the systemic forces perpetuating these injustices?

De La Torre begins by observing the nature of global corporations like Nike, Walmart, and Apple and how they operate in a global economy. One thing is clear: corporations are driven primarily by profit. De La Torre notes that many economists harken back to Scottish moral philosopher Adam Smith's idea of self-interest as the basis for corporate behavior: "It is not from the benevolence of the butcher, the brewer, or the baker from whom we expect our dinner, but from their regard for their own self-interest."[20] As noted above, conservative economist Milton Friedman brings this idea into the context of modern corporations by saying that the only social responsibility of corporations is to make as much money for the shareholders of the corporation within the bounds of the law. Wages and other benefits are not based on what a worker needs to live reasonably but on a corporation's desire to increase profits (*DEM* 73). Corporations provide those benefits that are required by law, but they are taking their marching orders from the corporate boards, not the workers. Thus, corporations are always in search of the cheapest labor markets and the least restrictive legal regulations in order to maximize their profits.

But what does it mean to stay within the bounds of the laws of society? Which laws should they follow? The laws of the country where their products are made? Or the laws where the products are sold? Given the effort on the part of Nike and other global corporations, the focus has been on the local laws, where wages are cheaper and worker support in terms of unions and safety protections are minimal. Many corporations, like Nike, thought that was enough, even in the face of human rights groups' arguments to the contrary. This is not surprising to De La Torre. While corporations have been granted legal personhood by US courts, they are "soulless" persons (*DEM* 237), which raises the question of whether they can be expected to follow moral principles in their practice. "If a corporation decides that its first responsibility is to create profits for its stockholders, then it may need to redefine what is just and ethical in order to allow the maximum profit to be made" (*DEM* 237). From a corporate perspective, marginalized workers are a commodity to be bought and sold on the global labor market, providing a pool of cheap labor to maintain low costs to corporations and consumers

---

[20] Adam Smith, *An Inquiry into the Nature and Causes of the Wealth of Nations*, vol. 1, ed. R. H. Campbell, A. S. Skinner, and W. B. Todd (Oxford: Clarendon, 1976), 13; quoted in *DEM,* 234. De La Torre wrongly connects this with the notion of greed expressed by Gordon Gekko in the film *Wall Street*. As a moral philosopher, Smith's concept is connected to a community where the social context would provide moral limits to the extent of community members' self-interest. It may be true that Gekko and others have taken this to an extreme and that it is reflective of the reality that the individualism of the modern capitalist economy has lost sight of those communal connections.

(*DEM* 73). We can see evidence of this kind of thinking in the Nike case above; other global corporations do the same. As one Apple executive acknowledged when issues emerged at the factories in China with which Apple subcontracts to produce its products: "We've known about labor abuse in some factories for four years, and they're still going on. Why? Because the system works for us."[21]

What is the system that works for them? De La Torre contends it is neoliberalism, and any Christian ethical response to workplace injustices must begin with comprehending its dynamics.[22] At its heart, neoliberalism has generated a new world order where global finance capitalism, global markets, and their agents—corporations, the International Monetary Fund (IMF), and the World Bank, dominated by the United States and its European allies—dictate the terms for social and political order around the world. While this has been beneficial for many in developed countries, because of the steady flow of goods and services from developing countries to their shores, the effect on workers who are marginalized at home and abroad has led to reductions in wages, compromised safety standards, and increased poverty. Most of the benefits of the global economy have gone to capital and very few to labor. As corporations have shifted their production and factories from the United States to Central America and Asia, many of the jobs that provided access to a middle-class standard of living for high school graduates without college degrees have disappeared, leaving only non-unionized, lower-wage service jobs. The impact on workers in developing countries is even more problematic. While some people may make higher wages than they were able to make previously, they are still poverty wages, and the jobs are without adequate safety and environmental standards, or opportunities for collective bargaining.

In addition, neoliberal policies have undermined social safety nets that were sacrificed for the sake of the global market's need for cheap labor, reducing the standards of living even further. Workers who rely on welfare policies to meet basic needs are vilified, requiring labor force participation even for the meager benefits they provided. In the meantime the bulk of the welfare in the United States is given to corporations, called corporate welfare, in the form of subsidies and tax breaks, seen most prominently in recent corporate bailouts by taxpayers of mismanaged corporations and banks deemed "too big to fail." De La Torre points out that critics of neoliberalism are not opposed to globalization, because that is our current reality. Rather, the criticism is aimed at the neoliberal policies and structures that have had a negative impact on humanity, particularly the marginalized, because they claim only one way of operating is right. "Neoliberalism . . . has created a parasitic relationship whereby the poor of the world sacrifice their humanity to serve the needs, wants, and desires of a privileged few" (*DEM* 66). Some people go so far as to say that neoliberalism and its devotion to free markets has the characteristics

---

[21] In Duhigg and Barboza, "In China, Human Costs Are Built into an iPad."

[22] The next few paragraphs draw from De La Torre's discussion of neoliberalism in *DEM* 65–71.

of a religion, including dogmatic beliefs, a rigid ethos, and rituals.[23] It is a "vast idolatrous cult of the great god Capital, creator and father of so many lesser gods: money, the free market, and so on."[24]

Although Nike is the focus of the case study, De La Torre highlights similar corporate responsibility concerns with Walmart, which employs thousands of marginalized workers in the United States and abroad. Except in states where minimum wage laws are set above poverty wages, Walmart wages are low enough that their employees qualify for public welfare benefits. Walmart has also been accused of taking advantage of many of these workers by having them work "off the clock" to keep them from getting overtime pay, which amounts to wage theft. Female employees have filed sexual discrimination charges against Walmart for disparities in pay and for preferring less-qualified male employees for promotion opportunities. The corporation has been accused of child labor law violations because it did not give time for breaks or meals, the latter to the tune of tens of thousands of violations each week. In response, it stopped employees from clocking out, which eliminated the ability to determine who was not receiving breaks. When workers seek to unionize, organizers claim that Walmart fights their efforts by intimidating and firing supporters. One union organizer claims: "They go after you any way they can to discredit you, to fire you. It's almost like a neurosurgeon going after a brain tumor: We got to get that thing out before it infects the rest of the store, the rest of the body" (*DEM* 244). Their anti-union tactics also affect other unionized workers in the retail industry, where employers demand wage and benefits concessions to compete with Walmart. De La Torre calls this the "Walmartizing" of America: "In effect, Walmart, the nation's largest corporate employer, is lowering the living standards for everyone by aggressively and artificially keeping wages depressed for the sake of profit" (*DEM* 245).

Given that Walmart is a global corporation, the impact of such marginalization of workers is felt worldwide. Walmart was accused of bribing public officials in Mexico to skirt or change laws so that they could open stores with little resistance. Even when caught, De La Torre says it was still worth it to the company to break the law because the repercussions did not have an adverse effect on its balance sheet or business model (*DEM* 246). The worst offense was a fatal fire in a factory in Bangladesh that made garments for Walmart. Walmart officials had resisted efforts to improve fire and safety at this and other factories. Even though the improvements would have meant minimal cost, Walmart officials noted, "It is not financially feasible for the brands to make such investments."[25] In the face of exposés regarding the practices, Walmart, like Nike, holds up the fact that it has "strict codes" for its

---

[23] See David R. Loy, "The Religion of the Market," *Journal of the American Academy of Religion* 65/2 (Summer 1997): 275–90.

[24] Leonardo Boff and George Pixley, *The Bible, the Church, and the Poor*, trans. Paul Burns (Maryknoll, NY: Orbis Books, 1989), 144.

[25] See Steven Greenhouse, "Documents Indicate Walmart Blocked Safety Push in Bangladesh," *New York Times*, December 6, 2012 (quoted in *DEM* 247).

suppliers, while ignoring the many violations of those codes when confronted with the realities on the ground (*DEM* 250).

Can anything be done about injustices perpetrated by global corporations? Many workers who have been harmed by corporate practices that place profit over people seek redress in the legislature and the courts. However, this is more difficult in today's political climate and because, De La Torre notes, the current Supreme Court in the United States is the most pro-corporate court since WWII, giving corporations the right to free speech (*Citizens United v. FEC*), which allows them to spend countless amounts of money in lobbying and campaigning, and protecting them from class action and human rights litigation (*Dukes v. Walmart*) (*DEM* 235). In this context, De La Torre suggests that the notion of corporate responsibility focused on making profit over people generates an ethical vacuum that will only continue the abuses noted above. "When the heads of corporations increase their wealth at the expense of the labor pool because they have the power to control wages, the corporation, even though it is an artificial person, is acting immorally" (*DEM* 233).

A biblical and theological analysis of the situation of the marginalized at the hands of global corporations leads De La Torre to declare that "neoliberalism is incapable of incorporating the basics of Christianity" (*DEM* 84). For example, one of the things he finds ironic is that despite the injustices that Walmart's labor policies inflict on many of its workers, nationally and internationally, some of its top officials are held up as having certain personal virtues of piety and generosity—attending church regularly and providing charitable contributions to their religious communities. However, these personal Christian virtues do not provide comfort to the marginalized being cheated of their wages or prohibited from organizing and forming unions. Reflecting the emphasis of Hispanic ethics on orthopraxis, right practice, over orthodoxy, right belief, De La Torre writes: "Just as faith without works is dead (James 2:20), right virtues without right praxis is meaningless" (*DEM* 251). He is also critical of those Christians who see the unfettered market as a good that all people should accept. In this view, maximizing profits and wealth is seen as a virtue, and competition separates the "sheep" from the "goats." Economic losers lack the ethics to manage their own lives properly, and failure as a worker means one lacks the personal ethics or moral duty to manage one's life well. Such Social Darwinist thinking, De La Torre contends, is not reflective of the gospel's concern and commitment to the poor and the marginalized (*DEM* 251).

Like progressive evangelicals, De La Torre finds Jesus's teaching to be applicable to the current situation. Two of Jesus's parables stand out to him. The first is the parable about two stewards who were placed in charge of their master's household. One fulfilled his ethical obligations to the master: to continue the work assigned to him and to treat his fellow servants well. The other chose to ignore his responsibilities while the master was away and treated his fellow servants terribly. The former was rewarded, the latter was punished (Mt 24:45–51). De La Torre says this parable denotes what the ethical responsibilities are for those with power over workers. The problem is that these new corporate stewards often mirror the behavior of the punished steward by contributing to the impoverishment and poor treatment of the disenfranchised (*DEM* 251).

The second parable is that of the vineyard owner who hires laborers throughout the day to work in his vineyard but, at the end of the day, decides to pay them all the same wage regardless of when they started working for him (Mt 20:1–16). Some might consider this unfair to those workers who started earlier in the day. But De La Torre challenges that view:

> To read this parable from the margins, from the perspective of the poor, is to recognize that the vineyard owner—that is, the employer—has a responsibility toward the laborers, a responsibility that goes beyond what traditional capitalist thinking defines as just. Jesus was aware of the laborer's plight. He fully understood that poverty prevented those who were created in the image of God from participating in the abundant life he came to give. In his parable of the vineyard owner, Jesus attempts to teach economic justice so that all can have life abundantly.[26]

If we put this parable into the context of minimum wage workers today, the failure to get a good job or any job is not always the fault of the worker, as some might claim; it is the problem of a system that claims it is fair to pay workers "market wages"—wages that are too low to meet their basic needs of food, shelter, and clothing. It is the failure of an economic system that says some percentage of the workforce must be unemployed to keep the economy from "overheating," losing sight of the social, economic, and psychological effects being part of that percentage has on the unemployed. Reading the Bible from the margins, the lesson for those who live under an economic system that advocates market wages as fair wages or cheers when corporations lay off workers to increase profitability is redefining what economic justice is. According to scripture, workers should be treated humanely and justly (Deut 24:14–15) and receive a living wage to enable them to live a decent life, not one trapped in an endless cycle of poverty. "It did not matter how many hours a laborer worked, what mattered was that at the end of the day, she or he took home a living wage so that the entire family could survive for another day. The worker's responsibility was to labor, and it was the employer's responsibility to ensure that the employee left with enough."[27]

De La Torre also draws from the biblical prophetic tradition to highlight the problems with current labor market exploitation. The prophet Amos condemned the abuses of Israel for the way it treated the poor and marginalized and promised divine judgment:

---

[26] Miguel De La Torre, "The Parable of the Vineyard from the Margins," June 7, 2012, drmigueldelatorre.com.

[27] Ibid.

> because they sell the righteous for silver,
>   and the needy for a pair of sandals—
> they who trample the head of the poor into the dust
>   of the earth,
>   and push the afflicted out of the way. (Am 2:6–7)

De La Torre suggests a similar occurrence is happening in our efforts to bolster corporate leaders and shareholders through lower taxes because they are the job creators in the world. What is overlooked is the *way* in which the profits are made and the bonuses paid, which are a result of their efficiency in reducing the number of workers needed at the lowest possible wages. "Westerners get to buy $100 sneakers because the poor of the earth make them at slave wages. . . . In effect, they sell the poor for a pair of sandals" (*DEM* 253).

De La Torre contends that corporations who contribute to the poverty and poor working conditions of workers in favor of economic markets are complicit "in establishing and maintaining institutionalized violence" (*DEM* 252). Violence is not just the physical force that is sometimes used to keep sweatshop workers in line. Rather, it is anything that keeps workers from living a decent life, which is the purpose of Christ's coming, that is, "I came that they may have life, and have it abundantly" (Jn 10:10). Violence is built into the structure of the corporation any time the working poor are prohibited from meeting their basic needs in favor of profits for the officials and stockholders. Reducing workers to expendable commodities results in their dehumanization; they become nonpersons "who are prevented from living the abundant life promised to them by Christ" (*DEM* 239). "Like Christ," De La Torre claims, "the marginalized of the earth die so that those with power and privilege can have life abundantly" (*DEM* 85). This is not what Jesus's sacrifice was supposed to mean. Christ's crucifixion is God's identification with the poor, who are disenfranchised from economic subsistence, and it is judgment on, not an affirmation of, economic structures that perpetuate their marginalization.

What praxis would De La Torre suggest that Christians engage in to address the economic justice issues he raises? Consistent with his understanding of Hispanic ethics as a "feet-on-the-ground" ethic, he contends that Christians should work in solidarity with the marginalized and disenfranchised—the workers—to ensure that they are central to any deliberations about moral rights, which he understands as positive rights that include the duty of others to assist in their fulfillment.[28] One of those moral rights should be a wage that supports basic needs for human fulfillment, which places a duty on corporations to pay a living wage (*DEM* 232). If they refuse, Christians should

---

[28] *Positive rights* refer to those social and economic rights, such as health care and education, which create entitlements that others are obligated to fulfill. *Negative rights* refer to those civic and political rights, such as free speech or freedom of assembly, with which others should not interfere.

stand with workers in their efforts to change minimum wage laws to bring workers out of poverty, as some states have recently done. Like progressive evangelicals, De La Torre argues that Christians should also advocate for a balanced international economic system that bolsters the empowerment of poor and marginalized workers through collective bargaining, union activity, and fair-trade agreements in the face of global corporations like Nike or Walmart that would exploit their labor for lower prices and corporate profits. De La Torre would affirm the "civil initiatives" of human rights groups, such as United Students against Sweatshops and the Interreligious Labor Coalition, who have engaged in consumer-education campaigns to draw attention to the injustices perpetrated against workers by global corporations, such as Nike, Walmart, and Apple, and have pressured them to change their ways by providing better wages and working conditions for workers.

So, De La Torre understands that any ethical feet-on-the-ground praxis geared to dismantling global injustices must begin by drawing attention to the reason people are hungry, poor, or destitute in the first place: the economic injustice of neoliberal practices that dehumanize them as just another commodity to be used for the benefit of the elite. Such exploitation, De La Torre claims, runs counter to the Spirit of God and all "the biblical texts that call for workers to be treated humanely and justly" (*DEM* 252).

RESOURCES

Discussion Questions

1. If you were CEO of Nike, how would you have responded to the claims that your company is engaged knowingly or unknowingly in unjust labor practices? Would your response have been different than Nike's actual response? If so, what values or beliefs motivate your response? What are the values and beliefs that underlie the responses that progressive evangelical ethics and Hispanic ethics give to this case?

2. One of the arguments in support of cheap labor is that it not only provides lower prices for the poor consumers in this country but also provides needed economic development for poor families in the countries where the factories are located. What do you think about this argument? Do you agree or disagree? What are the presuppositions in this position?

3. The chapter claims that consumerism on the part of affluent Americans is a principal factor in the problems associated with sweatshop labor. Should American consumers adjust their buying practices to foster better working conditions elsewhere? In what ways can they do this? Does the Christian social ethics of either tradition discussed above suggest that Christians have a moral responsibility to become aware of their consumption habits?

4. Stassen and Gushee and De La Torre contend that the extremes of inequality generated by liberal capitalism are unjust and should be confronted and addressed. Do you agree with their position? If not, why not? Is extreme economic inequality a problem that should be addressed, or is it just the way the system works? If you think it is a problem, what steps do you think need to be taken to overcome such inequality?

5. Fast-food workers in this country claim that increasing the minimum wage they are paid to $15 per hour ($31,500 per year for full-time work) would go a long way toward allowing them to live decently. What do you think about this claim? Would you support this change? How might the Christian ethical positions above stand on this issue?

Activities

1. Do an analysis of this case from a situation ethics or a womanist ethics perspective. Compare the conclusions you think they would reach with those from the two perspectives in this case analysis. In what ways are they similar? In what ways are they different? Which approach, in your opinion, addresses the case most comprehensively?

2. Do some research on issues related to ethical consumption and fair trade. Then visit your college bookstore or speak with your athletics department to see where they purchase their clothing apparel and uniforms. Ask about the values or other considerations that go into the decisions about which company or companies they buy from. Is worker justice a concern? Do they purchase from organizations that are committed to fair trade and fair treatments of workers in the factories that make their clothing and shoes? If not, share the research you have done with them to educate them on these issues. Consider starting a chapter of United Students against Sweatshops on your campus.

3. Engage in a research project on the issue of worker justice on your campus. You can either duplicate a research project already done by a previous scholar or it may be original. This might include administering a questionnaire, doing interviews, conducting an experiment, writing up a participant/observation research project, collecting and analyzing self-generated data, or the like. Most original research projects should begin with a review of the appropriate literature. After conducting the research, write it up as you would any research paper to share with your class.

4. Do an analysis of a religious social justice organization that seeks to address the unfair working conditions of low-wage workers, such as Interfaith Worker Justice. Arrange a visit or call the organization to find out the mission and purpose of the organization, the population it serves, or the issues it addresses, and how it goes about its work. Focus on the values or beliefs that motivate the work. Then write a report on the organization that is not merely descriptive but also analytical, in that the report shows the connectedness

among mission, beliefs/values, and organization. Moreover, you should include a critique of the organization from your perspective.

5. Lead a presentation and discussion on a film that deals with sweatshop labor (review the list below for ideas). This can be done inside class (with the instructor's permission) or outside class with students who are not necessarily enrolled in the class. Make connections between the ethical arguments in this class and the moral perspective present in the film. Consider recording the discussion (with the permission of the participants) and creating a podcast to share online.

Readings

Barrera, Albino. *Biblical Economic Ethics: Sacred Scripture's Teaching on Economic Life*. Plymouth, UK: Lexington Books, 2013. This theological synthesis of the findings of scripture scholars and ethicists on what the Bible teaches about economic life includes themes about care for the poor, generosity, wariness over the idolatry of wealth, the inseparability of genuine worship and upright moral conduct, and acknowledgment of an underlying divine order in economic life.

Featherstone, Liza. *Students against Sweatshops*. New York: Verso Press, 2002. This book chronicles the development of United Students against Sweatshops and its efforts against sweatshops on college campuses. The group's efforts have also led to a more broadly based engagement with issues of social justice and provide a potential model for transnational student/worker solidarity.

Finn, Daniel K. *Christian Economic Ethics*. Minneapolis: Fortress Press, 2013. Finn explores the implications of the historical account of Christian views of economic life for twenty-first-century economic life.

Gutiérrez, Gustavo. *A Theology of Liberation: History, Politics, and Salvation*. Maryknoll, NY: Orbis Books, 1988. This classic text on liberation theology provides the framework for challenging the political and economic conditions of the poor from a Christian theological and ethical perspective.

Henderson, James W., and John Pisciotta, eds. *Faithful Economics: The Moral Worlds of a Neutral Science*. Waco, TX: Baylor University Press, 2006. This volume explores the relationship between Christianity and economics, arguing that the two can and should be integrated. While no single Christian perspective drives the book, the authors do share in common a belief that scholarship shaped by Christian commitments is entirely appropriate and should be an integral part of the professional life of Christian economists.

Novak, Michael. *The Catholic Ethic and the Spirit of Capitalism.* New York: Free Press, 1993. Novak challenges the individualistic Protestant ethic that Max Weber says is at the heart of the rise of capitalism and contends that Catholic social thought, which has had difficulty coming to grips with capitalism, provides a better understanding, with its emphasis on cooperation, social initiative, creativity, and invention.

Sider, Ron. *Rich Christians in an Age of Hunger: Moving from Affluence to Generosity.* Sixth edition. Nashville: Thomas Nelson, 2015. This revised and updated edition of Sider's text—the first edition was published in 1978—explores the current realities of hunger through a biblical lens. He provides biblical principles for addressing hunger and practical suggestions for doing so.

Timmerman, Kelsey. *Where Am I Wearing? A Global Tour to the Countries, Factories, and People That Make Our Clothes.* Hoboken, NJ: John Wiley and Sons, 2009. This book is a journalist's account of his efforts to understand the forces, processes, economics, and politics at work in the garment industry.

Wogaman, J. Philip. *Economics and Ethics: A Christian Inquiry.* Minneapolis: Fortress Press, 1986. Wogaman explores here the nature of economic ethical judgments, who makes them, and on what values they are based. After looking at economic problems and human values and the way in which they are made, he asks whether there is a theological basis for social priorities.

Audiovisuals

China Blue. Teddy Bear Films, Inc., 2005. Directed by Micha Peled, this documentary takes the viewer inside a blue-jeans factory, where workers are trying to survive a harsh working environment. When the factory owner agrees to a deal with his Western client that forces his teenage workers to work around the clock, a confrontation becomes inevitable. Shot clandestinely in China, under difficult conditions, this is a deep-access account of what both China and the international retail companies don't want us to see—how the clothes we buy are actually made.

Made in L.A. Independent Television Service (ITVS), Semilla Verde Productions, 2007. Directed by Almudena Carracedo and Robert Bahar, this documentary follows the story of three Latina immigrants working in Los Angeles garment sweatshops as they embark on a three-year odyssey to win basic labor protections from a mega-trendy clothing retailer.

Maquilapolis. Independent Television Service (ITVS), 2006. Directed by Sergio De La Torre and Vicky Funari, this documentary highlights the working conditions in the *maquiladoras,* massive sweatshops often owned by the world's largest multinational corporations and located just across the US border in Mexico.

The True Cost. Life Is My Movie Entertainment, 2015. This documentary, directed by Andrew Morgan, explores the workers behind the fashion industry and the negative effects on their well-being and the environment in which they live.

Triangle: Remembering the Fire. Blowback Productions, 2011. Directed by Daphne Pinkerson, this HBO documentary deals with the infamous fire of March 15, 1911, in New York City, in which 146 employees of the Triangle Shirtwaist Company, most of them women, were killed because exits were locked. The tragedy led to the creation of modern health and safety laws and laid the foundation for aspects of Roosevelt's New Deal.

What Would Jesus Buy? Palisades Pictures, Warrior Poets Releasing, LLC, 2007. Directed by Rob VanAlkemade, this documentary/comedy examines the commercialization of Christmas in America while following Reverend Billy and the Church of the Stop Shopping Gospel Choir on a cross-country mission to save Christmas from the Shopocalypse. The film also delves into issues such as the role sweatshops play in America's mass consumerism and the big-box culture.

4

Medicine and Health Care

CASE STUDY:
STEM-CELL RESEARCH
AND THE MORAL STATUS OF THE EMBRYO

In 1998, a breakthrough occurred when researchers, led by James Thomson at the University of Wisconsin-Madison and financially supported by the Geron Corporation, first developed a technique to isolate and grow human embryonic stem cells (hESC) in cell culture. What is so special about embryonic stem cells? Stem cells are the raw material from which all the body's mature, differentiated cells are made.[1] Stem cells give rise to brain cells, nerve cells, heart cells, pancreatic cells, and others. Embryonic (also called pluripotent) stem cells can develop into all the cell types of the body.[2] Adult stem cells— which is a misnomer because they reside in infants and children as well—are stem cells that reside in already developed tissue and are thus more specialized and less versatile. Embryonic stem cells can replicate themselves over and over for a very long time in a laboratory environment. They have the potential to replace cell tissue that has been damaged or destroyed by severe illnesses. Researchers believe that understanding how stem cells develop into healthy and diseased cells will assist the search for cures for diseases such as Parkinson's, Alzheimer's, diabetes, and more.

There are two sources of embryonic stem cells: excess fertilized eggs from IVF (in vitro fertilization) clinics, and therapeutic cloning (somatic cell nuclear transfer or SCNT, the technique used for creating Dolly the Sheep). Couples who are having trouble naturally conceiving children may choose IVF as an alternative, although the procedure is expensive and many couples who would like this option cannot afford it. Unlike artificial insemination, where sperm

---

[1] International Society for Stem Cell Research, "Stem Cell Basics," http://www.isscr.org/.
[2] Ibid., "Stem Cell Facts."

79

is placed in the uterus to impregnate eggs within the woman, IVF combines the eggs and sperm outside the body in a laboratory. Five to six days after fertilization has occurred, the most promising embryos or blastocysts are placed inside the uterus in the hope that at least one of them will implant itself in the uterine wall where the normal gestation process takes place. (At one time, the offspring were referred to as test-tube babies.) To be effective, IVF requires an excess number of eggs to be fertilized and frozen, most of which will not be implanted into the uterus. As a result, tens of thousands of frozen embryos are created and routinely destroyed when couples finish their treatment. Some estimate the number to be between five and thirty embryos for each successful implantation. These surplus embryos can be used to produce stem cells by extracting them from a five-to-seven-day-old blastocyst. Surplus embryos were the initial source of stem cells used in research.[3]

SCNT involves removing the nucleus of a donated egg and replacing it with the nucleus of a mature somatic cell (a skin cell, for example) from a patient and then injecting it back into the patient for tissue regeneration.[4] The benefit is that this minimizes the risk that the patient's body will reject the cell because it belongs to the patient. No sperm is involved in this process, and no embryo is created to be implanted in a woman's womb. The resulting stem cells can potentially develop into specialized cells that are useful for treating severe illnesses in the patient and for researching the origins of such diseases.

As one might imagine, the potential medical benefits of such research raised a great deal of excitement for researchers, the medical community, and for people suffering from diseases for which information from this research might provide clues and even cures. One well-known figure is Michael J. Fox, who is suffering from Parkinson's disease. The question was how this research would be funded. Although private funding led to the initial discovery of embryonic stem cells, many voices began to clamor for public support for the research. Others, however, were concerned with this research because it inevitably resulted in the destruction of a human embryo—an embryo created in a laboratory—and they did not feel that public funds should be expended for this morally dubious research.

The use and funding of this research entered the political realm first under President Bill Clinton. The National Institutes of Health (NIH) recommended federal funding for research on leftover embryos from IVF and for embryos created specifically for research purposes. President Clinton, sensitive to the moral objections to the latter NIH suggestion, restricted federal funding to research on leftover embryos only. In 1995, Congress passed a law (the Dickey-Wicker amendment on appropriations) that would not allow federal funding for any research that resulted in the destruction of human embryos, regardless

---

[3] R. G. Edwards, "IVF and the History of Stem Cells," *Nature* 413 (September 27, 2001): 349–51.

[4] J. Liu et al., "Human Embryos Derived by Somatic Cell Nuclear Transfer Using an Alternative Enucleation Approach," *Cloning and Stem Cells* 11/1 (2009): 39–50.

of the source. When President George W. Bush took office, he placed further restrictions on federal funding to those embryonic stem cell lines that already existed from IVF prior to August 2001 (of which nineteen were available).

Many congressional representatives, scientists, doctors, and others in the country saw this as an undue burden placed on this promising research. They asked President Bush to loosen the restrictions and even passed laws that would allow more funding for this research with the same restrictions that were in place under President Clinton. President Bush, however, vetoed the laws. Many states, especially California, sought to promote this research and even generated their own funding for the research that bypassed the federal government.[5] When President Obama came into office, he issued an executive order that lifted the ban on federal funding, indicating that his administration would vigorously support scientists who engaged in this research.[6] This was challenged in court, but the appeals court ruled that while the 1995 law prohibited the destruction of embryos it did not prohibit funding a research project using embryonic stem cells. While these laws and debates focused on federal funding of stem-cell research, no federal law has been passed that specifically outlaws embryonic stem-cell research. Some states have passed such restrictive laws.[7] Recently, the Trump administration ordered the NIH to prohibit funding for fetal tissue research.[8]

ISSUES AND CONCERNS

As one might imagine, both sources of embryonic stem cells raise ethical issues. For many religious individuals and groups, human life is created as soon as conception takes place, whether in the womb or in the laboratory, and thus is sacred, with equal moral standing as all human life. With the removal of the stem cells, the embryo is destroyed. In their view the deliberate destruction of the human embryo for any reason, whether IVF, abortion, or research, is killing—some say murdering—a fully human life at the earliest stage and undercuts the moral respect owed to all human life.[9]

Some proponents of embryonic stem-cell research question whether embryos existing outside the human body have any or the same moral status as human beings just because they are human. For one thing, they do not

---

[5] See Pam Solo and Gail Pressberg, *The Promise and Politics of Stem Cell Research* (Westport, CT: Praeger Publishers, 2006).

[6] Exec. Order No. 13505, 74 Fed. Reg. 10667 (March 9, 2009).

[7] See Nefi D. Acosta and Sidney H. Golub, "The New Federalism: State Policies regarding Embryonic Stem Cell Research," *Journal of Law and Medical Ethics* 44/3 (September 2016): 419–36.

[8] See Sara Reardon, "Trump Administration Halts Fetal-Tissue Research by Government Scientists," *Nature* 570 (June 5, 2019), 148.

[9] See Richard M. Doerflinger, "The Ethics of Funding Embryonic Stem Cell Research: A Catholic Viewpoint," *Kennedy Institute of Ethics Journal* 9/2 (1999): 137–50.

possess the same potential to become full human beings because they will never be implanted inside a woman, which is required for the embryo to develop. This does not mean, however, that they should be treated without any moral respect. They are human and have a certain relationship to their biological parents. Thus, they have some limited moral standing and should be treated with some measure of respect, not created or destroyed for frivolous reasons. But this does not mean that they should have the same moral respect as a fetus or a fully developed human being. Rather, because they are being created and used for morally significant reasons—to enable infertile couples to have children and to conduct research to alleviate human suffering—their destruction can be morally justified. Moreover, proponents highlight the fact that these excess embryos would be destroyed anyway. Using them for their potential benefit for understanding and possibly curing disease and for tissue regeneration outweighs concerns about their use in research.[10] Of course, opponents suggest that they never should have been created in the first place, knowing that some would be destroyed.

Related to the second source of embryonic stem cells, SCNT, is the issue of cloning. While SCNT does not involve the destruction of an embryo, there is concern that such technology might eventually be used for human cloning, which in their view violates the uniqueness of each human life given only by God. Moreover, funding such research could lead humanity down a morally "slippery slope" where human clones are created and used for spare parts by the cell donor, which is the stuff of science fiction books and movies such as *The Island* (2005). Proponents reject this scenario, suggesting that within proper ethical guidelines the benefits of SCNT for restoring human tissue or gaining knowledge about the development of diseases like cancer could generate a great deal of human good and reduction of suffering.

In 2007, Dr. James Thomson discovered a way to create stem cells without using embryos. Following research by Dr. Shinya Yamanaka of Japan, who won the Nobel Prize for medicine in 2012, all Dr. Thomson's lab had to do was add four genes to ordinary adult skin cells and the cells would turn into what looked just like stem cells. Stem cells generated by this method, known as induced pluripotent cells, or iPS cells, could then be made to mature into any type of adult cell in the body, a finding with obvious potential for medical benefits. While the ability to do this with human cells is just beginning to emerge, Dr. Thomson believes that the new technique would make the stem cell wars a distant memory.[11] One of the major advantages of iPS cells is their potential to create cell lines for a specific disease or an individual patient. "Disease-specific stem cells are powerful tools for studying the cause of a

---

[10] See Michael Sandel, "Embryo Ethics: The Moral Logic of Stem-Cell Research," *New England Journal of Medicine* 351/3 (July 15, 2004): 207–9.

[11] Gina Kolata, "Man Who Helped Start Stem Cell War May End It," *New York Times* (November 22, 2007).

particular disease and then for testing drugs or discovering other approaches to treat or cure that disease."[12] The development of patient-specific stem cells is also very attractive for cell therapy, as these cell lines are from the patients themselves and may minimize some of the serious complications of rejection and immunosuppression that can occur. While iPS cells share many of the same characteristics of embryonic stem cells, including the ability to give rise to all the cell types in the body, they are not the same. Scientists are exploring what the differences are, and what they mean. For one thing, the first iPS cells were produced by using viruses to insert extra copies of genes into tissue-specific cells. Researchers are exploring safer methods to do so. However, it is clear that cells taken from an individual are not necessarily safe for use in or as therapy for that same individual.

Not everyone agrees with Thomson's assessment regarding the cell wars. While the new technique, if successful in human trials, may not result in the destruction of human embryos, it might well result in reproductive human cloning. After all, Thomson admits that it was the cloning of Dolly the Sheep that got him interested in this area of research. Moreover, because research on iPS cells may be easier and cheaper, relatively speaking, concerns about donor privacy and control as well as equitable sharing of the profits between the donor and the corporations reaping financial benefits from the research might arise. Finally, even if reliance on embryonic stem cells dwindles because of the development of iPS cells, some contend that there are still important distinctions that will "preclude the former's total eclipse of the latter."[13]

The question of public funding also raises a significant question about the relationships between church and state, and religion and politics. What role should religious convictions play in determining funding for scientific research? In a Gallup poll most Americans believed that President Bush's decision to restrict funding was primarily due to his personal religious convictions (although a sizeable minority believed that politics also played a role).[14] Religious and ethical convictions are important and have come into play in trying to provide some safeguards over the creation and treatment of embryos. But should they be allowed to stop most public funding for research when over 60 percent of the population sees embryonic stem-cell research as morally acceptable? Most Americans polled did not think so, nor did Bush's successor, President Obama. The Trump administration's ban on use of fetal tissue from aborted fetuses by scientists supported by the federal government was made in part to please his anti-abortion supporters. But there has been no such ban on stem-cell research.

---

[12] International Society for Stem Cell Research, "Stem Cell Facts."

[13] Zachary Brown, "A Bulwark against Trump's Stem Cell Ban," *Scientific American* (July 2, 2019).

[14] Joseph Carroll, "Public Opposes President Bush's Veto on Stem Cell Research Funding," *Gallup News Service* (July 27, 2006).

NATURAL LAW ETHICS

The first question to ask from a natural law ethics perspective, especially given its relationship to Catholic social ethics, is about the morality of IVF, especially since so many of the embryos available for research come from extra embryos that will not be implanted. If IVF is considered immoral, then the question of the morality of research on this source of embryonic stem cells seems clearer. The Vatican's Congregation for the Doctrine of the Faith (CDF), which has the responsibility to promote and safeguard the doctrine on the faith and morals throughout the Catholic world, argues that the natural form of sexuality is through the mutual, self-giving love (the unitive or relational dimension of marriage) and sexual union of a man and a woman (the procreative dimension).[15] While some medical interventions in the process of fertility between married persons are morally acceptable, such as hormonal treatments for infertility or unblocking fallopian tubes, this is not the case for IVF because, they conclude, all techniques of IVF "proceed as if the human embryo were simply a mass of cells to be used, selected, and discarded," which amounts to a "blithe acceptance of the enormous number of abortions" and "leads to a weakening of the respect owed to every human being."[16] Thus, in the official view of the Catholic Church, IVF is morally impermissible.

Jean Porter understands the church's concerns surrounding IVF but is not inclined to agree on this issue.[17] She suggests that the use of IVF can express the unitive and procreative dimensions of sexuality and can be an expression of parental mutual, self-giving love. Medical interventions to overcome sterility can be seen as a manifestation of their love. All artificial interventions in the prevention or promotion of conception are "second best" in that they are not made through the sexual union of the man and the woman, but they cannot all be ruled out. Porter also suggests that the CDF document moves away from an older view of natural law in its affirmation of the more personalist view of sexuality developed since Vatican II (noted in Chapter 2 of this volume). Given her notion that the natural law has norms that are undedetermined, she suggests it is neither possible nor desirable to develop clear-cut moral prohibitions in the area of reproductive morality "given the central importance of the affective and relational for this dimension of human life" ("Human Need" 105).

---

[15] Congregation for the Doctrine of the Faith, *Instruction* Dignitas Personae *on Certain Bioethical Questions*, AAS 100 (2008).

[16] Ibid., II, 14, 16.

[17] The discussion of Porter's view on this issue draws on two essays: "Human Need and Natural Law," in *Infertility: A Crossroad of Faith, Medicine, and Technology*, ed. Kevin Wm. Wildes, SJ (Dordrecht, The Netherlands: Kluwer Academic Publishing, 1997), 93–106 (hereafter cited as "Human Need"); and "Is the Embryo a Person?" *Commonweal* (February 8, 2002): 8–10 (hereafter cited as "Embryo"); as well as *Nature as Reason: A Thomistic Theory of the Natural Law* (Grand Rapids, MI: Eerdmans, 2005) (hereafter cited as *NR*).

With this understanding of IVF as background, Porter begins with a theological framework when addressing the moral permissibility of stem-cell research (and the moral permissibility of abortion). In particular, she begins with the question of the ontological and moral status of the zygote/embryo. In other words, when does the zygote/embryo become a person in the fullest metaphysical and moral sense of that term so that it deserves the full moral protection accorded to other living persons? To put this in the language of scholastic thinkers such as Thomas Aquinas, when is the soul infused into the developing fetus? Some of that debate among Catholic theologians and ethicists today, she suggests, revolves around whether one believes in "immediate" or "delayed hominization." Immediate hominization refers to the notion that, at the moment of conception, the zygote/embryo is fully human, genetically distinct from its parents, and, if allowed to develop, will result in the birth of a child. The CDF contends, "This teaching remains valid and is further confirmed, if confirmation were needed, by recent findings of human biological science which recognize that in the zygote resulting from fertilization the biological identity of a new human individual is already constituted."[18] This is the official teaching of the Catholic Church, which perceives this to be obviously true. "The conclusions of science regarding the human embryo provide a valuable indication for discerning by the use of reason a personal presence at the moment of this first appearance of a human life: how could a human individual not be a human person?"[19] As such, the embryo deserves all the protections afforded to all human beings. Any willful termination of the life of the embryo, as happens with both stem-cell research and abortion, is tantamount to murder. "The human being is to be respected and treated as a person from the moment of conception; and therefore from that same moment his rights as a person must be recognized, among which in the first place is the inviolable right of every innocent human being to life."[20] The CDF claims that ethical principle, "which reason is capable of recognizing as true and in conformity with the natural moral law, should be the basis for all legislation in this area."[21]

But Porter suggests that what seems obvious to the church is not obvious to everyone else or even to all Catholic thinkers. Delayed hominization refers to the notion that while the zygote/embryo is surely human, distinct from its mother's body, it is not a person until a later stage in its development. Because rationality is central to what it means to be a human being, it makes sense that to be considered fully human the zygote/embryo must have the biological capacity for rationality ("Embryo" 9). Aquinas and other scholastics believed that God could not infuse a rational soul into a body that does not have the

---

[18] Congregation for the Doctrine of the Faith, *Instruction on Respect for Human Life in Its Origin and on the Dignity of Procreation: Replies to Certain Questions of the Day*, I, 1: AAS 80 (1988), 79.

[19] Ibid.

[20] Ibid.

[21] Congregation for the Doctrine of the Faith, *Instruction* Dignitas Personae, I, 5.

physical structure or capacity for rational functioning, which develops later in the gestation process; contemporary views of delayed hominization focus on the point when the developing embryo/fetus can be claimed to be identical to the person who will eventually be born (past the point of twinning). In the former case the time can be said to be roughly twenty weeks; in the latter, fourteen days. Obviously, where one stands on this question has implications for one's views regarding stem-cell research.

Where does Porter come out on this question? She asks: What are the qualities of personhood? Is it only in one's capacity for rationality? That is at least certainly a significant component of personhood. However, Porter goes further. When talking about the issue of abortion, she contends: "The identity of a human person does not just reside in her rational capacities. It is also grounded and manifested in her affective life, her bodily existence, and even in her social identity and her participation in a shared communal history. All of these are aspects of personal existence, and they all exercise a claim."[22] However, she understands that in the early stages of development a fetus has none of these qualities and therefore does not have the same moral status as a person that a fetus has in later stages of development. Thus, she concludes that she does support stem-cell research (and even some abortions) under certain circumstances ("Embryo" 10).

Porter argues that the strongest argument against abortion (and stem-cell research) is the principle of equality, which underlies the Golden Rule and is a fundamental norm for natural law, informing all our moral arguments (see natural law ethics in Chapter 1). If it could be shown that the fetus has the same moral status as fully developed human beings, then justifying abortion would be difficult. As Pope John Paul II argues in *Evangelium vitae*: "The mere probability that a human person is involved would suffice to justify an absolutely clear prohibition of any intervention aimed at killing a human embryo" (no. 60).[23] But, as noted above, Porter and many others challenge this view. The fetus, especially at the early stages of development, such as a five-to-seven-day-old blastocyst, does not have the same moral status because it is not a human person and therefore is not subject to the principle of equality in the way that fully formed persons would be. As a result, Porter contends that embryonic stem-cell research and abortion in some circumstances could be morally justified. It is important to recognize that the embryo is still human and deserving of respect in its handling and treatment. However, the actions involved in embryonic stem-cell research are not tantamount to murder as the magisterium—the teaching authority of the Catholic Church—and some conservative Catholics claim ("Embryo" 9).

The second issue for Porter is the purpose of stem-cell research (and even abortion). For Porter, this is where the teleological element comes into play in natural law ethics—our actions ought to correspond to some ideal end or

---

[22] Jean Porter, *Moral Action and Christian Ethics* (Cambridge University Press, 1995), 123 (hereafter cited as *MA*).

[23] Quoted in Porter, "Embryo," 10.

paradigm for a particular living creature, including humanity (*NR* 49–50). The purpose of these ends is to promote flourishing for each creature, person, or society. This is a different teleological approach than the utilitarian calculus noted in the discussion of situation ethics. The ends are not the greatest good for the greatest number. Rather, the ends Porter has in mind relate to the ideal end for each creature, which she speaks about in terms of well-being, flourishing, and happiness. What are the ends being sought by stem-cell research (and abortion)? For advocates, the ends are the well-being of humanity—the potential development of therapeutic cures that would alleviate human suffering from diseases or organ failures, as well as the well-being of the woman and her family. If one accepts that the principle of equality does not fully apply to the zygote/embryo in the early stages of development, then the rational ends and norms associated with such research can ethically justify this action. These ends and norms can also justify abortions in some instances, including saving the mother's life and eliminating some of the hardships many women experience. Porter contends that we must take seriously "the suffering of the countless women and their families who find themselves faced with pregnancy in difficult circumstances" (*MA* 121). While the fetus in early stages of development deserves reverence and protection, it does not fall under the principle of equality in the same way. Thus, the fetus's claim to such protections can be overridden in some cases to overcome human suffering.

The third issue in embryonic stem-cell research is its implications for public policy. Porter notes how the Catholic Church objected to Senator Orrin Hatch's (R-Utah) support for stem-cell research funding on the grounds that he was attempting to have Mormon values determine public policy and laws. However, Porter argues, this is exactly what many citizens claim the Catholic Church is seeking to do. She contends that there are other moralities with some validity that should come into play here. Based on her understanding of natural law, all human beings have some capacity to distinguish right from wrong, good from evil. It is not the sole province of those of Christian faith. This capacity opens the door for people who do not share the Christian faith to find common ground with Christians. If Catholics think their perspective is appropriate, they cannot assert it; they must convince others of its merits. The challenge for Catholics is to find ways to communicate their beliefs effectively, which requires some dialogue and some willingness to justify those beliefs in language and ideas that resonate with those of others ("Embryo" 10).

Porter contends that the Catholic Church has done a poor job of developing such communication. Blanket assertions—that because the zygote/embryo has the potential to develop into a human person it is therefore is fully human, and that any opinions to the contrary merely contribute to the "culture of death" in our society—have not been convincing. In fact, Porter argues, most people, including many Catholic thinkers, question whether the embryo does have the same status. Therefore, the Catholic Church cannot expect everyone to agree with, nor should it attempt to push, its perspective onto others who disagree with it in the area of public policy. She writes: "It is fair to say that our efforts in this case have largely failed. We have not convinced our fellow citizens that embryonic stem-cell research is morally wrong because we have not convinced them that the embryo, from the first moment of its existence, is a human person in the fullest sense, with the same right to life as anyone else" ("Embryo" 8). We cannot simply translate the tenets of Catholic faith into public policy. She thinks others are not convinced because what the church is saying is not convincing—it needs a more systematic argument. The arguments drawn from the scholastic tradition pose the same challenge that many folks in the debate share: that the early-stage embryo is not a human person in the fullest sense. Just as Catholics do not want other religious beliefs forced upon them through public policy, they cannot expect others to allow Catholics to do it to them. Instead, Porter contends that Christians must engage with their fellow citizens in genuine dialogue to resolve the differences in their views of what constitutes the ethical treatment of embryos (*NR* 373).

SITUATION ETHICS

As we look at this issue, let us recall that for situation ethics the key base point is the concrete situation, the objective set of circumstances in which moral agents make their choices and decisions. Before one can know whether one has done the right thing, the good thing, or the loving thing, one must understand the situation at hand in all its complexity. In *Humanhood: Essays in Biomedical Ethics*,[24] Joseph Fletcher expanded his situation ethics to cover the issues of genetic engineering, fetal research, and abortion, all of which fit well with the case before us on the ethics of stem-cell research. In his book Fletcher focuses a great deal on IVF and embryonic research.

Fletcher rejects legalism of any sort on these issues—whether the legalism of natural law or conservative evangelical ethics—that deduces certain rules or prescriptions that are universal and therefore must be applied in all cases. He calls the legalistic view the "law of divine monopoly," which suggests that only God has any control over human reproduction. Fletcher puts the question of the ethics of all biomedical research this way: "Are we to reason from general propositions and universals, or are we to reason from empirical data, variable situations, and human values?" (*HH* 81). He argues for the latter, that is, "the acquisition of useful know-how in medicine's effort to save and improve human life" (*HH* 104). As his approach makes clear, we cannot rule such embryonic stem-cell research out of bounds just because of some preset or a priori principles. Rather, he argues, "the radical openness of situation ethics is such as to declare that the direct taking even of an innocent life might, under some circumstances, be morally licit" (*HH* 52).

---

[24] Joseph Fletcher, *Humanhood: Essays in Biomedical Ethics* (Buffalo, NY: Prometheus Books, 1979) (hereafter cited as HH).

Fletcher disagrees with those who suggest that laboratory reproduction is no longer human procreation, as we saw in the Catholic Church's perspective; even those who favor some forms of IVF see it as "second best." Fletcher writes: "Man is a maker and a selecter and a designer, and the more rationally contrived and deliberate anything is, the more human it is. . . . The real difference is between accidental or random reproduction and rationally willed or chosen reproduction" (*HH* 87–88). Reproduction that results from sex between a man and a woman may be more pleasurable, "but with our separation of baby making from lovemaking, both become more human because they are matters of choice, and not chance" (*HH* 88). And choice, Fletcher argues, is essential for ethical action: "Whatever we are compelled to do is amoral" (*HH* 91).

Moreover, he dismisses the arguments of those who think that such efforts will result in some form of tyranny, as envisaged by dystopian novels like Aldous Huxley's *Brave New World*. In Huxley's book the leaders of the New World Order seek to maintain stability and order in society by controlling reproduction and engaging in genetic and environmental manipulation to produce certain classes of people with limited freedoms who willingly assume their predetermined positions in society. While Fletcher is concerned with any kind of tyranny, he claims genetic research will not lead to tyranny, as some fear; rather, tyranny begins in the political realm, not the biological one (*HH* 86). What he means is that in Huxley's novel it was the political tyranny of trying to control all elements of society that led to the other forms of tyranny. Once the political tyranny was established, the society was enabled to engage in other forms of tyranny. He contends that with proper ethical oversight—and this is crucial—there is no reason to assume that reproductive and genetic research will result in such tyranny. If we can justify the ends, then we can justify the means.

As noted in the case study and discussed in the previous section on natural law ethics, a key issue in the debate is the moral status of the embryo: Is the embryo at the time of conception a full human person with the same dignity, sanctity, and right to life as all human persons? Fletcher suggests that to answer this question adequately we must decide two issues: (1) What is the essence of a person? and (2) When is a human being a person? Regarding the essence, Fletcher highlights three options. The first, as we saw in the discussion of the Catholic perspective, is that life or vitality is the essence of human life. Wherever life is present, a human organism is a person, generally at fertilization or conception (although some have argued even before the egg and sperm come together because they also are "alive"). The second is that the presence of a soul is what makes a person, referred to previously as "ensoulment." For some Christians, such as Aquinas, the soul or *animus* enters after conception (in the second trimester); for others, such as the magisterium of the Roman Catholic Church, the soul enters immediately at conception. The third option, which is Fletcher's position, is that the essence of a person is that person's rational capacity. "Before cerebration comes into play, or when it is ended, in the absence of the synthesizing or *thinking* function of the cerebral cortex, the person is nonexistent; or, put another way, the life which is functioning biologically is a nonperson" (*HH* 134). He would agree with Porter that persons are more than rational beings, but he suggests that rationality is critical for any other function of persons, whether in the case of a five-to-seven-day-old blastocyst or someone who experiences brain death.

Clearly, the question of *what* makes a human a person, the essence, has implications for *when* a human becomes a person. Rather than a "sanctity of human life" argument, Fletcher offers a quality-of-life argument. "When does a fetus become human (the better term is 'personal')?" He might disagree with Porter about when this takes place, but clearly it has not yet developed in a five-to-seven-day-old blastocyst.

He also rejects the notion that embryos have rights. In his view the only things that can validate our humanistic concerns and person-centered values are needs. "Needs are the moral stabilizers, not rights. . . . Rights are nothing but a formal recognition by society of certain human needs, and as needs change with changing conditions, so rights should change, too" (*HH* 89–90). Moreover, he contends that underlying needs is some understanding of human values. "To speak of needs is to speak of human values. . . . If medical care can use genetic controls preventively to protect people from disease or deformity, or to ameliorate such things, then let the so-called right to be born step aside" (*HH* 90). From his view the actions are moral "as long as they are tailored to a loving concern for human beings" (*HH* 91).

Like Porter, Fletcher's argument is teleological, although he follows a more utilitarian line of argument. Does embryonic stem-cell research "add to or take away from human welfare" (*HH* 84)? In his perspective the only ends that can be justified are results, and those results that contribute to human well-being are good—in particular, our obligations to future generations. When Fletcher reviews the science associated with embryonic research, he notes that there are a great number of people who are suffering. He sees the promise that embryonic research holds to help relieve that suffering. The questions he raises include whether the benefits outweigh the costs and how to determine the most loving thing to do. Also, we do have a variety of embryos available for this research. We have the technology to do it. He is not in favor of what he calls the "capacity-fallacy," which suggests that just because we can, we should. "Science deals with the possible and probable, but ethics deals with the preferable" (*HH* 89). Thus, what are important in his view are the ends sought and the underlying values to those ends; they should be the foundation for choosing to engage in this type of research. We must ask, what is the motivation? If the motivation is to help others and to improve human welfare, to bring about the most good for the most people (our "neighbors"), then he sees the action as morally permissible. Given the potential embryonic stem-cell research has for therapeutic cures and for aiding our attempts to eradicate diseases that cause a great deal of suffering, he would support the research.

Fletcher resorts to the same type of moral argument when considering the morality of cloning, whether of animals or humans. If the cloning of some humans can be shown to provide some significant benefit to the community, and the respect owed to all human beings is guaranteed, he sees no reason why cloning technology should be forbidden out of hand. Whether such cloning for therapeutic or reproductive purposes is ethical would depend upon the situation. For example, he indicates that some forms of cloning in healthy people "to compensate for the spread of genetic diseases and to elevate the plus factors available in ordinary reproduction" might be a good thing (*HH* 85). He rejects the notion that a cloned person would be a carbon copy of the parent, because personalities are not shaped simply by genotypes but also by environments. He understands there is a danger of tyranny, but, as we noted above, the genetic engineering does not lead to dictatorships; rather, the dictatorship is already in place, and this leads to the tyranny.

Fletcher also addresses the question of funding for such research, whether by government or private donors. He argues that an effort to restrict funding based on a narrow religious view about what human life is, and when it begins, is a violation of the First Amendment protection of actual persons who have freedom of religion (and freedom from the religious dictates of others). Fletcher contends: "Homogenization of opinion would be a disaster to science as well as to medical care and treatment if any particular set of pre- or meta-ethical assumptions about personhood and humanhood in fetal life were to be given a monopoly force by law, or by funding work which must be done exclusively according to only one system of ethics and rules" (*HH* 99). He would also disagree on whether any one "faith" stance, whether held by just one tradition or even if all are in agreement, would be best. There will always be some who have a different perspective, and all those perspectives should be honored in law. Any attempt to enact one faith stance into law would be a violation of the First Amendment and religious freedom. He notes, "If rules are imposed by law or public agencies, somebody is frustrated, one group or another. In matters of this kind there is great wisdom in the old adage, the best government is the least government" (*HH* 103). This is not a matter to be decided by government fiat. He argues for a postnatal definition of a person in law, much as he suggests was articulated in *Roe v. Wade* by the Supreme Court. He says this is because other views are "only a matter of private faith and belief, and it is morally unjust to impose private beliefs upon others who do not share them. To do so violates the First Amendment of the Constitution which guarantees religious freedom and freedom of thought" (*HH* 137).

Thus, Fletcher would agree with Porter regarding the need for Catholics to dialogue with non-Catholics regarding what constitutes the good, providing solid reasoning for their arguments. He understands that many religious moralists, such as some Catholics and conservative evangelicals, would like a "one-faith, one-morality order," claiming that stem-cell research and abortion violate the natural law that is binding on all people (*MR* 106). But relying on the magisterium or a legalistic view of scripture would violate what he calls the *consensus communis* (consensus of the community) on these issues that occur in a democratic society.

RESOURCES

Discussion Questions

1. Does the creation of iPS cells, which can be generated from adult skin cells rather than embryonic stem cells, change the nature of the ethical debate, as James Thomson claims? In what ways? Would Porter or Fletcher agree?

2. President George W. Bush allowed federal funding for already established embryonic cell lines but prohibited it for new ones. Do you think he was right to do this? If he can justify the use of already established embryonic cell lines and support it with federal funding, how does this differ morally from supporting research on embryonic stem cells from frozen embryos that will be created through IVF, the excess of which will ultimately be destroyed? What would the two Christian social ethics models above say about this?

3. Should religious motivations be the primary determiner of public policy decisions? Porter and Fletcher suggest that they should not. Why not? How do you balance the different religiously motivated positions in this debate?

4. Fletcher rejects the argument that somehow laboratory reproduction is unnatural, meaning that it does not occur as a result of sexual intercourse between a man and a woman. In fact, he suggests that it is more human because it is "willed, chosen, purposed, and controlled." Do you agree or disagree? Why?

5. Porter and Fletcher question the full moral status of a five-to-seven-day-old blastocyst. What is the basis for their claims? How are their views similar? How are they different? Do you agree with them? Why or why not?

Activities

1. Do an analysis of this case from the perspective of feminist or womanist ethics. Compare and contrast the conclusions that perspective might draw with those from the two perspectives in this case analysis. In what ways are they similar? In what ways are they different? Which approach, in your opinion, addresses the case most comprehensively?

2. Watch several films from the list below that highlight some of the ethical issues associated with stem-cell research, cloning, and others (*The Island* and *My Sister's Keeper* are particularly good examples). Analyze the films to discern the approach the filmmaker takes on the moral issue in question. How are the ethical issues illustrated? Where do the films fall short in raising the ethical concerns? How would their perspective differ from those of the Christian social ethical traditions discussed above?

3. Religious and theological perspectives influence public policies on laws and funding associated with stem-cell research and abortion. Organize a debate on the merits and liabilities of religious influence on public policy in this area. Draw from the discussion above to make your case.

4. Create a piece of artwork (a poem, painting, sculpture, video) to demonstrate your learning on either stem-cell research or the moral status of the embryo. The object is to convey some ideas, thoughts, or feelings through the use of symbols, which enables you to demonstrate that you understand the ethical issues associated with this subject matter. These may be shared with the class, or they may be shared only with the professor. In addition to the artwork itself, attach a brief (two to four pages) written statement that explains the purpose of the artwork, what you were seeking to demonstrate in its creation, and how you have attempted to accomplish your goal.

5. Review the Pew Research Center's Forum on Religion and Public Life to see where different Christian denominations stand on the issue of embryonic stem-cell research. Note the similarities and differences, and make a report to your class.

Readings

Holland, Suzanne, Karen Lebacqz, and Laurie Zoloth, eds. *The Human Embryonic Stem Cell Debate: Science, Ethics, and Public Policy.* Cambridge, MA: MIT Press, 2001. This book considers the many ethical issues involved in human embryonic stem-cell research, including the nature of human life, the limits of intervention into human cells and tissues, and the meaning of our bodily existence.

Meilaender, Gilbert. *Bioethics: A Primer for Christians.* Third edition. Grand Rapids, MI: Eerdmans, 2013. A theologically informed treatment of such issues as abortion, assisted reproduction, genetic research, and human experimentation, this book also includes a section on the need to protect Christian conscience in the practice of medicine.

Peters, Ted. *The Stem-Cell Debate.* Minneapolis: Fortress Press, 2007. This book challenges people of faith to think critically about the science of stem cells and regenerative medicine, tracing the ethical debate to three very different moral frameworks and illustrating the legitimate concerns of each.

Waters, Brent, and Ronald Cole-Turner, eds. *God and the Embryo: Religious Voices on Stem Cells and Cloning.* Washington, DC: Georgetown University Press, 2003. The contributors to this book discuss ethical issues associated with stem cells and cloning from a spectrum of Christian voices—liberal Protestant, evangelical, and Roman Catholic.

Wildes, Kevin, ed. *Religious Faith and Psychological Needs in Infertility.* Dordrecht, The Netherlands: Kluwer Academic Publishers, 1997. A diverse group of clinicians, theologians, and philosophers are brought together here to examine the use of reproductive technologies in light of the Roman Catholic moral tradition and recent teaching.

Audiovisuals

Hope. Ambler Films, IDream Motion Pictures, 2008. This Ambler film raises the question of whether one can support stem-cell therapy for an injured family member if it goes against one's religious beliefs.

The Island. DreamWorks Pictures, 2005. Directed by Michael Bay and starring Scarlett Johansson and Ewan McGregor, this futuristic film illustrates the ethical difficulties of creating and maintaining human clones to be used for body parts should the original person need them.

My Sister's Keeper. New Line Cinema, 2009. This film, directed by Nick Cassavetes and starring Cameron Diaz and Alec Baldwin, highlights the story of one daughter's attempt to earn medical emancipation from her parents, who until now have relied on their youngest child to help their leukemia-stricken older daughter remain alive.

Stem Cell Revolutions. Scottish Documentary Institute, 2013. Directed by Amy Hardie, this documentary interviews leading stem cell scientists, including Nobel laureate Dr. Shinya Yamanaka, and charts the history and scientific evolution of stem-cell research, including current clinical developments.

Stem Cells: The Early Research. PBS, 2005. Written by Julia Court, this NOVA scienceNOW segment explores the promise and potential of the emerging field of stem-cell research, as well as the maelstrom of emotion and politics that engulfs it.

Terra Incognita: The Perils and Promise of Stem Cell Research. Kartemquin Films, 2007. This documentary relates Dr. Jack Kessler's experience of changing his research on stem cells for diabetes to research using embryonic stem cells on spinal cord injuries after his daughter was paralyzed in a skiing accident.

5

Economic and Social Inequality

CASE STUDY:
DEFERRED ACTION FOR CHILDHOOD ARRIVALS (DACA)
AND IMMIGRATION

Zoila Pelayo received a letter in fall 2019 from Immigrations and Customs Enforcement (ICE) telling her that the agency was filing to reopen her deportation case, which had been closed eight years earlier. Pelayo was brought to the United States from Mexico without documentation when she was six years old. Now thirty-three, and having never been in trouble with the law, she was living with her husband and two young children in Tucson, Arizona. "I never thought they would reopen my case," she said. "I feel like I'm an American. . . . If they send me back to Mexico what are my kids going to do without me? What am I going to do without them?" Pelayo isn't the only one facing that question. The Trump administration, in its efforts to pursue undocumented immigrants, is moving to deport members of a group that seemed until a few years ago the most protected: DACA recipients.[1]

DACA refers to the Deferred Action for Childhood Arrivals program, which was introduced by the Obama administration in 2012 as a stopgap measure in response to the failure of the US Congress to implement a comprehensive immigration policy. "DACA is an exercise of prosecutorial discretion, providing temporary relief from deportation (deferred action) and work authorization to certain young undocumented immigrants brought to the United States as children."[2] These Dreamers, as they are called, get their name from

---

[1] Bob Ortega, "ICE Reopening Long-Closed Deportation Cases against Dreamers," *CNN Investigates* (December 21, 2019).

[2] American Immigration Council, "Fact Sheet: The Dream Act, DACA, and Other Policies Designed to Protect Dreamers," https://www.americanimmigrationcouncil.org/research. To be eligible, DACA applicants have had to meet the following requirements: arrived in the United States before turning sixteen and under the age of thirty-one on June 15, 2012; continuously resided in the United States from June 15, 2007, to

a legislative effort in 2001 called the DREAM Act (Development, Relief and Education for Alien Minors Act), which would have provided a pathway to US citizenship to those undocumented youth who go to college and/or serve in the military while maintaining a clean record. The bill enjoyed bipartisan support and came close to being enacted in 2010 when it passed in the House of Representatives but fell just five votes short of the sixty needed to avoid a filibuster in the Senate. The Obama administration's executive action allowed certain undocumented young people to register for the program every two years, enabling them to go to school or to work without fear of deportation; it did not, however, provide a path to citizenship. When initiating the program, President Obama remarked: "These are young people who study in our schools, they play in our neighborhoods, they're friends with our kids, they pledge allegiance to our flag. They are Americans in their heart, in their minds, in every single way but one: on paper."[3] The majority of public opinion agreed with that sentiment.

In November 2014, President Obama announced an expansion of the DACA program that would have increased the population eligible to apply for employment authorization to people of any current age who had entered the United States before the age of sixteen, and who could demonstrate continuous residence in the United States since January 1, 2010. On February 16, 2015, just two days before the program was scheduled to begin, Texas and twenty-five other states were able to secure a temporary court injunction ultimately suspending the expansion of the program from going into effect. This action prompted the Obama administration to go to federal court. In *United States v. Texas*, the Fifth Circuit ruled in favor of the states. The case was referred to the US Supreme Court, whose 4–4 split vote let the lower court ruling stand, thus maintaining the original DACA program but not the expansion.

In September 2017, the Trump administration rescinded the original DACA program when ten states threatened to sue to eliminate the program. President Trump claimed that it was the legislative rather than the executive branch of government that enacts laws, and that the Obama administration had usurped its authority. Rather than ending the program abruptly, the Trump administration would allow those applications in the pipeline to be processed

---

the present; were physically present in the United States on June 15, 2012, as well as at the time of requesting deferred action; entered without inspection before June 15, 2012, or any previous lawful immigration status expired on or before June 15, 2012; either in school, have graduated, or obtained a certificate of completion from high school, have obtained a general education development (GED) certificate, or are honorably discharged veterans of the US Coast Guard or the US Armed Forces; and have not been convicted of a felony, significant misdemeanor, or three or more other misdemeanors occurring on different dates and arising out of different acts, omissions, or schemes of misconduct and do not otherwise pose a threat to national security or public safety.

[3] President Obama, "Remarks by the President on Immigration," June 15, 2012.

and those currently in the program to renew their status for an additional two years. No new applications, however, would be accepted. At the end of the two-year cycle, the program would end, and no more work permits would be issued. President Trump's stated goal was not to punish the young people in the program but rather to force Congress to "finally act."[4] In early 2018, two federal judges issued injunctions against the Trump administration's efforts to terminate the DACA program and required that it continue to allow renewal requests beyond the two-year cycle. In fall 2019, the Supreme Court agreed to hear the challenge to DACA brought by the states and heard oral arguments in November focused on the legality of the program and the prerogative of the administration to end it, which it would decide in June 2020. In the interim, ICE indicated that all DACA recipients whose deportation cases were administratively closed because of the program could expect to see them reopened. On June 18, 2020, the Supreme Court ruled 5–4 that the Department of Homeland Security (DHS) in its rescission (revocation) of the program "failed to consider the conspicuous issues of whether to retain forbearance and what if anything to do about the hardship to DACA recipients," failures that raise "doubts about whether the agency appreciated the scope of its discretion or exercised that discretion in a reasonable manner."[5] Thus, the program was remanded back to DHS for reconsideration.[6] The ruling did not, however, say anything about the legality of the program. Thus, the reprieve for Zoila Pelayo and other Dreamers may be short lived.

ISSUES AND CONCERNS

People for and against continuation of the DACA program use both pragmatic (economic and social) and justice (legal and moral) arguments in support of their position. Supporters suggest that the country has already made a substantial investment in many of these young Dreamers through public health care, public assistance, and public schools. They have earned their high school diplomas, trade school certification, and college degrees. Many have gone on to secure better-paying jobs, to establish businesses, and to purchase homes, all of which contribute to state and local tax bases and economies. Some are medical professionals who have worked on the front lines of the fight

---

[4] President Donald J. Trump, "Statement from President Donald J. Trump: Immigration," Statements and Releases, September 5, 2017 (hereafter cited as "Immigration").

[5] *Department of Homeland Security et al., v. Regents of the University of California et al.* 591 U. S. 29 (2020).

[6] In response to the June 2020 Supreme Court decision, President Trump tweeted: "The Supreme Court asked us to resubmit on DACA, nothing was lost or won. They 'punted,' much like in a football game (where hopefully they would stand for our great American Flag). We will be submitting enhanced papers shortly in order to properly fulfil the Supreme Court's ruling & request of yesterday."

against the most recent pandemic.[7] They have gotten driver's licenses, which makes our roads and communities safer. Others have joined the ranks of the military and fought on behalf of the country. They are already assimilated into our society, and for most, English is their only language. Deporting them would mean throwing all those investments away. Moreover, deportation itself is expensive and would cost taxpayers additional money. By allowing them to stay, either through maintaining the DACA program or passing the current version of the Dream Act, they could continue to contribute billions of dollars to the economy and to society, providing stability for them, their schools, their employers, and their communities.

Opponents suggest that some of the benefits highlighted above are burdens on rather than benefits to society. Providing health care, public assistance, and education to illegal immigrants has been at the expense of local communities and taxpayers, especially when the current emphasis on multiculturalism rather than assimilation requires additional resources to accommodate their cultural and language needs.[8] While many may take jobs that citizens find undesirable, this is not true across the board. Because of their educational achievements at taxpayers' expense, they compete for available jobs, thus contributing to the unemployment of citizens with similar educations and background. The Trump administration argues that their availability for jobs, combined with the presence of other undocumented workers, creates looseness in low-wage labor markets that undermines employer incentives to raise wages. In other words, "when the supply of workers goes up, the price that firms have to pay to hire workers goes down," a claim that economists are divided over.[9] Even though there are restrictions on eligibility for the DACA program, keeping this program might encourage others to come here illegally to seek work permits, furthering the immigration crisis we currently experience and adding to our already overburdened public assistance, public health care, and public school systems.

The legal questions DACA raises are another consideration. In the oral arguments of the Supreme Court there was debate about whether the decision

---

[7] Adam Liptak writes that twenty-seven thousand Dreamers worked in health care in 2020 ("'Dreamers' Tell Supreme Court Ending DACA during Pandemic Would Be 'Catastrophic,'" *New York Times,* March 27, 2020).

[8] National Academies of Sciences, Engineering, and Medicine, *The Economic and Fiscal Consequences of Immigration* (Washington, DC: National Academies Press, 2017).

[9] George Borjas, "Yes, Immigration Hurts American Workers," *Politico* (September/October 2016). The Trump administration cites the work of Borjas for its arguments, but Borjas says it only highlights half the truth and does not consider the economic benefits overall. The Economic Policy Institute argues that the opposite would be true: "Ending DACA and forcing these young workers out of the formal, regulated labor market, thus making them easily exploitable, will not help American workers, it will do the opposite" (Daniel Costa, "Ending DACA Lowers Wages and Tax Revenues, and Degrades Labor Standards," EPI Working Economics blog (September 5, 2017).

to establish the program violated the Constitution, which places authority for immigration laws in the hands of Congress, not the president. President Trump noted in his decision to rescind DACA that President Obama knew he shouldn't make immigration policy unilaterally, "and yet that is exactly what he did, making an end-run around Congress and violating the core tenets that sustain our Republic" ("Immigration"). Yet allowing the Trump administration to eliminate the program would suggest that the executive branch does have more legal authority than opponents believe. For some, the continued presence of these Dreamers raises concerns about criminal activity and threats to national security posed by the presence of noncitizens. The Center for Immigration Studies, an organization that says it is "low immigration, pro immigration," notes that many Dreamers have committed work-related crimes such as Social Security fraud, forgery, and falsifying identification cards.[10] Some Dreamers have lost their program status because of criminal activity or involvement in gangs. Others contend, however, that this only proves that the safeguards in the program regarding illegal activity are working, and that national security is strengthened when everyone in the country lives openly and contributes to society.

Regarding the ethical issues associated with fairness and justice in this case, opponents claim that DACA gives amnesty to lawbreakers and encourages others to cheat the system, as demonstrated by the recent surge in unaccompanied minors seeking to enter illegally. President Trump argues: "Before we ask what is fair to illegal immigrants, we must also ask what is fair to American families, students, taxpayers, and jobseekers" ("Immigration").[11] Some worry that if we leave DACA in place, it will encourage further demands on behalf of illegal immigrants, leading ultimately to totally open borders. By contrast, supporters argue it would be unfair and morally wrong to eliminate DACA because these young people are innocent and blameless. They were brought to the United States as children, and our society does not generally hold children morally accountable for their parents' actions. The government should treat them as victims, not offenders. Deportation to a country they never knew with languages they do not speak would amount to cruel and inhumane punishment, especially if the dangerous conditions that led their parents to leave have continued.[12] The DACA program invited these Dreamers to come out from the shadows and trust us. Turning on them violates that

---

[10] Ronald W. Mortensen, "DACA: Granting Amnesty to Dreamers Committing Crimes While Abandoning Their Victims," Center for Immigration Studies, cis.org, March 10, 2017.

[11] As an example of the Trump administration's efforts to focus on citizens, the US Department of Education under Secretary DeVos ruled that noncitizens, such as the Dreamers, could not receive emergency funds that are part of the coronavirus pandemic response for colleges and universities.

[12] Thiru Vignarajah, "Deporting Dreamers Is as Cruel and Unusual as It Gets," *Seattle Times,* November 12, 2017.

trust, and this is not who we are as a society.[13] Others argue that the presence of these students and workers in key industries, especially health care, contributes not only to the creativity and talent of our workforce but also to its diversity, which could have a significant impact on the care of underserved and immigrant populations.[14]

The case also raises concerns about the rights of citizens versus the rights of undocumented immigrants. When discussing the language of rights, it is important to make a distinction between negative rights and positive rights.[15] What is the basis for distributing those rights? Is it because we are citizens of a country or because we are persons? Most legal scholars would agree that the rights granted by the Constitution are based on personhood and jurisdiction. Persons living in the United States, legally or not, have the same basic rights. For example, in the case of public education for undocumented children, the Supreme Court ruled in *Plyler v. Doe* that if children who are citizens have access to a free public education, the Fourteenth Amendment requires that undocumented children should as well, because government cannot deny them equal access under the law unless "it furthers some substantial state interest," which the Court ruled was not the case. Of course, opponents of providing rights such as education to undocumented immigrants believe that doing so would undermine the economic and political stability of our society. The Supreme Court majority in this case argued that the reverse would be true: "We cannot ignore the significant social costs borne by our Nation when select groups are denied the means to absorb the values and skills upon which our social order rests."[16]

DACA defenders agree with the assertion that rights should be based on personhood and not on citizenship. The program is in keeping with the heritage of the United States as a nation that treats immigrants fairly and equally and makes special efforts to reach out to young people. This sentiment is expressed by some of President Trump's Christian evangelical supporters. Evangelical Pastor Tony Suarez, a member of Trump's evangelical advisory board, argues: "Since we first joined the advisory board, we told the president that if you're going to build a wall then you must also build bridges: bridges of compassion, bridges of mercy to understand the plight of these undocumented children."[17] Moreover, the American tradition as

---

[13] George Bradt, "The Moral, Ethical, and Pragmatic Case for DACA," *Forbes* (October 6, 2017).

[14] See D. Zaidi and M. Kuczewski, "Ending DACA Has Pragmatic and Ethical Implications for US Health Care," *Hastings Center Report* 47/6 (November 2017): 14–15.

[15] As noted in Chapter 3, *positive rights* refer to those social and economic rights, such as health care and education, which create entitlements that others are obligated to fulfill. *Negative rights* refer to those civic and political rights, such as free speech or freedom of assembly, with which others should not interfere.

[16] *Plyler v. Doe* 457 U. S. 230 (1982).

[17] National Public Radio, "Christians and DACA," *Morning Edition*, September 7, 2017.

a sanctuary for exiles dictates that we allow these innocent immigrants a chance to move on with their lives and not cast them off as refugees without a homeland. This coincides with the Christian tradition's ideals of welcoming the stranger and love of neighbor with support coming from Christians across the religious spectrum. As do some other religious leaders, Terri Hord Owens, general minister and president of the Disciples of Christ, claims that "DACA . . . recipients have followed the calling of God in Jeremiah 27:9 to 'seek the welfare of the city to where I send you'; and our faith compels us likewise to support the well-being and healing of those who offer their gifts generously to our nation."[18]

HISPANIC LIBERATIVE ETHICS

The analysis of this case from the Hispanic liberative ethics approach draws upon Miguel De La Torre's hermeneutical circle and from his *The US Immigration Crisis: Toward an Ethics of Place*,[19] which broadly explores the ethical implications of US immigration policy that undergirds the development of DACA. As noted previously, Hispanic liberative ethics is a contextual approach to Christian ethics drawing from the lived religious, cultural, ethnic, and social realities of Hispanics living in the United States, particularly the immigrant Hispanic community. Social location is important for a contextual ethic. Not only has De La Torre visited Latinx immigrants at the border, walking their trails and documenting the injustices they face, but his solidarity with this population and with DACA recipients has a personal dimension to it: for a good part of his early life, he was an undocumented person brought here from Cuba by his parents.

De La Torre begins by engaging in some historical analysis and asks how this and other immigration issues have emerged in the first place. Why are so many undocumented Latinx immigrants drawn to the United States, and why do they stay? He notes how anti-immigration forces believe they come with their children to take away jobs and to avail themselves of our public and social services. More sympathetic voices say they come to find the American dream for themselves and their families. But both narratives are erroneous, De La Torre argues. The undocumented presence in the United States is not immigrants' attempt to force themselves upon an unwilling host country; rather, it is the result of political, social, and economic conditions created, in good measure, by US trade and foreign policies from the nineteenth through the twenty-first centuries that have left them insecure and unable to provide for their families (*TEP* 151). Two policies that have contributed to this

---

[18] Reverend Terri Hord Owens. "Thoughts on Deferred Action for Childhood Arrivals (DACA) in the US," September 5, 2017.

[19] Miguel De La Torre, *The US Immigration Crisis: Toward an Ethics of Place* (Eugene, OR: Cascade Books, 2016) (hereafter cited as *TEP*).

situation the most are "gunboat diplomacy" and the North American Free Trade Agreement (NAFTA).

When thinking about those undocumented young people coming from Central America, a historical analysis reveals the impact of gunboat diplomacy, which refers to the close ties between American corporate and consumer interests in having the goods they desire and the use of the military and the CIA to advance those interests. A prime example De La Torre cites is the United Fruit Company's banana industry in Guatemala, where the company owned most of the land and the CIA engineered a coup in 1954 to install a new political leadership more friendly to its economic interests. The creation of "banana republics" was a result of these interventions in the political and economic conditions in these countries to ensure the flow of goods and services to the United States, while generating "poverty, strife, and death" for the citizens there (*TEP* 69). If we are serious about understanding why people from El Salvador, Honduras, and Guatemala are crossing our borders today, we must recognize that "they come to escape the violence and terrorism our foreign policy unleashed in order to confiscate their resources and cheap labor" (*TEP* 66).

A more significant policy that contributed to the rise of Mexican undocumented immigrants was the North American Free Trade Agreement (NAFTA).[20] The goal of NAFTA, which included Canada, the United States, and Mexico, was to promote the free flow of goods and services among the countries with limited tariffs on some agricultural and other products. The agreement, De La Torre argues, had a negative impact on workers in Mexico and the United States. For example, because of the corn subsidies given to US farmers, they were able to sell their corn at a lower price, rendering subsistence corn farmers in Mexico unable to compete. The agreement also allowed US corporations to move factories from the United States to Mexico along the border in search of cheaper labor and tax breaks, which created *maquiladoras* (factories). Raw materials would come to Mexico from the US tariff free, and the finished products would be produced in the factories and then shipped back to the United States and taxed on the "value added" to the product. Because corn farming in Mexico was no longer profitable, many of the farmers went to work in these factories in cities where unemployment was high, which kept wages depressed. Eventually, many corporations in search of even cheaper labor began to shift production to countries in Asia, leaving workers on both sides of the border at a disadvantage, having to compete against each other and workers in the global labor market, who are often paid a fraction for the same work (*TEP* 29). Even though many factory jobs in the United States went overseas in search of cheaper labor markets and less restrictive labor laws, work in the United States under minimum wage laws paid

---

[20] The trilateral agreement came into force in January 1994. This law has been superseded by the United States Mexico Canada Agreement (USMCA) that was finally ratified in March 2020. The new agreement provides some additional labor protections for each country.

more than in Mexico. The result was an influx of immigrants from Mexico, documented and undocumented, into the United States in search of better opportunities. Although many in the United States try to scapegoat Mexican migrants, including DACA participants, for the US immigration crisis, the real culprit, De La Torre claims, is NAFTA, "a consequence of what immigration experts call the 'push-and-pull' factor. The economic condition existing in the immigrant's homeland, due in part to our corn subsidies, 'pushes' them out, while the US need for cheap labor 'pulls' them in" (*TEP* 32).

Social analysis of the case reveals other economic and social costs of immigration and deportation. The economic threat of moving jobs to Mexico has forced workers in the United States to agree to reductions in wages and benefits and has undermined union recruitment efforts. Yet even after agreeing to the cuts, the jobs went south anyway, generating misplaced resentment toward Mexican immigrants (*TEP* 30). "Anti-immigrant sentiments correspond to the downward mobility faced by many middle-class Euromericans due to the globalization of the economy. Rather than holding economic elites responsible for the upward transfer of wealth, the immigrant became a scapegoat and was presented as a threat" (*TEP* 41). De La Torre notes that the cost of removing undocumented immigrants, including DACA recipients, would be prohibitively expensive. By some conservative estimates, the cost would run from $400 to $600 billion and would take many years to accomplish. The removal of these undocumented immigrants would also lead to a drop in real gross domestic product (GDP) by as much at $1.6 trillion, because many of the jobs that are important to the economy in agriculture and the service sector, which many Americans refuse to take, would go unfilled. In addition, new courts and detention camps would need to be constructed to deal with the volume of cases that would result (*TEP* 86).

The social costs to the immigrants and the stigma of being labeled as illegal can be problematic. The term *illegal* implies that they are criminals and inherently bad persons, a characterization perpetuated by Donald Trump in 2015, who said: "When Mexico sends its people, they're not sending their best. They're sending people that have a lot of problems, and they're bringing those problems with them. They're bringing drugs. They're bringing crime. They're rapists. And some, I assume, are good people."[21] The same is true with the word *migrants,* which has come to denote inferiority and a lack of skills and education, no matter how far from the truth that is (*TEP* 75). More problematic still is the racist bias that underlies these labels. De La Torre claims, "The current social, economic, and political structures are undergirded with the recognition that only white lives matter" (*TEP* 77). Whenever persons of color, brown and black, seek some level of equality in the institutions that affect them, powerful whites, who are the most privileged in society economically, socially, and politically, rewrite themselves into the national narrative as victims and accuse those seeking equality of "playing the race card" or as

---

[21] Donald J. Trump, "Presidential Announcement Speech," June 16, 2015.

"race hustlers" (*TEP* 83). Unfortunately, as we have seen in the debate over DACA and immigration, men who are not economically privileged have been encouraged to seek upward mobility for themselves and to blame their inability to achieve it on brown and black people who are "stealing their jobs and depressing wages, thus preventing them from achieving their rightful place in society" (*TEP* 85). The result is a society that perpetuates inequality to the benefit of the powerful and to the detriment of the rest.

Furthermore, although much of the focus on immigration has been on the geographic border between the United States and the south, the social and psychological borders for the undocumented can be even more devastating. The DACA program allowed these young Dreamers to come out of the shadows and contribute to society, but the threatened elimination of the program and subsequent deportation is generating a great deal of anxiety. Dreamers are losing access to educational and other public services that not only benefit them but, some argue, the whole society.[22] De La Torre contends that the physical borders that many had to cross to come to the United States at great peril to themselves and their families continue to live on in the borders the powerful have constructed: "the borders . . . between legitimacy and illegitimacy, the borders between economic class and poverty, the borders between acceptance and rejection, the border between life and death" (*TEP* 71).

Staying true to his Christocentric ethics, De La Torre's biblical and theological analysis in this case leads him to extend his understanding of the incarnation of God in the life and work of Jesus the Christ. Where earlier we noted that the incarnation was God's self-identification with the poor, being born in humble circumstances, in this case the poor that God self-identifies with are the undocumented. Drawing from the Gospels' portrayal of Jesus's early life, he notes that Jesus and his family also had to flee the oppressive circumstances they found in the Roman Empire; thus, Jesus assumed the role of the disenfranchised and marginalized, and he remained in that role during his earthly ministry. So, as Christians ponder their responsibilities in this context, De La Torre writes, "if we want to see the face of Jesus, all we need to do is gaze into the face of the undocumented," including those in the DACA program (*TEP* 155, 157). Just as God always sides with and intervenes to liberate the marginalized (Ex 23:9), so must Christians of all stripes stand in solidarity with the undocumented in their struggle for justice and an immigration policy that treats them with the dignity and respect they deserve.

De La Torre connects the importance of solidarity with the marginalized with two biblical narratives: the salvation narrative in the Gospel of Matthew (Mt 25) and the parable of the Good Samaritan (Lk 10). In the first instance, entry into the kingdom of heaven depends on the treatment given to the hungry, the thirsty, the sick, the naked, the prisoner, and the alien. Those who treat these marginalized sufferers well are welcomed into the

---

[22] For example, during the coronavirus pandemic the Education Department refused colleges and universities their requests to use federal stimulus money for needy DACA program participants.

kingdom; those who ignore them or treat them poorly are not. In this case, De La Torre notes, "the undocumented crossing the borders are usually the hungry, the thirsty, the naked, and of course the alien; because they are often the sick due to the hazards of their journey, and when caught by the Border Patrol become the prisoner" (*TEP* 155). Our immigration policies and the decision to end the DACA program suggest that we are treating them poorly. The parable of the Good Samaritan, which De La Torre suggests might be renamed in this context the "parable of the Good Illegal Alien,"[23] offers a moral example of how to treat them well. "To be faithful to the parable of the Good Samaritan means we must care for all we find in the wilderness who are hungry, thirsty, and naked—regardless of documentation," even if it means arrest and imprisonment (*TEP* 55).

Christians who support the Dreamers highlight the ethical principle of hospitality. "The virtue of hospitality becomes our religious or civic duty to assist (bring salvation to) these poor unfortunate souls, for after all, there go I but by the grace of God" (*TEP* 153). While certainly an important biblical concept embedded in the notion of welcoming the stranger, the problem with hospitality in this case, De La Torre argues, is that it implies that the "house" belongs to the one who practices this virtue, who is sharing resources with the "other" who has no claim to the possession. Given his analysis of the ways in which the United States has destroyed these Latinxs' livelihoods through our economic and foreign policies in their homelands, perhaps it is time to talk about the principle of restitution. What do we owe to these Latinxs whose livelihoods we have destroyed with our economic and military might? "Maybe the ethical question we should be asking is not 'why' are they coming, but how do we begin to make reparations for all we have stolen to create the present economic empire we call the United States?" (*TEP* 159).

For De La Torre, affirming the theological claim that God has a preferential option for those who face oppression and injustice requires a "feet on the ground" presence and praxis with those who are undocumented, working with them in solidarity to achieve the respect and justice they deserve. One such practice, as we noted in Chapter 1, is civil initiative. De La Torre came across this concept when he researched and worked alongside activists on the border who were seeking to protect the human rights of undocumented immigrants. From their perspective it is not the Dreamers or other undocumented immigrants who are violating the law. Rather, it is the US government and its agents failing to live up to their international commitments and responsibilities. They are the ones engaged in civil disobedience of these international laws to which they had agreed and ratified. "When this occurs, it falls upon civil society to provide protection to the victims of human rights violations, not as an act of civil disobedience, but as an act of civil 'initiative,'" an ethical concept developed and implemented during the Sanctuary Movement, which

---

[23] De La Torre, *The Politics of Jesus: A Hispanic Political Theology* (Lanham, MD: Rowman and Littlefield, 2015), 37.

recognizes that "international duties transcend individual obligations to obey national states" (*TEP* 122–23).

Proponents of civil initiative contend that those who practice it are called to

1) neither evade nor seize police powers, but stand ready to be arrested, and if they are, demand a trial by jury; 2) be truthful, open and subject to public examination; 3) strive toward being catholic, protecting the rights of the abused regardless of their ideology or their political usefulness; 4) seek to be dialogical, treating government officials as persons, not simply adversaries, in the hope of reaching a reconciliation that does not compromise human rights; 5) remain germane to the needs of the oppressed to be protected and not simply focus on media attention; 6) be volunteer-based and operated; and 7) community centered. (*TEP* 123)

In addition to providing sanctuary, another civil initiative is the practice of placing food and water along migrant trails. De La Torre worked with No More Death, a humanitarian organization consisting of faith and community groups. They identify the trails that migrants use to cross the border and leave necessities so that immigrants do not die of hunger or thirst. They recognize that such actions are considered violations of federal laws, but they are willing to face the consequences of their action to provide aid that might save lives.

To these practices on behalf of immigrants and Dreamers, De La Torre adds his ethical practice of *para joder* ("screwing with"). When one cannot overcome oppressive structures, then one screws with them to create chaos or disorder and to highlight their injustice (*TEP* 102). De La Torre also talks about how his ethics of *para joder* has had an impact on some of the praxis going on in relationship to this case. An example he gives is when ministers stood up during a deportation hearing and read scripture to highlight their faith and to bring the injustice of what was going on to light. An ethics of *para joder* provides imaginative ways to draw attention to unjust structures until we finally succeed in changing those structures.

WOMANIST LIBERATIVE ETHICS

To review this case from the perspective of womanist liberative ethics, we draw primarily from two works by Emilie Townes: *Womanist Ethics and the Cultural Production of Evil* and "Black Womanist Consciousness: Economic and Border Thoughts."[24] Like Hispanic ethics, womanist ethics explores the

---

[24] Emilie Townes, *Womanist Ethics and the Cultural Production of Evil* (New York: Palgrave Macmillan, 2006) (hereafter cited as *CPE*); idem, "Black Womanist Consciousness: Economic and Border Thoughts," *Interpretation* 74/1 (2020): 9–14 (hereafter cited as "Consciousness"). Limited reference is also made to Emilie Townes, "Ethics as an Art of Doing the Work Our Souls Must Have," in *Womanist Theological Ethics: A Reader*, ed. Katie Geneva Cannon, Emilie M. Townes, and Angela D.

lived realities of those who experience marginalization and oppression in the face of structures and systems that deny them their full humanity and justice. Townes identifies these structures as one dimension of the cultural production of evil. "Exploring evil as a cultural production highlights the systematic construction of truncated narratives designed to support and perpetuate structural inequities and forms of social oppression" (*CPE* 4). Resolving our immigration crisis and the situation of the Dreamers requires first and foremost a thorough social analysis of the racial, class, and psychological dynamics of their experiences and the social policies that contribute to their marginalization ("Souls" 44). With this descriptive account of the issue as a backdrop, we can then draw upon the insights of womanist ethics to identify critical moral values—the prescriptive element—in order to identify possible solutions to the crisis.

Townes's analysis of our immigration issues, which she labels "a hot mess" and "a fresh hell," highlights important features about the crisis. She rejects the argument that the immigration debate is one about sovereignty or security, as some have claimed. Rather, the crisis is a humanitarian one, where the real debate is not what is happening to migrants but "what is going on in us." "We have allowed the ideas of 'post truth' and 'alternative facts' that began as laughing points to be turned into policy points that have become legal points such that some of us need not apply for justice or mercy" ("Consciousness" 14). The profile of recent migrants and Dreamers is less about young men, women, and seasonal workers than about families who are seeking asylum from Central America, fleeing the violence, poverty, and political corruption that have made some parts of these countries uninhabitable. As De La Torre argued above, the reasons for these conditions, Townes contends, are a result of US economic and foreign policies in this region. Our previous policies have failed, and we must address this crisis as a refugee crisis, "rather than casting brown bodies as a threat to national security or the reason why we refuse to offer a living wage to millions of workers or the alleged cause of the rise in crime in the USA" ("Consciousness" 15). Building a wall will not resolve the issue, no matter how high or long we make it. Fixing the problem requires that the entire region work together to address the problems that failed economic and foreign policies have created. Townes suggests that what is going on in rejecting asylum seekers such as the Dreamers is part of what she calls a "fantastic hegemonic imagination" that we all share:

This is an imagination that encourages us to see one another through stereotypes and innuendos. It is an imagination that is arrogant about our ignorance and denies that we are often afraid of what we do not know or understand and hesitant to take on educating ourselves because

---

Sims, 35–60 (Louisville, KY: Westminster John Knox Press, 2011) (hereafter cited as "Souls"), which was the primary basis for the development of the womanist ethics tradition in Chapter 1.

it just might mean that we will have to open up our hearts, minds, souls, bodies, communities, religious homes to a full-blown spring cleaning of the spirit. In other words—we will have to change. (*CPE* 15)

One of the things Townes believes we must change is our understanding of race and racism. Like many theorists, Townes rejects the notion that race is an essential dimension of our being, determined by biology and genetics; rather, she sees race as a social construction that tends to privilege some groups (whites) and disadvantage others (persons of color). A major issue in society reflected in this case is what she calls "uninterrogated coloredness," which is "a complicated and interstructured set of social meanings that are always being transformed by political struggle" (*CPE* 75).[25] This is especially an issue among whites who do not see how whiteness is not colorless but is also a social construction; it shapes not only how they see brown and black persons in a negative light but also allows them to ignore the extent of their power and privilege (*CPE* 60). For Townes, such racialization "confers social significance to coloredness to an inordinate degree . . . a thoroughgoing yet often unconscious color caste system on degrees of darkness and lightness" (*CPE* 64). When uninterrogated, whites see their values, beliefs, and privileges as normal, and everything else as an exception. That is why when whites talk about race, they do not think about themselves but only about persons of color, often using stereotypes or coded language to suggest that they do not have the same moral qualities that whites have. As a result, whiteness tends to link people to a position of racial dominance (*CPE* 65). Even white claims that we are all the same "under the skin" suggest "that failures to live into this sameness and achieve it is the fault of colored peoples" (*CPE* 69). The irony in the case of the Dreamers is that many of them have worked hard to achieve that "sameness" by educating themselves, working hard, and assimilating fully into their communities, everything the DACA program has asked of them. Yet this has not been enough to grant them permanent status. Instead, Townes argues, if we are to address fully the immigration issue and the situation of Dreamers, we need to interrogate all forms of coloredness to get at the interstructured nature of oppression, structures she labels as evil.

In addition to race, a second dynamic in this immigration debate that contributes to oppression is the issue of class. Like De La Torre, Townes notes how powerful whites have sought to shift the narrative regarding immigration toward concerns about the costs of dependency on government largesse or competition for working-class jobs. She laments the way a Trump administration immigration official, Kenneth T. Cuccinelli II, recast the poet

---

[25] Many people see the 2020 riots in cities across the United States in response to more African Americans being killed at the hands of police as an example of the interstructuring of oppression. The violence in the cities is a response to the racial and economic violence being perpetrated by those in power, violence that has become more evident with the disproportionate negative effect of the coronavirus on brown and black populations.

Emma Lazarus's message on the Statue of Liberty to immigrants coming to our shores, "The New Colossus." Instead of "Give me your tired, your poor, your huddled masses yearning to breathe free," it was modified to "Give me your tired and your poor who can stand on their own two feet, and who will not become a public charge."[26] Such comments only fuel the perception that immigrants are here only to avail themselves of the social benefits the United States provides, benefits that Townes argues are sorely lacking for most citizens and immigrants alike, especially since Congress enacted the Personal Responsibility and Work Reconciliation Act (1996) during the Clinton administration, which overemphasized individual autonomy, personal responsibility, and rejection of dependency in the distribution of welfare benefits. Images of the "welfare queen" and the "black matriarch" have been used by powerful elites to justify reductions to the social safety net and to fuel racial animosity and working-class resentment. Missing in these policies, however, is clear recognition of "the structural evil and/or inequities" present in society. "Stressing personal responsibility while detesting dependency often wedges the diversity of human isness into a stultifying and in some cases death-dealing homogeneity that is healthy only for a precious (and elite) few" (*CPE* 123). Good values are important, but so is the need for public policies that stop blaming the victim and address the structural inequalities, such as low wages, lack of affordable housing, and disparities in educational resources that generate poverty and dependency in the first place (*CPE* 117).

A third consideration when discussing the lived realities of immigrants and Dreamers is the psychological harm they experience. As a Christian social ethicist Townes usually understands the issues of racial discrimination, economic instability, and a host of other social problems as social and theological issues. But now, she sees that many of the acts of injustice toward immigrants and Dreamers take place within a matrix of uncertainty with profound psychological effects. We place all the responsibility for change on them without acknowledging the stress and trauma they have already experienced. By demonizing them, we ignore the violence they have experienced in the countries they have fled and at the hands of our immigration policies, inflicting further psychological harm by piling "these stressors and trauma they engender high and deeper" ("Consciousness" 15). Townes likens what we are doing with children who come on their own or are separated from their families at the border to what occurred during slavery "when children became pawns: caged, expendable, unaccounted for except for on the tote boards of slave bills of sale" ("Consciousness" 15). In many ways the Dreamers in this case are pawns, caught in the throes of uncertainty, while politicians debate questions about how diverse and welcoming our society should be.

---

[26] It is difficult not to see the racial undertones in the same official's suggestion that the message referred to those immigrants coming from Europe. See "'Huddled Masses' in Statue of Liberty Poem Are European, Trump Official Says," *New York Times*, August 14, 2019.

In the face of these descriptive elements of the issue, womanist ethics offers several prescriptive possibilities. The first relates to the notion of liberation. By accepting God's liberation of humanity for freedom and relationship with God, we are then free to establish loving relationships with others and to transform the structures that perpetuate the injustices in our society ("Souls" 41). For Townes, a womanist agenda for justice relies on the gospel message that God is on the side of oppressed peoples. "Justice is the notion that each one of us has worth, and that each one of us has the right to have that worth recognized and respected. In short, justice lets us know that we owe one another respect and the right to our dignity" (*CPE* 135). Such dignity has long been denied in the United States for persons of color, as evidenced by the numerous structural inequities and social policies that continue to inflict harm, limit opportunities, and deny them the basic resources needed to live fully human lives. To achieve the justice we seek requires more than reform; it requires transformation of our understanding of the common good, which for Townes is "having the social structures on which all depend work so that they benefit all people as we strive to create a genuinely inclusive and democratic social and moral order" (*CPE* 137). Justice affirms public policies that recognize positive rights to human dignity and well-being. Of course, as we noted earlier, a womanist ethic "cannot be content with a justice that addresses only a particular person's or group's wholeness" ("Souls" 42). Rather, the prescriptive element of womanist ethics looks beyond its own community to expose the way that others suffer injustice, and partners with them to create communities that work for justice for all, however incomplete it may be. In the context of the immigration debate this includes the immigrants and Dreamers from our southern borders who, after overcoming tremendous obstacles and hardships to come to this country and to make a life here, find themselves denied the respect and dignity they deserve as persons and are in constant threat of deportation.

Advocacy for justice is part of the prophetic task Townes associates with womanist ethics. Like the prophets Micah and Amos, people of faith need a "heart that beats for justice" (*CPE* 136).

> When faced with the humanity of what we do when we would build a wall instead of opening a door, a Black womanist consciousness reminds us that we are not to be the poster children of the status quo and that we must turn to a bone-deep faith—its depths *and* its shallows—and recognize that if we have a faith that only rests on the familiar and the known, this does not get us to the radical reordering of the new heaven and new earth we are to seek to proclaim and work with God to bring in (Isa 65:17; Rev 21:1). ("Consciousness" 15)

Instead, a womanist ethic is "unapologetically confrontive" regarding the injustices that persist in society, not in an adversarial sense but in a manner that is willing to engage others in dialogue, in a relationship among equals, to find ways to understand and affirm diversity.

This points to the second prescriptive element in womanist ethics: reconciliation. Just as God has reconciled with us, our response must be to seek reconciliation with others and with the whole of creation. Part of the reconciliation, Townes contends, must begin with ourselves. We must come to grips with who we are in order to achieve the moral agency we need to address the issue of immigration and the situation of the Dreamers.

> Most importantly for the conversation on immigration, how can we love our neighbor as we love ourselves if we do not know the very basics of who we are? A Black womanist consciousness insists on this self-knowledge so that we can reach outside of ourselves rather than to continue to use the same dubious moral playbook to guide our actions. If we continue to refuse to dig deep into who we are, our consciousness, we will, at best, only come up with updated versions of the same beliefs and practices that got us in the immigration conundrum (among others) to begin with. ("Consciousness" 16)

Reconciliation also requires that we find ways to include those with whom we disagree, part of the pastoral element of womanist ethics. Townes argues that it is important to recognize "the humanness of being human," which attends to "the need to care for the people behind the institutions" ("Souls" 43). We may be inclined to vilify the immigration officials and ICE agents who are beginning the deportation process for Dreamers like Zoila Pelayo because it violates our understanding of what a just solution to their precarious situation requires. While it is important to call attention to the injustice, a pastoral approach that seeks reconciliation with all concerned will find ways to engage even those responsible for immigration law enforcement in respectful dialogue. Townes writes: "If our moral standards are so rigid that we have no room for grace, then we fail to allow for human failings and weaknesses—even our own" ("Souls" 43). Seeking justice for the Dreamers requires that we hold personal and social transformation in tension.

Womanist ethics calls for Christians to engage directly with the work of promoting justice for the Dreamers and other immigrants. There are many Christians who express empathy for their plight, but "empathy is not the same as lived experience" (*CPE* 112). Dismantling the systems that support structural evil must be a group effort. Doing so requires building coalitions among likeminded people seeking transformation that moves us "beyond the wounds of injustice" ("Souls" 42). Townes recognizes that this can be frightening because "we know that loving and caring for others and ourselves interrupts the mundane and comfortable in us and calls to us to move beyond ourselves and accept a new agenda for living" (*CPE* 163). Townes contends that to live their faith deeply, members of faith communities who are seeking justice must be there as witnesses and disciples to make sure "no one is alone or caged or marked as less than." They must be supportive of those who left their homes in search of a safer and better life. Townes identifies several strategies people of faith can be engaged in to support justice for Dreamers and other immigrants. These include:

> Lobbying our elected officials to protect the rights of migrants and Dreamers; pressuring the government to process asylum claims with diligence and fairness so that migrants and Dreamers are not left in uncertainty or locked away in detentions centers; working to see that migrants are being protected from exploitation and abuse by their employers or by traffickers; and remembering that "migrant" or "asylum seeker" are temporary names—they do not reflect the person behind the label, and it is that person to whom we must fight for at all the borders that get constructed in our society.[27]

All these efforts require a strong sense of hope in one another and in the God of liberation, who enables our ethical action in the world to transform unjust societies and structures. In this transformative experience we name "the oppression of our lives and our institutions for what they are—sinful—and demand that we work with God for a new thing—the reign of God in all of life" ("Souls" 42).

RESOURCES

Discussion Questions

1. Should those who came illegally as children be deported if they lack documentation? Should they be able to get a driver's license, attend school, work? Should they be granted a path to citizenship? Why or why not?
2. What is the difference between a negative right and a positive right? In the issue of immigration, how should we balance the human rights of immigrants and Dreamers against the legal rights of citizens?
3. Does De La Torre's own experience as an undocumented immigrant shape his position on the issue of immigration? Is personal experience an appropriate lens for ethical issues, or should ethical frameworks be more objective? How would Townes respond?
4. Hispanic liberative ethics and womanist liberative ethics speak out against the racial, economic, and psychological barriers that have been erected by powerful, primarily white, elites to limit opportunities for persons of color

---

[27] Emilie M. Townes, "Displacement and Trauma," plenary session, Migration and Border Crossings conference, Decatur, Georgia, February 2019.

to achieve justice and to fuel white working-class resentment toward them. Do you agree with their assessment? Why or why not?

5. Both of the Christian social ethical traditions above contend that when one seeks God in the face of issues of justice, one will find God on the side of the marginalized and the oppressed. What is the basis for this claim? Does this mean that God has no concern for others? Or is their claim that unless Christians are working to establish justice for all, then they are not living up to what it means to claim the name Christian? Do you agree or disagree?

Activities

1. Select one of the books from the reading list below that is not discussed in the chapter to address the following questions in a report or a review: How does the author understand the issue from a Christian perspective? What are the strengths of the author's view? What is missing from the analysis? How does it compare to the views expressed in this chapter?

2. Do an analysis of a Christian social justice organization that works on immigration issues, such as Catholic Charities Immigration and Refugee Services or Evangelical Immigration Table. Gather information regarding the underlying values and beliefs of the organization and analyze how well the structure (ethos) reflects the organization's purpose (worldview). Present your findings in a written or oral report.

3. Watch two of the documentaries listed below. Compare and contrast the filmmakers' views on the issue of immigration and/or DACA. What are the ethical issues they raise for the viewer? What solutions, if any, do they offer for the US immigration crisis? How do they compare to those offered by the Christian ethical traditions discussed above? Share your analysis in a class presentation or written report.

4. Do an analysis of this case from the perspective of natural law or evangelical ethics. How would those traditions approach this case? What ethical norms would they bring to this issue? How would they be similar to or different from Hispanic and womanist ethics? Share your findings with your classmates.

5. Write two or three papers (three to five pages each) giving your ethical responses to the issues related to the Dreamers and/or immigration. The thoughts should be original; they should not merely restate what others have said. These may be distributed to the entire class if you wish. They should be tightly focused and each should address a single topic; they should be logical and well written.

Readings

Amstutz, Mark R. *Just Immigration: American Policy in Christian Perspective.* Grand Rapids, MI: Eerdmans, 2017. The author offers a succinct overview and assessment of current immigration policy and argues for an approach to the complex immigration debate that is solidly grounded in Christian political thought.

González, Karen J. *The God Who Sees: Immigrants, the Bible, and the Journey to Belong.* Harrisonburg, VA: Herald Press, 2019. Written by an immigrant advocate, this book recounts her family's struggles as they emigrate from Guatemala to California and Florida and uses stories of refugees and immigrants in the Bible to remind Christians how God demonstrated love toward marginalized people and how they are called to do the same.

Heimburger, Robert W. *God and the Illegal Alien: United States Immigration Law and a Theology of Politics.* Cambridge, UK: Cambridge University Press, 2018. This book asks where migrants stand within God's world and how authorities can govern immigration with Christian ethics. The author tracks the emergence of the concept of the illegal alien in federal US law while exploring Christian ways of understanding belonging, government, and relationships with neighbors.

Heyer, Kristin E. *Kinship across Borders: A Christian Ethic of Immigration.* Washington, DC: Georgetown University Press, 2012. Heyer chronicles the failure of current immigration policies in the United States that have generated border death, prolonged family separation, and the creation of an underclass, none of which meet the ethical norms of Christianity.

Audiovisuals

Little America. 2020. Apple TV. This streaming series, produced by Lee Eisenberg and inspired by the true stories featured by *Epic* magazine, goes beyond the headlines to look at the funny, romantic, heartfelt, inspiring, and surprising stories of immigrants in America.

New American Girls. Latino Public Broadcasting, 2014. This documentary series, directed by Mitchell Teplitsky and Betty Bastidas, follows three teenage girls (of Mexican, Peruvian, and Indian descent) brought to the United States by their parents at a young age as they describe their experiences as undocumented residents who feel American.

Pursuing the Dream. Brave New Films, 2017. Part of a series of short films on immigration and refugees, this documentary, directed by Robert Greenwald, looks at the protections provided to undocumented immigrants through DACA and the threats they face from intensified deportation actions.

Trails of Hope and Terror. V1 Educational Media, 2016. Written by Miguel A. De La Torre, this documentary attempts to explain why immigrants come, allowing the undocumented to speak for themselves and for their allies to speak in solidarity with them.

What Happens to a Dream Deferred? Michigan State University, 2018. This short documentary, directed by Scott Boehm, is an intimate portrait of a day in the life of two DACA recipients, José Adrián Badillo Carlos and Osvaldo Sandoval, graduate students at Michigan State University whose lives were thrown into limbo after the Trump administration rescinded the DACA program on September 5, 2017.

Which Way Home. Bullfrog Films, 2009. This Academy Award–nominated film, directed by Rebecca Cammisa, follows several unaccompanied children as they journey through Mexico en route to the United States on a freight train called *La Bestia*.

6

Environment

CASE STUDY:
KEYSTONE XL PIPELINE

The Keystone Pipeline is a 1,210-mile pipeline system developed and built by the energy corporation TransCanada, now known as TC Energy, which will transport oil known as diluted bitumen (derived from tar sands) from Alberta, Canada, and the northern United States to refineries in the Midwest and Gulf Coast. While parts (phases I and II) of the pipeline are already under construction or in operation, the construction of those parts of the pipeline from Alberta, Canada, to Steele City, Nebraska, known as the Keystone XL Pipeline (phase III), has come under dispute by environmental and indigenous groups.

The company claims that the construction of the pipeline will "lead to thousands of new jobs, billions in economic stimulus and enhanced North American energy security."[1] But the "State Department environmental review estimated that Keystone would support 42,000 temporary jobs over its two-year construction period—about 3,900 of them in construction, the rest in indirect support jobs, such as food service. It estimated that it would create about 35 permanent jobs."[2] Moreover, since the corporation made no promises that the oil sent through the pipeline would actually be going to the United States, some suspect that it would be sold on the open market with much of it heading to China, which has invested heavily in the tar sands oil extraction industry in Canada. Moreover, the pipeline would allow oil currently refined and sold in the Midwest to move to the Gulf, resulting in increased consumer costs.

However, the main objections to the pipeline are the environmental concerns raised by the construction of the pipeline, which include the risk

---

[1] TC Energy, "TC Energy to Build Keystone XL Pipeline," news release, March 31, 2020.
[2] Coral Davenport, "Keystone Pipeline Pros, Cons and Steps to a Final Decision," *New York Times,* November 18, 2014.

of oil spills along the pipeline and higher greenhouse-gas emissions that oil extracted from tar sands generates compared to those from the extraction of conventional oil. Initially, the proposed pipeline would have crossed the Sandhills wetland ecosystem in Nebraska (the company has since proposed a route that would avoid this area) and the Ogallala Aquifer, one of the largest freshwater reserves in the world. A pipeline spill in this area would not only pollute the air and critical water supplies, but it would also harm migratory birds and other wildlife. The Ogallala Aquifer, which spans eight states, provides drinking water for two million people and supports billions of dollars in agriculture production in those states. A major leak, such as one from a pipeline transporting the same type of oil that affected the Kalamazoo River in Michigan—and which, after four years and the cost of nearly one billion dollars continues to plague that region—could ruin drinking water and have disastrous effects on the Midwestern economy. In addition, indigenous communities along the proposed route worry about the damage to sacred sites and the possible negative health effects any leak might cause in their communities. Health issues are also a concern at the points of extraction and refinement of the oil, populated primarily by indigenous and poor communities, which the expansion of the pipeline would generate. Proponents of the Keystone XL Pipeline suggest that the proposed pipeline would be the safest ever constructed and that the benefits of the expansion outweigh the minimal risks. Opponents disagree, especially since the first Keystone pipeline spilled over 383,000 gallons of oil into the wetlands of North Dakota in October 2019.[3]

The other major environmental concern raised by opponents of the pipeline is the impact the extraction of this type of oil will have on global warming. The Environmental Protection Agency (EPA) estimates that the pipeline has the potential to increase carbon emissions by twenty-seven million metric tons of carbon dioxide, which the National Resource Defense Council suggests is "the equivalent of seven coal-fired power plants operating continuously or having 6.2 million cars on the road for 50 years."[4] In spring 2011, environmental activist Bill McKibben asked highly respected NASA climate scientist James Hansen what the impact of the pipeline would be on the environment. Hansen replied that it would be "game over for the planet."[5] He stated that "moving to tar sands, one of the dirtiest, most carbon-intensive fuels on the planet," is a step in the wrong direction and flies in the face of the US commitment to a clean-energy economy. Critics counter this argument by suggesting that the alternative—coal-fired electricity plants—generate nearly forty times more greenhouse-gas emissions. Moreover, if the corporation ships the oil to the western coast of Canada, the oil will still be burned, and the impact will be the same. While the decision by British Columbia to refuse

---

[3] Elizabeth Wolfe and Brian Ries, "The Latest Keystone Pipeline Oil Leak Is Almost 10 Times Worse Than Initially Thought," CNN, November 20, 2019.

[4] See National Resources Defense Council, "Tar Sands Facts: The Keystone XL Tar Sands Pipeline Hinders Climate Change Progress," 2012.

[5] See Jane Mayer, "Taking It to the Streets," *New Yorker* (November 21, 2011).

to allow a pipeline through its territory for environmental reasons initially placed a hold on the future of the tar sands industry, the recent decision by the Canadian Supreme Court to declare the legislation by British Columbia unconstitutional opens the door for renewed battles between proponents and opponents of the pipeline there.[6]

The Canadian government has spent millions of dollars promoting the benefits of the pipeline to US members of Congress. During the Obama administration the Republican-controlled House of Representatives passed legislation that sought to bypass the president's approval of the pipeline, which current law requires because it crosses international borders, but the Democrat-controlled Senate did not take up the measure. President Obama agreed to allow the construction of the pipeline from Steele City, Nebraska, to Cushing, Oklahoma (phase IV), to go forward. Regarding phase III, however, he said, "Allowing the Keystone pipeline to be built requires a finding that doing so would be in our nation's interests. Our national interest would be served only if this project does not significantly exacerbate the problem of carbon pollution."[7] Given the glut of oil on the market at the time, reductions in energy costs, and the improving job market there was not much economic incentive to approve the pipeline. Moreover, considering the president's commitment to address global climate change, he indicated that he would veto any attempt by Congress to push through legislation to approve it. There was concern that President Obama's resolve could change if he found it necessary to use approval of the pipeline as a bargaining chip with Republicans for other budgetary concessions, suggesting that the issue over the pipeline is more political than anything else.

President Obama eventually vetoed the pipeline in 2015, but after the 2016 election, which gave Republicans control of all three branches of government, President Trump signed an executive order in January 2017 approving the pipeline. However, in November 2018, a US district judge issued an order blocking construction of the pipeline until the State Department could conduct further study of its impact on the environment. A month later the same judge ruled that TC Energy could not do preparatory work for the pipeline, thus pushing the earliest start date for construction to 2020. The most recent court decision (in December 2019) allows for preconstruction efforts on the part of TC Energy until the case is resolved in the courts. On March 29, 2020, President Trump reissued a permit for the pipeline to continue, replacing the previous permit he had issued, which he asserted was an exercise of his presidential authority and not subject to judicial review.[8] In response, TC Energy has said it will continue the pipeline project, expecting it to enter

---

[6] Andrea Germanos, "Canada's Top Court Rejects BC Bid to Halt Trans Mountain Tar Sands Project," Common Dreams, January 17, 2020.

[7] President Barack Obama, speech, Georgetown University, Washington, DC, June 25, 2013.

[8] White House Office of the Press Secretary, "Subject: Presidential Permit," pool reports, March 29, 2020.

service in 2023.[9] In April 2020, a federal judge ruled that the project could not proceed until the more thorough permit process was completed. In July 2020, the Supreme Court upheld that ruling.

Opponents continue to challenge the project, including asking Democratic presidential candidates to pledge to revoke the permit issued by President Trump, to stop construction on the pipeline on their first day in office, to send the project back "to relevant federal agencies to undergo legitimate environmental review and Tribal consultations," to reject any project that would "exacerbate our climate crisis," and to protect tribes, farmers, and ranchers from "eminent domain abuse."[10] Former Vice President Joe Biden, the 2020 Democratic presidential nominee, announced he would rescind Trump's permit because of the potential harm it would cause.[11] Opponents also claim that, in addition to the continued lawsuits over eminent domain seizures, the decision to move forward with the project is problematic because all the necessary federal, state, and local permits have not been secured. Moreover, continuing the project will exacerbate the public health crisis from the coronavirus pandemic by sending workers into communities that are unable to handle the public health threat. A final concern opponents raise is that the creation of pipeline worker "man camps" will lead to increased crime and sexual violence against indigenous women.[12]

ISSUES AND CONCERNS

As we can see, for many the debate surrounding the Keystone XL Pipeline (and other issues such as hydraulic fracturing or hydrofracking for natural gas resources) revolves around which human concerns should take precedence: economic or environmental. Some contend that these are inseparable in many ways. For example, what good is caring for the environment if people do not have enough resources—jobs, income, housing, and so on—to care for themselves, especially in an economy with high unemployment? What good is a focus on the economic benefits of the pipeline when the environmental devastation ultimately undermines the foundation for all economic goods, namely, the natural world?[13]

---

[9] TC Energy, "TC Energy to Build Keystone XL Pipeline," news release, March 31, 2020.

[10] Mark Hefflinger, "Take the 'NoKXL Pledge," Bold Nebraska, August 13, 2019.

[11] Matt Viser and Dino Grandoni, "Biden Says He Would Revoke Permit for Keystone Pipeline," *Washington Post,* May 18, 2020.

[12] See "CANCEL KXL: Halt All Keystone XL Construction Due to Coronavirus Public Health Emergency," petition, actionnetwork.org.

[13] Interestingly, there is a similar debate at present (2020) regarding the coronavirus pandemic between reopening the economy and protecting the health of those at risk of contracting and dying from the virus.

Many see the problems as technical in nature. Can we develop and use technology to release nature's resources for human benefit in ways that do not generate environmental problems? Few raise questions about the positive impact that industrial development has had on human flourishing and the role that oil and gas have played. But where is the tipping point when such technology generates unintentional consequences that are devastating for both humans and nature? Have we reached the limits of the earth's ability to absorb carbon emissions, as environmentalists claim? Or are the new extraction technologies for oil and gas and the emissions controls on burning them developed to the extent that we can feel more secure about their use?

In this line of questioning the value of the natural world is largely instrumental. Our concern for the environment is driven by human need and interest and thus has an anthropocentric and utilitarian ring to it. Many environmentalists, however, are biocentric or ecocentric in their approach to environmental issues. They contend that we should care for the natural world not simply because of its extrinsic value to humanity but because it has its own intrinsic value.[14] Some go so far as to suggest that all of earth's living creatures have equal intrinsic worth.

In the Keystone XL Pipeline case there are clashes among a variety of interests and claims. Corporate economic interests are one example—they have invested a great amount of resources with the expectation that there will be substantial return on their investments (profit, increased shareholder investment, and so on). Then there are the economic interests of those landowners who are willing to lease their lands for money, especially when small family farms are not as income producing as they were in the past. Local communities seeking economic development and tax revenue to sustain their workforce and their infrastructure also have a stake. Indigenous groups want to protect their historic and sacred lands as well as the lifestyle of living off the land to which they are accustomed. Tribes, farmers, and ranchers want the government to stop abusing eminent domain—the practice of governments or their agents taking private property deemed necessary to the public interest—even though they are financially compensated for these seizures. People and communities closely tied to the points of extraction and refinement of the oil have a dual stake in economic benefits (jobs) and concerns about the health effects on their communities. Environmental groups are worried about potential damage to ecosystems should a leak or spill occur; more important, they fear the effects that burning this type of fuel will have on the earth's climate, which they contend is already at its breaking point. All interested parties also appeal to future generations: corporations, landowners, and communities cite the need for jobs for young workers and revenue to sustain educational institutions; indigenous communities worry about the loss of their cultural heritage; and environmental groups focus on the need for a

---

[14] See Anne Rea and Wayne Munn, "The Value of Nature: Economic, Intrinsic, or Both?" *Integrated Environmental Assessment and Management* 13/5 (September 2017): 953–55.

living environment for future generations, which for some environmentalists includes the nonhuman world affected by these developments, both in terms of living creatures as well as ecosystems and the interactions among various creatures with their habitats. Considering current fears about global terrorism, let us not forget national geopolitical interests in increasing domestic energy production to reduce dependence on foreign oil from countries and governments that have generated harms.

NATURAL LAW ETHICS

If we are to view this case from the perspective of natural law ethics, it is important to begin with the base point that is most important from that perspective: theological convictions. These convictions undergird their valuation of the natural world and human rationality, the role of human agency and its limits in relationship to nature, the moral norms that would be operative as they approach this case, and the situations embedded in it. The two key theological convictions, as noted in Chapter 1, are the doctrine of creation and the understanding of what it means for humanity to be created in the image of God (Imago Dei).

Jean Porter contends: "The scholastic concept of the natural law could only have emerged within a context that was friendly to the idea of nature and optimistic about the capacities of the human intellect to understand and appropriately value the natural world."[15] With an understanding of the doctrine of creation that sees the world as "an intelligible and good reflection of God's loving will," one that provides all creatures with some "purposeful existence proper to it" (*NR* 135), it is clear that a natural law perspective affirms the intrinsic goodness of nature. She writes, "The intelligibility of natural processes in terms of intrinsic causal principles was invariably correlated with some idea of natural goodness . . . and good in terms that are intrinsic to natural processes themselves—that is to say, not instrumentally, by reference to extrinsic desires and needs" ("Defense" 21). In other words, the nonhuman world has value that cannot be limited merely to its value for human purposes. She does not argue this from a biocentric position, as some environmentalists do, but from a theocentric framework in which the value of the nonhuman world is acquired through its creation by God. Each creature has an end or *telos* toward which it moves in order to flourish in a meaningful way.

---

[15] Jean Porter, "In Defense of Living Nature," in *The Ideal of Nature*, ed. Gregory Kaebnick, 17–28 (Baltimore: Johns Hopkins University Press, 2011), 18 (hereafter cited as "Defense"). References also made to Porter's texts, *Natural and Divine Law: Reclaiming the Tradition for Christian Ethics* (Grand Rapids, MI: Eerdmans, 1999) (hereafter cited as *NDL*); and *Nature as Reason: A Thomistic Theory of the Natural Law* (Grand Rapids, MI: Eerdmans, 2005) (hereafter cited as *NR*).

At the same time, the doctrine of creation as revealed in Genesis places humanity at the pinnacle of that creation and thus as having dominion over that created order, which, Porter notes, includes a "correlative claim that nonhuman entities were created and continue to exist for the sake of human welfare" ("Defense" 22). Human flourishing depends upon the use of the natural world for human ends. The resources derived from nature enable self-preservation, a fundamental natural law. Just because the natural world has intrinsic value created by God, which humanity must respect, does not mean that all individual creatures have the same value. Moreover, human flourishing goes beyond survival and requires the ability to work purposefully and creatively and to demonstrate the same type of creativity exemplified in God's creative activity. The natural world provides the raw materials out of which human achievements in work and technology arise.

This tension within the natural law tradition and its understanding of the doctrine of creation—which affirms the intrinsic goodness of nature beyond its instrumental value for human ends and the dominion human beings have over nature—raises the question of whether or not this tension can be resolved in ways that provide direction for cases where human and natural interests conflict, as they do in the Keystone XL Pipeline case. Porter suggests that there is a scriptural counter-narrative to dominion that gives the nonhuman natural world value in the context of God's creative and providential care. She suggests that in this context the concept of dominion

> would be nothing more (or less!) than the privilege of participating in, fostering, and safeguarding the independence and operations of natural processes, enjoyed by men and women because we are capable of grasping and appreciating what these mean, and what their true value is. This privilege emphatically would not be understood as a license to usurp God's ultimate authority over creation, or much less as a mandate to despoil and distort the nonhuman world in pursuit of our own aims. ("Defense" 24–25)

This understanding of the relationship between humanity and nonhuman nature is connected to the second theological conviction: the Imago Dei. Human beings are images of God in a distinctive sense. As noted above, it affirms their place at the pinnacle of creation. The Imago Dei also highlights the importance of human agency, and the human person "as a free and self-determining agent . . . enjoying certain powers on the basis of his or her capacities for choice and self-direction" (*NDL* 359). At the same time, however, because humanity has the intellectual capacity to understand and value the natural world rightly, we also have a responsibility toward that world. As we saw in the discussion of natural law in Chapter 1, all creatures have certain ends toward which they aim. These ends place limits upon our ability to do as we please. Humanity has the responsibility of enabling the nonhuman world to attain its ends. These intelligibilities in nature "inform and constrain human life" (*NDL* 69). This suggests that the use of natural resources must always be with an eye toward their sustainability, not simply for the consumptive needs of humanity but also for the flourishing of the natural world itself.

These ends are part of the source of moral norms, the next base point. Two fundamental moral norms in the natural law tradition are self-preservation and do no harm. However, these broad norms are underdetermined. The expectation is that human beings who have the capacity to reason will together seek out those ways and actions that promote the preservation and flourishing of all creatures, human and nonhuman, and minimize the harm done to them. When we think about the flourishing of the nonhuman world, we do not necessarily mean each creature. We eat meat, fish, grains, and vegetables for food. We use trees and other natural resources to construct human habitats. In the competition for resources some individuals will not survive. The real question is about the harm being done to entire species. If human action results in wholesale destruction of ecosystems and the species that depend upon those ecosystems, the natural law tradition would contend that the norms of self-preservation and do no harm must place constraints on human action.

We also cannot forget the role that the virtues play here. The virtue of charity in the natural law tradition calls upon human beings to extend our concern and commitment to justice beyond ourselves. So, for example, if the extraction of oil from tar sands is causing harm to indigenous and marginalized communities, there is a special concern for them. We must be partial toward these groups in order to ensure that justice prevails. This is the foundation of the Catholic notion of the preferential option for the poor. But the commitment to charity also pushes us to defend the living natural environment. In our deliberations we must consider the impact of the extraction, transportation, and burning of tar sands oil upon other creatures and their ecosystems.

As we analyze this case, all sides are concerned about the flourishing of humanity. Those in favor of building the pipeline speak about the economic benefits, however disputed, that the pipeline will bring to the communities affected by it. Not only would this provide resources for people currently affected but it would also provide resources to build the infrastructure of schools, economic development, and so on needed for future generations. However, there is conflicting information about the economic benefits that the pipeline will generate: there will be some jobs, but most are temporary; some who lease land will get benefit; and local governments often provide tax incentives, so the economic benefit of taxes is limited. The natural law tradition would hold that in evaluating the building of the pipeline we should not focus only on what it does for jobs and economic development. We must also look at its implications for the planet. Of course, where they would differ is that these considerations on the environment and sustainability are not solely for the benefit of humanity but also for the flourishing of the nonhuman world.

Thus, we cannot look at the building of the pipeline purely from an economic standpoint. We must look at it from a broader perspective, not only including all of those currently affected by the pipeline, human and nonhuman, but also future generations of both. There is conflicting information about the impact of this type of fossil fuel on the environment. The oil industry says it is better than coal-fired plants, and there is evidence to support that claim. Moreover, the industry claims that the pipeline will be the safest ever built, ostensibly minimizing the risk of a spill that would damage ecosystems.

One could argue that thinking narrowly of human well-being is a case of disordered or sinful understanding. Rather, the doctrine of creation pushes us to look beyond ourselves and think of other creatures as well. In particular, the virtue of charity forces us to think in terms of the relationship with God and not of ourselves, and this moves us out of the narrow anthropocentric focus. Not taking into consideration the good of nature is a flaw, even though we do it all the time.

The question is whether the flourishing of the nonhuman natural world is a basis for human action either positively (action to promote the flourishing of other creatures) or negatively (action that restricts the harm being done). Porter suggests that it is with respect to the ends or flourishing intrinsic to those creatures. Take migratory birds, for example. Such birds need ecosystems that are conducive to their well-being. Human action that destroys those ecosystems ultimately inhibits their flourishing. As part of God's created order, it is particularly important for human beings to be conscious and aware of those realities and thus act in such ways as not to harm those creatures. Porter might say that the decision on the part of TC Energy to move the pipeline away from the Sandhills region is a responsible and appropriate human action. Of course, this was not done for the sake of the creatures but for the sake of making sure the pipeline gets built.

The question emerges as to whether human beings can contribute to their own well-being in ways that also protect the well-being of other creatures. Clearly, environmental energy policies that seek forms of energy significant for human flourishing that also mitigate or minimize the obstacles to the flourishing of other creatures and the natural world in general make good ethical sense. But how much truth is there in the claim that if we continue to extract oil from tar sands, refine it, and burn it, it will be "game over" for the planet? The EPA gives some data. If environmentalists are correct, then the natural law tradition would agree that we should not build the pipeline, especially given the current economic climate of a world oil glut and improving job market. They would go so far as to suggest that we need to stop the extraction of this kind of oil; that it has only a limited and short-lived value for humanity; that it would affect future generations negatively; and that the

time, money, and investment spent in this industry would detract from invest-
ing in other renewable, nonpolluting sources of energy that would do less
to harm the environment and might promote other economic development.

Who is being harmed by the construction of the Keystone XL Pipeline?
On the one hand, if the pipeline is constructed safely and never leaks,
and the impact on the environment is negligible, one could argue that no
one is being harmed or that it is less harmful than the coal-fired plants it
might replace. Burning oil from tar sands may generate less pollution than
coal-fired electricity plants, but that does not mean there is no impact. The
cumulative effect of burning fossil fuels has generated a great deal of damage to the world, both human and nonhuman. We need to take the broader
perspective of questioning whether we need to do something decisive about
the problem to ensure the future flourishing of all of creation. This could
run into conflict with the human need for self-preservation. Human beings
need financial resources in order to promote human flourishing. If the economic benefits presented by proponents of the pipeline are accurate, then
one could contend that they ought to proceed. But this raises the question
of what constitutes human flourishing. Economic well-being is not a sufficient condition for measuring this.

This is where Porter begins to acknowledge that what is needed today
is collective action. The debate over the Keystone XL Pipeline brings into
sharp relief the dangers of doing things in the same way. The extraction,
refinement, and consumption of fossil fuels and the economic systems in
place that facilitate and make this happen have brought us to the point of
no return. What is required is significant change in the systems in place,
which individual actions by themselves cannot accomplish. Opponents of
the pipeline are suggesting this very thing. We need to defend the living
nature of which we are a part.

Porter acknowledges that given the focus of natural law theory on individual actions, there may be limits on what this moral theory can do. What
is required to address the problems we are faced with is collective action that
addresses systems and institutions. While limited, however, natural law ethics
may provide us with "a renewed sensibility, shaped by a deeper appreciation
for the value and integrity—and, perhaps, the divine origins—of living nature" ("Defense" 26). This may provide the motivation and political will to
carry out the needed changes to destructive systems. Humanity understands
its potential for natural destruction, and we can no longer hide behind the
Genesis-based notion of dominion. Through collective action we must act
"in defense of living nature" ("Defense" 25).

In the face of conflicting data, the natural law tradition would uphold the
norm of do no harm; if there are other ways of ensuring human flourishing
and happiness, then the economic issues are not the only ones. Rather, given
that there are other ways to promote the energy needs of the human population that theoretically would not result in as much harm to the environment,

and that there are other ways to conserve so that the energy needs are not as devastating, the rush to build the pipeline is morally problematic.

FEMINIST LIBERATIVE ETHICS

As we review this case from a feminist ethics perspective, we should recall some important base points that are relevant for this case study. First, feminist ethics rejects any of the theoretical dualisms that have contributed to gender, racial, and class divisions and environmental exploitation. In the realm of sexuality and social justice, there is no mind/body split to support male superiority; in the realm of environmental ethics, there is no spirit/nature dualism to support the anthropocentric, total dominance of humanity over our natural environment. Rather, we are our bodies. We are embedded in our social and natural environments in and through our bodies, and this constitutes our dignity and intrinsic value. Beverly Harrison writes:

> Within a feminist liberation theological vision, we stress that this planet, indeed the whole cosmos that we inhabit, is not merely a gracious home. It is an interactive web of life that is as much a part of us as we of it. The wholistic theological vision of total interrelationship we insist upon makes it inconceivable that nature, with its resources for abundant life, can be conceived as something external, as something merely to be manipulated and dominated. (*JM* 173)[16]

Considering this reality, we cannot resort to some world of abstract principles to make rational, ethical decisions about significant social issues. We must make those in the nitty-gritty of the everyday life in which we are enmeshed. As she reviews our interactions with nature, Harrison claims that given our "ravenous" consumption of natural resources, including the nonrenewable oil and gas resources central to this case study, humanity has indeed been insensitive to our environments, and the dirty emissions from tar sands oil or the possible leaks have the potential to make matters worse (*MC* 174).

Second, relationship is central to human experience. Harrison rejects the concept of the autonomous individual unencumbered by social relations evident in the individualism promoted by the social and economic forces affecting our lives. Instead, feminists highlight the ways we are enmeshed in relationships with one another, which generates an interdependence in human

---

[16] Harrison's perspective on this issue is drawn from Beverly W. Harrison, *Making the Connections: Essays in Feminist Social Ethics*, ed. Carol S. Robb (Boston: Beacon Press, 1985) (hereafter cited as *MC*); and idem, *Justice in the Making: Feminist Social Ethics* (Louisville, KY: Westminster John Knox Press, 2004) (hereafter cited as *JM*).

society, an interdependence Harrison claims is also part of our engagement with our natural environments, a part of "our bodies, ourselves." "From a feminist perspective, we are all sensuous and embodied beings, separated from the cosmic whole and from others of our species-being only by the fragile skin that separates us from each other and the created and creative processes of nature of which we are a part" (*JM* 173). We must overcome what she calls the "life-denying forms of spirituality" that continue the dualism of matter and spirit. For Harrison and other feminist ethicists, the divine/human encounter occurs as much in our mundane interactions with one another and with nature through our work and the meals we share together as it does in prayer (*MC* 75). That is why feminists insist on a "holistic, relational approach to nature," one that assumes a "nonexploitative attitude" and recognizes nature's intrinsic value, because our well-being is intertwined, and because of that interrelatedness our environment is imposing moral claims on us (*MC* 175).

Third, the feminist ethics conception of justice is substantive, not procedural. A procedural view of justice suggests that if we have the appropriate principles in place, then the outcomes from the implementation of those principles are fair.[17] Harrison argues that this is often not true, especially when those in power determine what those principles are. Instead, a substantive view of justice attends to the needs of the most disadvantaged, which are too often denied because of sexist, heterosexist, racist, and classist institutional barriers erected by those with power and privilege. As a Christian ethicist she understands justice as rightly related persons and communities under God, which from a biblical perspective is demonstrated through concern for the least well-off and includes the needs of both humanity and nature. "A theologically based Christian ethic of ecojustice cannot aim at anything less than a social policy that takes special account of the effects of that policy on those already most disadvantaged in society" (*MC* 177). Justice requires that we address the lived realities of those experiencing inequities and work against those institutional arrangements that perpetuate them. When thinking of ecojustice, the negative impact on the poor, the disenfranchised, and nature must take center stage. "This is an uncompromising assumption of feminist liberation theology. We can affirm human dignity until we are blue in the face, but if we do so from a theological perspective that divides material and spiritual well-being, our moral rhetoric will be vacuous." Human dignity happens only "when we are deeply and richly related to one another" (*JM* 174–75).

Feminist ethics also advocates the need for social theory and analysis to look concretely at the lived realities of those affected by social policies and institutional arrangements. One candidate for analysis is the nature of political economy in the context of global capitalism. The dynamics at play in our political economy are shaping all our lives, including our relationship with the

---

[17] See, for example, John Rawls, *A Theory of Justice* (Cambridge, MA: Harvard University Press, 1971).

planet, and not necessarily for the better. In Harrison's view a serious critique of political economy and the way in which it promotes economic injustice is needed to address the issue meaningfully (*JM* 158). Our current political economy assumes that the ideology of free market and profit maximization are essential for the economic well-being of societies and people. The role of government is to generate the political stability required for the smooth operation of this system. But the structural changes generated to produce these benefits fail to include economic and ecological harms for many people and the planet in these calculations, such as cyclical unemployment, poverty, and pollution (*MC* 72). Harrison contends that when we rely solely on this system of political economy, "we collude in masking the way the massive political-economic structures of late capitalism shape the social problems such as racism, sexism, or classism and we allow these powerful institutions to continue to be unresponsive to the social consequences of their actions" (*MC* 78).

Moreover, Harrison is concerned about the ways in which economic forces have come to dominate our politics in this system. She notes how in our society corporations have better political rights than citizens. "The state is now far more an instrument of corporate will than it is of the will of the people" (*JM* 178). This dynamic can clearly be seen in the case of the Keystone Pipeline. The Obama administration allowed for some segments of the pipeline to be built, in part because of corporate pressure to do so. President Obama resisted the XL extension, but his successor, who has strong ties to global corporations, reversed course and issued the permit. For Harrison, this reflects her view that we are locked in a corporate-statist situation that contends that nothing can be done in the face of inexorable market forces, especially when economic growth and creation of jobs is at stake. The question she asks is, "How do we gain some access to make change in this massive cooperative corporate-statist venture?!" (*JM* 181). We do this by bringing critical social analysis to the arbitrary way in which these unjust structures have been developed and imposed and by encouraging more direct participation in shaping social policy by those who have been excluded. "We who love democracy need to begin to create alternative political constraints on a now global economic productive system that does not have to give a damn bit of attention to what people need" (*JM* 159).

This question about how one creates those alternatives gives rise to an analysis of power and the ways it is understood and used. Feminist ethics rejects a conception of power as "power over," which has been so prevalent in debates regarding energy policy: the power of corporate-statist ventures over natural resources, energy production, and land. Rather, feminists support a mutual, reciprocal view of power, shared by those affected by social policies, especially in situations where there are conflicts of interest. Unfortunately, much social policy is forged in a context where power is not shared or mutual but inequitably distributed. Policy debates are often framed by business and government interests as addressing economic needs: worker needs for jobs, consumer needs for cheaper oil, and local community needs for taxes to pay for public services. These arguments have been central in the debate over the construction of the Keystone XL Pipeline. The problem for Harrison is that, in such arguments, "there is no room for substantive questions of social justice and ecological well-being in the ongoing process of shaping and implementing public energy policy" (*MC* 182). This has certainly been prevalent in the Trump administration's efforts to promote the pipeline while at the same time rolling back any environmental regulations deemed burdensome to the fossil-fuel industry, including Obama-era emissions rules for power plants and vehicles; rules governing clean air, water, and toxic chemicals; and participation in the Paris Climate Accord.[18] A feminist emphasis on shared power would enable these other ethical and environmental concerns to become part of the social policy decision-making process, which is the goal of critical ethical analysis. "To me, the point of all critical social theorizing of society is to enable more movement in the direction of participation in shaping social policy. We need more movement in the direction of shaping communities, so they are habitable for human beings and our cohabitants in the environment and on planet Earth" (*JM* 158).

Harrison recognizes that including other voices in debates on policy decisions may in some instances be zero sum: some interests cannot be accommodated fully when other interests conflict with them (*MC* 176). The question then becomes whose interests in policy debates should take precedence. She rejects those who argue for free-market solutions to energy policies because, as discussed above, it is usually the corporate-statist group in power that gets to determine what they are and the least well-off are the losers in these policy debates (*MC* 181). In the Keystone XL Pipeline case the confluence of corporate and governmental interests, including those of Canada, China, and the United States, are readily apparent. Without the court's interventions their interests would have prevailed already. But given the commitment of feminist ethics to the marginalized, when a conflict of interest like this occurs, the focus should be on those remedies that adequately address the ecojustice concerns of the least advantaged. In the context of this case the least advantaged include poor communities of color, who bear the brunt of the pollution in their communities from refining this oil; Native American communities, who fear disruption of their sacred lands and potential water pollution from leaks; and the species of birds and other animals that would suffer loss of habitat should a significant leak occur. TC Energy's promise that this would be the safest pipeline in the world does not assuage these concerns considering the recent leaks in other pipelines, especially since the cost of environmental damage is seldom absorbed fully by the corporations, but rather by taxpayers, citizens, and other species (*MC* 189).

---

[18] See Nadja Popovich et al., "The Trump Administration Is Reversing 100 Environmental Rules: Here's the Full List," *New York Times,* July 15, 2020.

Harrison is not suggesting that environmental concerns should override all economic interests, such as jobs and cheaper oil, which low-skilled workers desperately need. She understands the way in which high energy costs have a negative effect on people at the bottom end of income distribution, whose wages are set by the market and are often well below a living wage. Lower gas prices are beneficial to low-income people who must drive to work, often in automobiles that are older and less fuel-efficient and for whom energy costs consume a larger share of their income. But part of the reason for this disparity is because the United States has provided the bulk of its tax incentives and public investments to the fossil fuels and automobile industries (including costs of roads and highways) instead of major investments in public transportation, which would have reduced both transportation costs for the poor and harmful emissions from fossil-fuel consumption (*MC* 185). What she does challenge is the ways these industries have used the threat of loss of jobs, cuts in production, and increased costs to reject regulations that require better efficiency or more investment in renewable energy. In truth, investments in solar and other renewable sources of energies are job creators that pay living wages while also protecting the environment. In addition, she wants to add a global justice perspective to social policy by noting how overconsumption of energy resources by the First World has a negative impact on the economic health of developing countries. In this context, and given her feminist commitment to the least advantaged, she argues that the costs associated with efforts to protect the global environment through conservation efforts and investments in alternative renewable energy sources should be borne primarily by the developed world (*MC* 184–85). In her view, these are the kinds of initiatives that bring concerns about social justice and ecological well-being to the table and make "unaccountable power more accountable to broader public well-being" (*MC* 189).

In the face of this power imbalance Harrison calls for a praxis of resistance (*JM* 183). In relationship to corporations that dominate many of these debates, she advocates for creating structures of accountability internal to corporations with publicly elected corporate boards, rather than the private and self-serving way those boards are currently elected. Doing so would enable those with concerns about social justice and environmental issues to be at the table when such decisions are made. She also suggests that we require energy corporations to pay the actual social costs of their production. We need a clearer understanding of how wealthy nations controlled by the wealthy few are exploiting poor nations, and also an international system of justice that would hold them accountable for their economic crimes (*JM* 217).

This praxis of resistance would applaud the grassroots efforts on the part of Native American and environmental activists to stand up to the power of the corporate-statist groups behind energy developments like the Keystone XL Pipeline. In addition, Harrison advocates for massive education of the public about the intricacies of what a just social-energy policy would look like, one that affirms a quality of life and substantive justice for all. She understands that the "powers that be" will do what they can to label ecojustice perspectives as extreme, utopian, or socialistic (*MC* 189).[19] But, Harrison argues, there is too much at stake for the least advantaged, for future generations, and for the habitability of the planet to relinquish our efforts to ensure that these broader societal interests are represented fairly in energy policy decisions. "As Christians, we have no choice but to accelerate our involvement, working together with coalitions of persons engaged in these concerns" (*MC* 190).

In the end, feminist ethics, like the natural law tradition, would affirm that the building of the pipeline should not focus only on what it does for jobs and economic development. Given the ecological threats posed by the burning and extraction of this oil, the potential damage to ecosystems should the pipeline leak, and the possibilities for addressing both the issues of employment and protecting the environment through major investments in renewable energy sources such as wind and solar, Harrison would reject the continuation of the pipeline. For Harrison, like Porter, the rejection of the pipeline would demonstrate that humanity takes seriously the moral claims that our inter-relatedness to the nonhuman world has on us. Our focus on climate change and sustainability is not grounded only in a concern for how these issues impact humanity, but also reflects our commitment to the flourishing of the nonhuman world.

RESOURCES

Discussion Questions

1. In this case study both natural law ethics and feminist ethics raise the question of which concerns should take precedence: economic or environmental. Do the economic benefits outweigh the long-term environmental impact of greenhouse-gas emissions associated with burning this type of oil? Porter and Harrison suggest they do not. Do you agree with their position? Why or why not?

2. The case highlights the potential danger of a pipeline rupture on the health and well-being of families, communities, and ecosystems. Should these be only corporate-statist decisions, or do communities, citizens, and government have a legitimate and moral role in determining what is built in their neighborhoods?

---

[19] A recent example is the characterization of the Green New Deal introduced by Senator Ed Markey (D-MA) and Representative Alexandria Ocasio-Cortez (D-NY) in February 2019, of which one critic writes: "The Green New Deal seeks to use the issue of the environment to impose a grand vision for a planned society—one with high taxes, less choice and even more reliance on politicians in Washington, D.C. America deserves a better, freer future than that." David Ditch, "The Green New Deal Is a Lousy Deal for Americans," The Heritage Foundation (February 19, 2019).

3. Harrison claims that the pollution costs of the extraction and refinement of this oil tend to fall upon the poor and marginalized and is a form of environmental racism and classism. Do you agree with her assessment? If not, what is missing in her argument?

4. Both Porter and Harrison claim that nations have legal and moral obligations to protect our shared natural environment for future generations. How do they suggest those obligations should be enforced? What do you think about their recommendations?

5. In many ways the questions raised in this case center around the limits of sovereignty in a global society in the age of climate change. When should national and international interests in reducing carbon-based emissions trump free trade in the global marketplace? Who should make those decisions?

Activities

1. Do an analysis of this case from the model of conservative evangelical ethics. Compare and contrast the conclusions you draw regarding climate change and the burning of fossil fuels with those from the two perspectives in this case analysis. In what ways are they similar? In what ways are they different? Which approach, in your opinion, addresses the case most comprehensively?

2. Engage individually or with a group in an environmental action. This activity involves analyzing an environmental problem and taking appropriate action to try to improve it. This is not merely action but *informed* action with a research component, a strategic component, and an action component. Students should present a formal report (written, oral, or multimedia) that details what they did, what they found, why they did it (religious/ethical reasoning), what the impact of the action was, and what they learned from the experience.

3. Do an analysis of a religious environmental organization such as Eco-Justice Ministries or National Religious Partnership for the Environment. Visit a local chapter or review the group's mission and purpose to gather information regarding the underlying values and beliefs of the organization, and analyze how well the structure (ethos) reflects the organization's purpose (worldview). Present your findings in a written, oral, or multimedia report.

4. Identify another environmental issue, such as hydrofracking or the availability of clean water, and write a case analysis of it. Be sure to develop the case clearly, including a good sense of the issues and concerns it raises. Challenge your fellow students to use the Christian ethical positions in this chapter to discern what their ethical stance would be on this issue.

5. Hold a forum on campus on Pope Francis's encyclical *Laudato si'* (*On Care for Our Common Home*). Be sure to identify the spiritual and moral challenges that he says the current ecological crises we face pose for us. Include presenters who support the positions taken by the pope as well as presenters who raise critical challenges to them.

Readings

Bauman, Whitney. *Religion and Ecology: Developing a Planetary Ethic.* New York: Columbia University Press, 2014. Bauman calls attention to the historical, political, and ecological influences shaping our understanding of nature, religion, humanity, and identity, and collapses the boundaries separating male from female, biology from machine, human from more than human, and religion from science, encouraging readers to embrace hybridity and the inherent fluctuations of an open, evolving global community.

Gottlieb, Roger S., ed. *Morality and the Environmental Crisis.* Cambridge, UK: Cambridge University Press, 2019. In this book the author argues that the environmental crisis creates an unprecedented moral predicament: how to be a good person when our collective and individual actions contribute to immeasurable devastation and suffering. Drawing on an extraordinary range of sources from philosophy, political theory, global religion, ecology, and contemporary spirituality, he explores the ethical ambiguities, challenges, and opportunities we face.

Harris, Melanie L. *Ecowomanism: African American Women and Earth-Honoring Faiths.* Maryknoll, NY: Orbis Books, 2017. In this book Harris argues that African American women make distinctive contributions to the environmental justice movement in the ways that they theologize, theorize, practice spiritual activism, and come into religious understandings about our relationship with the earth.

Martin-Schramm, James, Daniel T. Spencer, and Laura A. Stivers. *Earth Ethics: A Case Method Approach.* Maryknoll, NY: Orbis Books, 2015. Using a case method approach, the authors introduce new topics in environmental ethics—including hydraulic fracturing, greenhouse gases, food consumption, and resource stewardship—and revisit traditional topics in environmental ethics while expanding beyond a specifically Christian hermeneutic.

McFague, Sallie. *Blessed Are the Consumers: Climate Change and the Practice of Constraint.* Minneapolis: Fortress Press, 2013. This book emphasizes the practice of restraint. Rooted in the ancient Christian notion of kenosis, or self-emptying, restraint is the only possible path forward, the author suggests, for a world bent on consumption and overuse.

McKibben, Bill. *The End of Nature.* New York: Random House, 2006. McKibben argues that the survival of the globe is dependent on a fundamental, philosophical shift in the way we relate to nature, addressing such issues as the greenhouse effect, acid rain, and the depletion of the ozone layer.

Pope Francis. *Care for Creation: A Call for Ecological Conversion.* Maryknoll, NY: Orbis Books, 2016. In the encyclical *Laudato si'* Pope Francis provides an outline of the values and principles allowing us to live together in our common home and lays out his comprehensive vision of integral ecology. He calls for a profound conversion of values that involves a new understanding of our relation to God's creation, both the earth and its creatures, as well as our fellow human beings.

Audiovisuals

Above All Else. Fiege Films, 2014. Shot in the forests, pastures, and living rooms of rural East Texas, the film follows David Daniel as he rallies neighbors and environmental activists to join him in a final act of brinkmanship: a treetop blockade of the controversial Keystone Pipeline. What begins as a stand against corporate bullying becomes a rallying cry for climate protesters nationwide.

An Inconvenient Sequel: Truth to Power. Paramount Pictures, 2017. Directed by Bonni Cohen and Jon Shenk, this follow-up documentary addresses the progress made to tackle the problem of climate change and Al Gore's global efforts to persuade governmental leaders to invest in renewable energy, culminating in the landmark signing of the 2016 Paris Climate Agreement.

An Inconvenient Truth. Lawrence Bender Productions, 2006. Directed by Davis Guggenheim, this documentary highlights former vice president Al Gore's campaign to make the issue of global warming a recognized problem worldwide.

Before the Flood. Appian Way, 2016. Directed by Fisher Stevens and starring Leonardo DiCaprio, this documentary chronicles a three-year journey to every corner of the globe to document the devastating impacts of climate change, and it questions humanity's ability to reverse what may be the most catastrophic problem humankind has ever faced.

Gasland: Parts I and II. HBO Documentary Films, 2010, 2013. These documentaries directed by Josh Fox suggest that the gas industry's portrayal of natural gas as a clean and safe alternative to oil is a myth and that fracked wells inevitably leak over time, contaminating water and air, hurting families, and endangering the earth's climate with methane, a potent greenhouse gas.

Pipe Dreams. Vimeo on Demand, 2011. This film, directed by Leslie Iwerks and narrated by Daryl Hannah, follows the stories of farmers and landowners fighting to protect their land, their water, and their livelihood in the face of the efforts by TC Energy to build the Keystone XL Pipeline.

Snowpiercer. Moho Film, Opus Pictures, 2014. Directed by Bong Joon-ho, this science-fiction action film creates a future in which a failed climate-change experiment has killed all life except for the lucky few who boarded the Snowpiercer, a train that travels around the globe, in which a new class system emerges.

The 11th Hour. Appian Way, 2007. Directed by Leila and Nadia Conners and narrated by Leonardo DiCaprio, this documentary looks at the state of the global environment, including visionary and practical solutions for restoring the planet's ecosystems.

This Changes Everything. Klein Lewis Productions, 2015. Directed by Avi Lewis, this documentary draws from Naomi Klein's thesis in her book with the same title that our current capitalist system is contributing significantly to climate change. It brings her thesis to life through the stories of people living and working on the front lines of change.

7

Criminal Justice

CASE STUDY:
RACIAL DISCRIMINATION
AND THE EXECUTION OF TROY ANTHONY DAVIS

Troy Anthony Davis was a poor African American man accused and convicted of murdering a white, off-duty police officer, Mark MacPhail, in
Savannah, Georgia, on August 19, 1989. MacPhail was shot and killed
when responding to the cries of Larry Young, a homeless man who was
being beaten outside a Burger King. Davis maintained his innocence from
the start. At the trial that took place in August 1991, two years after the
incident, the prosecution called several eyewitnesses to the shooting who
said Davis was the shooter, although others were not sure; two witnesses
testified that Davis had confessed to them. The defense only called six witnesses, including Davis. Davis testified that he had fled the scene before
any shots were fired.[1] The jury of seven African Americans and five whites
deliberated on August 28 for less than two hours and convicted Davis of all
charges brought against him. The prosecutors asked for the death penalty.
Davis maintained his innocence to the jury, but after seven hours of deliberation the jury recommended the death penalty and the death sentence
was imposed on August 30.

  The death sentence triggered an automatic appeal, a process that would
last for twenty-two years. His first appeals were denied, and the first execution order was issued in March 1994. Davis and his lawyers from the
Georgia Resource Center (GRC), a small nonprofit law office that provided
free representation to indigent, death-sentenced Georgia prisoners in state
and federal proceedings, began habeas corpus proceedings in state court,
alleging that he had been wrongfully convicted and that his death sentence

---

[1] Jan Skutch, "Davis: I Fled before Shots Fired," *Savannah Morning News,* August
28, 1991.

was a miscarriage of justice because some of the witnesses had been coerced by the police in their testimony. Just as they were preparing their appeal, the GRC in 1995 lost 70 percent of its funding and thus was unable to do the kind of investigating and tracking down of witnesses required for an effective representation.[2] The state courts denied Davis's petitions in November 2000, saying these issues should have been raised at trial.

In 2001, Davis filed an appeal with the federal courts. All but three of the witnesses against Davis had recanted all or part of their testimony, some claiming that they felt pressured by the police to identify Davis as the shooter. Other witnesses swore affidavits indicating someone else had confessed to the murder. But these were rejected because they should have been introduced earlier in the appeals process. Many legal experts blame ⊠the Antiterrorism and Effective Death Penalty Act of 1996, which limits death row inmates from presenting evidence later in the appeals process that could have been presented at trial, for limiting the ability of wrongfully convicted persons to prove their innocence.

Davis's first appeal to the US Supreme Court was denied in June 2007, and he was scheduled for execution on July 17. By this time the Davis case had generated widespread interest, especially on the heels of the decision by Governor George Ryan of Illinois (2003) to commute death sentences there because of how many men had been wrongfully convicted. People from around the globe had asked for clemency from the governor of Georgia, including former president Jimmy Carter, South African Bishop Desmond Tutu, and Pope Benedict XVI. Amnesty International argued that while it did not know if Davis was guilty of the crime, there were sufficient questions raised to halt what might ultimately be a miscarriage of justice. A stay of execution was granted by the Georgia Supreme Court in order to hear testimony on the claim of mistaken identity. The court ruled 4–3 against the appeal, favoring the original testimony over the new. The chief justice, who was in the minority, dissented, troubled by the categorical rejection of the new testimony by the court's majority.

A second execution date was set for September 2008. A US Supreme Court stay halted the execution shortly before it was scheduled to take place. However, in the end the US Supreme Court chose not to hear Davis's petition. Another stay was granted by the 11th Circuit Court of Appeals, and oral arguments took place in December 2008 before a three-judge panel. In the interim, thousands signed a petition asking for the death sentence to be commuted. In a 2–1 decision issued in April 2009, the panel rejected Davis's petition. The 11th Circuit Court again issued a stay so that Davis could appeal once again to the US Supreme Court. In August 2009, the Supreme Court ordered the Savannah district court to "receive testimony and make findings of fact as to whether evidence that could not have been obtained at

---

[2] Brendan Lowe, "Will Georgia Kill an Innocent Man?" *Time* (July 13, 2007).

the time of trial clearly establishes innocence." The reasoning put forward by Justice John Paul Stevens for this order: "The substantial risk of putting an innocent man to death clearly provides an adequate justification for holding an evidentiary hearing."

A two-day hearing was held and presided over by Judge William Moore in June 2010. In July he issued his ruling, in which he stated that while executing an innocent man would violate the Constitution, Davis was not innocent. The recantations by the witnesses did present some minimal doubt, but it was not enough to overturn the jury verdict. Moreover, because the defense did not bring the other person who was thought to be the shooter to court, the testimony to that effect was hearsay and not admissible. Again, Davis appealed to the US Supreme Court in January 2011, but the appeal was dismissed without comment in March of that year. In May 2011, Amnesty International, People of Faith against the Death Penalty, and the NAACP gathered over 660,000 signatures on a petition to the Georgia Board of Pardons and Paroles asking it to commute Davis's death sentence. Law enforcement officials and the MacPhail family continued to believe that Davis was guilty and that only Davis's execution would establish justice and uphold the law. The board set a new execution date of September 21, 2011.

All last-minute appeals were ultimately denied. Davis's last words to the MacPhail family and the witnesses were the following:

The incident that happened that night was not my fault. I did not have a gun that night. I did not shoot your family member. But I am so sorry for your loss. I really am—sincerely. All I can ask is that each of you look deeper into this case, so that you really will finally see the truth. I ask my family and friends that you all continue to pray, that you all continue to forgive. Continue to fight this fight. For those about to take my life, may God have mercy on all of your souls. God bless you all.[3]

Davis was declared dead from lethal injection at 11:08 p.m. In response, Amnesty International issued this statement: "The US justice system was shaken to its core as Georgia executed a person who may well be innocent. Killing a man under this enormous cloud of doubt is horrific and amounts to a catastrophic failure of the justice system."[4] According to CNN, Davis's execution shocked the world.[5]

---

[3] John Rudolf, "Troy Davis' Last Words Released by Georgia Department of Corrections," *Huffington Post*, December 7, 2011.

[4] Amnesty International, "Troy Davis Execution a 'Catastrophic Failure of the Justice System,' Charges Amnesty International," September 22, 2011.

[5] Peter Wilkinson, "World Shocked by US Execution of Troy Davis," CNN, September 22, 2011.

ISSUES AND CONCERNS

The Davis case illustrates the ethical complexity involved in the criminal justice system, especially in death penalty cases. First, this case raises questions about police and prosecutorial misconduct, which has been shown to be involved in other cases where death row inmates were exonerated.[6] Affidavits by several of the witnesses in the Davis trial who recanted their trial testimony stated that they felt threatened by the police and prosecutors to provide testimony to Davis's commitment of the crime. One of the people to whom Davis supposedly confessed indicated later that he said what he did because of the pressure the police put on him: "The only way they would leave me alone is if I told them what they wanted to hear."[7] Several other witnesses said the same thing. Because the victim was a police officer, there was community pressure to solve the case. However, the prosecutors and the police department denied such allegations, and the courts supported their position, with Judge Moore calling the recantations nothing but "smoke and mirrors."[8]

The case also raises concerns about jury selection in capital cases. In death penalty cases, prospective jurors who are against the death penalty are often excluded for cause, which means they can be dismissed because they have conscientious objections to capital punishment. What this suggests is that only those willing to recommend the death penalty are included in what is known as a death-qualified jury, a setting that clearly favors the prosecution. There is substantial evidence that a death-qualified jury is more likely to recommend conviction than one that is not.[9] If this is the case, then some question whether it is ethical "to allow any defendant-victim of a tainted verdict of this sort to be executed."[10]

The Davis case also highlights concerns about eyewitness testimony and inadequate legal representation, especially for the poor, which the Innocence Project argues is systemic in death penalty cases it has defended.[11] One of the witnesses at trial stated right after the shooting that he would not be able

---

[6] "[In 2018] official misconduct and perjury/false accusation were the leading factors contributing to wrongful homicide convictions—79 percent of which involved police and/or prosecutorial misconduct and 77 percent (52 cases) of which involved perjury or false accusation. Both factors were present in more than two-thirds of homicide exonerations." Equal Justice Initiative, May 5, 2019.

[7] Amnesty International, "'Where is the justice for me?': The Case of Troy Davis, Facing Execution in Georgia," February 2007.

[8] Trymaine Lee, "Troy Davis' Execution Eve Sees Last-Minute Efforts to Save His Life," *Huffington Post,* November 20, 2011.

[9] F. P. Williams and M. D. McShane, "Inclinations of Prospective Jurors in Capital Cases," *Sociology and Social Research* 74/2 (January 1990): 85–94.

[10] Welsh S. White, "The Constitutional Invalidity of Convictions Imposed by Death-Qualified Juries," *Cornell Law Review* 58/6 (July 1973): 1178.

[11] See Innocence Project, "Eyewitness Identification Reform"; and Emily West, "Court Findings of Ineffective Assistance of Counsel Claims in Post-Conviction Appeals among the First 255 DNA Exoneration Cases," September 2010.

to identify the shooter but only the clothes he was wearing. By the time the trial came about he did identify Davis as the shooter. Another witness who did not recant his testimony has since been identified as the actual shooter. Davis's appeal lawyers have argued that his trial counsel failed to conduct an adequate investigation of all the state's evidence, including concerns about police coercion in witness testimony. The defense also only called six witnesses of its own to rebut the state's case.

Class and race are additional elements in this case. It is likely that part of the reason for the failure of his counsel at the trial is the limited amount of resources Davis could provide to pay for his defense. This also affected his chances in the appeals process. Death penalty appeals can be lengthy and costly. The poor and indigent do not have the resources to pay these costs. In fact, almost all death row inmates could not afford their own lawyers at trial. Davis did have the nonprofit Georgia Resource Center helping him, but substantial budget cuts limited the GRC's ability to track down witnesses. For some, the question of race may not be an issue, because seven of the twelve jurors were black. However, those who raise the issue of race look more systematically at the way in which the criminal justice system and the death penalty affects persons of different races. Over 75 percent of the murder victims in cases that result in the death penalty are white, even though only 50 percent of victims overall are white. Studies also show that African American defendants are three times more likely to receive the death penalty than white defendants when the victims are white.[12]

The issues of race and class also raise questions about the fairness of the entire criminal justice system.[13] Black males are six times more likely to serve time in prison than white males. They constitute over 35 percent of the prison population, even though they are less than 10 percent of the total population. Their jail sentences are often 20 percent longer than whites. Moreover, as the recent protests over the death of George Floyd seek to highlight, black Americans in 2019 were nearly three times more likely to die at the hands of police than white Americans, and one-and-a-half times more likely to be unarmed before their deaths.[14] While crime is committed by members of every socio-economic class, the poor experience higher rates of arrest, criminal charges, convictions, longer prison sentences, and denial of parole. While lately there has been some emphasis on white collar crime, the rich are often not caught, processed, or sentenced as severely as poor defendants. According to Jeffrey Reiman and Paul Leighton, "The rich get richer and the poor get prison."[15]

---

[12] Scott Phillips and Justin Marceau, "Whom the State Kills," *Harvard Civil Liberties-Civil Law Review* 55/2 (Summer 2020).

[13] See Michelle Alexander, *The New Jim Crow: Mass Incarceration in the Age of Colorblindness* (New York: The New Press, 2012).

[14] Willem Roper, "Black Americans 2.5X More Likely Than Whites to Be Killed By Police," Statista.com (June 2, 2020).

[15] Jeffrey Reiman and Paul Leighton, *The Rich Get Richer and the Poor Get Prison*, 10th ed. (New York: Pearson, 2012).

Finally, the case highlights different conceptions about what is just. Some contend that the American criminal justice system is based primarily on a retributive notion of justice. What this means is that when someone violates the law, the courts punish the offender with some type of retribution, usually jail time, which is thought to be equivalent to the offense committed. This view is often understood as "an eye for an eye." In death penalty cases the punishment includes the forfeiture of the guilty party's life. This was certainly the position of the prosecutors and the jury who sentenced Davis. It is also the position of the MacPhail family, who argued that Davis's execution was not about vengeance but about justice under the law.[16] Amnesty International and others questioned whether this was the case, especially given the doubt raised about Davis's guilt by the witnesses who recanted their testimony. When such doubt exists, carrying out an execution undercuts the justice people are seeking.[17]

Others advocate for a restorative notion of justice. Restorative justice looks at crime as a violation of people and relationships. Because we live in an interconnected world, one person's harmful actions create a rift in relationships not only between the immediately involved persons but also in the community. Moreover, crime inflicts harm on victims, which generates needs that may not have been there before. Such violations create guilt and obligations on the part of offenders to take responsibility for their offense and to make things right. It also places obligations on the part of the community to look at underlying causes and to provide for the needs of the victims. Justice, therefore, involves making things right for all. The victims, the offenders, and the community are stakeholders and cannot be excluded from the justice process as they are currently.[18] What is the relationship between restorative justice and the death penalty? Murder is the most despicable offense to relationships. In some respects it is the ultimate denial of the respect owed to all persons. There is no way to "make right" the crime of murder. Society must protect the social fabric from those who will not acknowledge their crimes, and it uses the criminal justice system to establish their guilt. Yet killing people to punish them must be avoided if there is another morally serious way to address their offense. A restorative justice approach suggests that more can be and is being done to recognize survivors' needs and the needs of co-victims while holding offenders accountable for their actions. Taking their lives eliminates the possibility for transformation and healing for the victims, for the offenders, and for the community that restorative justice seeks.

---

[16] Adam Van Brimmer, "MacPhail Family Readies for Next Act in Painful Tragedy," *Savannah Morning News,* September 19, 2011.

[17] Amnesty International, "Where Is the Justice for Me?"

[18] See Howard Zehr, *The Little Book of Restorative Justice* (Intercourse, PA: Good Books, 2002).

EVANGELICAL ETHICS

As we saw in Chapter 1, both the conservative and the progressive evangelical ethics traditions highlight the authority and central role that scripture plays in their ethical thinking. John Jefferson Davis calls the Bible "the only infallible and inerrant rule of faith and practice" and the "final court of appeals for ethics."[19] Glen Stassen and David Gushee contend that "the Bible is the 'sun' around which all other sources of authority are brought into orbit."[20] However, where conservative evangelicals like Davis tend to be rule oriented in their approach to scripture, progressives like Stassen and Gushee are Jesus centered. The result is a split among evangelicals on the issue of the death penalty in principle. Both look to the Bible for guidance; however, their understanding of what the Bible says regarding capital punishment is drastically different.

Davis contends that on the principle of whether capital punishment is morally appropriate today, Genesis 9:6 on the Noachic Covenant is the key scriptural passage (*EE4* 202). That verse reads:

Whoever sheds the blood of a human,
by a human shall that person's blood be shed;
for in his own image
God made humankind.

For Davis, capital punishment is an instance of retributive justice demanded by God. Davis suggests that the context of the verse indicates that this is a divine command (rather than a divine prediction of what will happen if someone takes the life of another); it is an imperative required by God as a reckoning for the destruction of the image of God in another person. It is also supported by other Old Testament passages, such as Numbers 35:16–21, which clearly indicate that murderers should be put to death.

Some would suggest that the Mosaic Covenant, of which the Numbers passage is a part, also requires the death penalty for kidnapping, rape, fornication, cursing a parent, and incest, to name a few. Why restrict this biblical interpretation to only murder? Davis makes the distinction between those laws given to Israel as part of the Mosaic Covenant in a theocratic state and those under the Noachic Covenant meant to apply to all humankind, which include also the continuation of the seasons (Gen 8:22) and the dread animals have toward humanity (Gen 9:2). "It follows that while the detailed provisions of the criminal code of Israel are no longer binding on the church, the

---

[19] John Jefferson Davis, *Evangelical Ethics,* 4th ed. (Phillipsburg, NJ: P&R Publishing, 2015), 3 (hereafter cited as *EE4*).
[20] Glen Stassen and David Gushee, *Kingdom Ethics* (Madison, WI: InterVarsity Press, 2003), 89 (hereafter cited as *KE*).

mandate of Genesis 9:6 requiring the death penalty for murder remains one of continuing validity today" (*EE4* 204).

What about New Testament passages that seem to suggest some modification of the death penalty? Davis points to three passages: John 7:53–8:11 (the woman caught in adultery); Romans 13:1–7 (with its emphasis on the civil magistrate wielding the sword); and Acts 25:11 (Paul's declaration that if he committed a capital offense, he would submit willingly to death). In the first passage Jesus challenges those who have brought the woman to throw stones if they are free from sin. When they all walk away, he tells her that he also does not condemn her but to sin no more. Davis suggests that what was at stake here was not the issue of abrogating the death penalty for adultery as part of the Mosaic Law; after all, Jesus had declared that he did not come to abolish the law but to fulfill it (Mt 5:17). His point was that the so-called witnesses had failed to act according to the law, which required that the man also be brought up on charges (*EE4* 206).

Some contend that what Paul is referring to in Romans 13:1–7 is the symbol of capital punishment and not its actual practice. Davis challenges that reading because the context also talks about other things the civil authorities can enact, such as the imposition of taxes. Paul was aware that the Roman authorities practiced capital punishment. So, his reference to the sword is not meant symbolically but practically as the instrument of capital punishment (*EE4* 206). Moreover, in Acts 25:11, Paul presupposes that some crimes are intrinsically worthy of death and that the authorities have the divinely sanctioned authority to implement it in those cases. Paul's challenge was that he had not committed such a crime; however, if the authorities could convict him of such, he would willingly submit to the punishment.

But doesn't this emphasis on the violent restraint of evil run counter to Jesus's emphasis on love and nonviolence, as some claim? On this point Davis suggests that in the latter case, the emphasis is on the salvation of the sinner, whereas the former is focused on the preservation of the world from evil: "God ordains the punishment in *time* of those whom he may in fact pardon in *eternity*" (*EE4* 207). In his view the Bible affirms the legitimacy of both. Thus, following his emphasis on contextual absolutism, which "holds that in each and every ethical situation, no matter how extreme, there is a course of action that is morally right and free of sin" (*EE4* 8), there is no disagreement between the Old Testament and the New Testament on the moral legitimacy of the death penalty. While the New Testament forgoes some elements of the Mosaic Law, the Noachic Covenant that applies to all humanity is still valid. "The New Testament, including the teaching of Jesus, does not overturn this basic mandate, but presupposes its continuing validity for nontheocratic societies" (*EE4* 207).

Stassen and Gushee have a different view of the biblical record. They agree that this should not be viewed as a New Testament versus Old Testament debate. However, they insist that "the direction of the Old Testament moves from the ancient practice of the death penalty toward its abolition" (*KE* 205).

Their fundamental orientation is toward Jesus's teaching and discipleship based upon that understanding of Jesus's teaching found in the Gospels; they are thus critical of evangelical ethicists who do not draw their understandings about the role of the Bible from the person and work of Christ and who do not employ the same prophetic hermeneutic that Jesus did (*KE* 97). Jesus's view of righteousness was prophetic and not legalistic, a righteousness that consisted of love, mercy, and justice, especially to the vulnerable.

Based upon this view they interpret the scriptural passages differently than Davis does. Rather than fencing off Jesus's teaching regarding the death penalty, they take Jesus's teaching as the key and interpret Genesis 9:6 through the lens of Jesus's teaching. They disagree with Davis's view that this verse is a command. Rather, they suggest it is a proverb, indicating what might be the likely consequences if one engages in violent actions: violence always begets more violence. The notion that all human beings are created in the image of God "strongly asserts God's command that we value the sacredness of the life of human persons" (*KE* 205). How could God command, therefore, that we sacrifice the life of those who have lost sight of this in others? They conclude that the value of human life works "to oppose actually carrying out a death penalty" (*KE* 206).

If one looks at Genesis 9:6 through the lens of Jesus's teaching, as expressed in Matthew 26:52, "All who take the sword, by the sword will die," this consequentialist framework makes sense. They would suggest that even in the Old Testament the penalties for certain acts, like murder, adultery, and others, are more to address the seriousness of the offenses, not meant as penalties always to be included. For example, Cain murdered his brother, and yet he was not killed in response. David committed adultery with Bathsheba and had her husband sent to his death, and yet the response of God through Nathan was for repentance and not for his death. Tamar committed adultery and was commended for her actions, not punished with death. They claim that in the entire Old Testament there is not one example where the death penalty was actually carried out (KE 202). Thus, they contend that the effort to affirm Genesis 9:6 as a foundation for the death penalty seems more like a desire to find biblical support for the American practice of the death penalty rather than a serious attempt to comprehend fully the biblical view of this violent practice.

Looking at Jesus's body of teaching, it is clear to Stassen and Gushee that Jesus emphasized a move toward nonviolence and a rejection of violence both for the individual and the civil authorities. They agree that Jesus affirmed the Law of Moses, but whenever he spoke about it he always omitted the parts that advocated violence. "He avoided the violent parts of the teaching so systematically that it must not be happenstance. Jesus' teachings are always consistent with the sacredness of human life and with initiatives to heal vicious cycles of killing" (*KE* 198). Rather, Jesus focuses on those practices that result in violence and murder, like fomenting rage, holding grudges, and the like. Moreover, he calls into question the whole practice of vengeful retaliation (Mt 5:39–42). Instead of hate, we are to love even our enemies (*KE* 198).

Regarding the story of the woman caught in adultery, Jesus was demonstrating a delicate balance between not condoning sin and showing mercy. He could not openly go against the Mosaic Law, not because he believed that it advocated the death penalty but because he knew that they were trying to trap him. In fact, Stassen and Gushee argue, it was because of Jesus's consistent message against violence that the accusers hoped he would oppose her execution even in the face of the law (*KE* 199). As a result, Jesus released the woman from the death penalty. Moreover, in their view, the followers of Jesus also repudiated the death penalty. All ten instances where the death penalty is threatened or imposed in the New Testament, such as the beheading of John the Baptist (Mt 14:1–12) and the stoning of Stephen (Acts 7), are considered unjust. Finally, Paul was not affirming the death penalty in Acts 25:11, as Davis claims, but rather his willingness to die on behalf of Christ.

In addition to the interpretation and authority of scripture, there is also the question of what principle of justice ought to govern the criminal justice system, retributive or restorative. As noted previously, retributive justice refers to the view that when one party violates the law or the norm, then there is an imbalance generated that must be restored by the courts. The retribution is usually some form of punishment. In this case it is the forfeiture of the life of the guilty party. Restorative justice refers to the notion that when one party breaks the law or the norm, there is a violation of people and relationships. This violation creates obligations to restore what was lost. Justice involves victims, offenders, and community members in an effort to put things right. This does not mean that punishment is not a part of the remedy, but rather that the goal is to restore the relationships that were broken by addressing the needs of victims and placing responsibility on the offenders for repairing harm.

When it comes to capital punishment, Davis affirms the norm of retributive justice. Whereas some Christians suggest that retribution is merely a form of revenge and should not be supported by Christians, Davis says their view is misguided. "Properly understood, retribution is a satisfaction of the requirements of justice, a restoration of a disturbed moral balance" (*EE4* 208). He agrees that personal feelings of hatred and revenge have no place in the administration of the death penalty but argues that scripture clearly distinguishes between that and the appropriate application of distributive justice. In fact, the affirmation of distributive justice in the Bible goes so far as to ensure that inappropriate punishments, such as excessive violence and torture, are prohibited. The punishment should only fit the crime—no more and no less. In the case of murder, the only punishment that can restore justice is the death of the murderer (*EE4* 208).

Davis points to the divine plan of salvation for evidence of divine sanction of retributive justice as a basis for capital punishment. It is a moral fact that some actions, such as sin and crime, deserve punishment in God's sight. God's sense of justice demands it. Fortunately, rather than inflict that punishment on humanity, God has enforced the standards of justice by mercifully assuming the punishment through the person and work of Jesus, often referred to as the penal substitution theory of atonement. Thus, Davis concludes, "capital punishment is actually the application on the human plane of the principle of retributive justice demonstrated by God himself in the cross of Jesus Christ" (*EE4* 209).

As one might surmise from the title of their chapter on the death penalty, "Restorative Penalties for Homicide," Stassen and Gushee contend that the appropriate notion of justice for the criminal justice system is restorative (not retributive) justice. Drawing from their understanding of what Jesus did, they emphasize that biblical justice delivers people from the hatred and violence that are so much a part of society. Justice from the biblical perspective has its focus on "deliverance of those in bondage and restoration to community" (*KE* 212). They agree that biblical justice does have a retributive dimension, punishment for wrongdoing; but the overwhelming direction is toward restitution and restoration. They speak about "transforming initiatives" that seek to end the cycle of violence that we get caught up in and that is perpetuated by the presence of the death penalty. Contrary to Davis, they have a different view of the divine plan of salvation. The direction is toward forgiveness and reconciliation. The death of Christ is the supreme example of the lengths God goes to in order to restore humanity to community with God. The last words on the cross were words of forgiveness, not judgment: "Father, forgive them for they do not know what they are doing" (Lk 23:34).

Even though there is a difference in principle on the morality of the death penalty between the two evangelical ethics positions, this does not mean that they would necessarily disagree on the case at hand. As Davis contends: "Good principles and good facts are both necessary for sound decision-making" (*EE4* 5). Davis does not address this case, but he does speak about some of the issues associated with this case. Regarding the issue of discrimination based on race and/or class, Davis agrees that discrimination and bias in the application of the death penalty are problems: "Discrimination in any part of the criminal justice system is a matter of serious concern" (*EE4* 211). However, he suggests that the problems are not as extensive as sometimes argued and often exaggerated. He points to statistics that suggest that white inmates make up the majority of death row inmates. Moreover, he might point out that in the Troy Davis case, seven of the jurors were black. He acknowledges that the wealthy often have the resources to skirt the law or to escape the penalties associated with breaking it. But does this mean that we must have perfection in the system before we can administer justice and punishment? He does not think so: "If a given principle is valid—whether capital punishment or some other principle of criminal justice—then imperfections of administration are justification not for the abolition of the principle, but rather for its reform and more evenhanded application" (*EE4* 211).

Regarding the question of whether we sometimes execute innocent persons, Davis argues that the existence of the appeals process, something quite evident in the Troy Davis case, would militate against eliminating the death penalty. "The proper administration of the death penalty is a display of divine justice and God's wrath on the wrongdoer" (*EE4* 212). If it could be proven that in Troy Davis's case the proper administration of the death penalty did not occur, he would be open to allowing Davis to live. However, given the extensive appeals process and the fact that he was repeatedly seen as guilty of the crime, Davis would question whether a miscarriage of justice had been done here.

As one might imagine, Stassen and Gushee would consider all instances of the death penalty unjust. At the beginning of their chapter on this issue they provide anecdotes of families of murdered victims who were seeking the death penalty to find some sense of release from the emotional toll, much like the sentiments expressed by the MacPhail family in this case. However, at least according to Stassen and Gushee, such release never comes; rather, their resentment kills their spirits, "making them into victims too" (*KE* 194).

Stassen and Gushee also disagree with Davis's assessment of the presence of racial or class bias in the implementation of the death penalty in this country. They point to numerous studies that illustrate how widespread such bias is. One such study points out that a black defendant is four times more likely to receive a death sentence than a white defendant (*KE* 210). Another study pointed out that key decision-makers in death penalty cases are almost exclusively white men. Moreover, they note that when the victim is white, the chances of receiving the death penalty are much greater than if the victim is black. This leads them to conclude that the justice system "treats the lives of whites as more valuable than those of blacks" (*KE* 211).

Discrimination by class is also prevalent in the administration of the death penalty. Citing their personal experiences in visiting death row inmates, Stassen and Gushee contend that most of the defendants "were strikingly poor" and note that even defenders of capital punishment admit that "no affluent person has ever been given the death penalty in US history" (*KE* 211). They contend that the data for mistaken death penalty convictions is greater than Davis believes, citing a study commissioned by the Senate Judiciary Committee of nearly forty-six hundred capital cases where serious reversible errors occurred in nearly seven out of ten cases. Such errors included incompetent defense lawyers, police, or prosecutors who did not share mitigating evidence with jurors. Moreover, they note that since 1900 there have been hundreds of cases where innocent people have been convicted and sentenced to die.

David Gushee is clear that these questions and concerns apply to the Troy Davis case. He signed a petition on September 21, 2011, which stated that the execution of Troy Davis was "a grievous wrong":

We oppose the death penalty for both principled and pragmatic reasons. In practice death penalty cases have been riddled with misdeeds like prosecutorial misconduct, police coercion of witnesses, misidentification of suspects, and not least racial prejudice—all of which seem to have played an appalling role in the Davis case, as they have in so many others.[21]

Gushee goes even further when he declares that our entire death penalty system is broken:

My personal take is that our criminal justice system does not demonstrate the capacity to administer the death penalty in a manner just enough to entrust it with this awesome power. Flaws that are bad enough in relation to lesser punishments rise to the level of the truly intolerable in relation to this ultimate punishment. These flaws crop up at every point in the administration of what passes for justice in the United States. . . . And none of this is to say anything about how dubious it is for those who claim to follow an unjustly executed Savior to look blithely on the execution of others.[22]

WOMANIST ETHICS

Considering this case from the perspective of womanist ethics requires that we keep in mind two key points from that tradition. First, an important source for womanist ethics is found in sociohistorical analysis: investigating the historical and contemporary events, persons, and cultural situations of the black community and the cultural contexts in which they live in order to discern the patterns of discrimination and oppression they have experienced. As Emilie Townes writes, "The contemporary scene did not emerge from a vacuum; it evolved historically and is immanently contextual."[23] Social scientists understand culture to be a pattern that embraces three interrelated dimensions: a worldview (a picture of how things really are or ought to be, embodied in symbols, myths, beliefs, and values); an ethos (ways of relating and behaving in relationship to one another reflecting that worldview); and

---

[21] GoPetition, "An Appeal to End the Death Penalty—Signed by Christian Theologians and Ethicists in the United States," October 4, 2011.

[22] David Gushee, "The Death Penalty System Is Broken," *Associated Baptist Press News,* May 13, 2014.

[23] Townes's analysis in this case is drawn from her following works: *Womanist Ethics and the Cultural Production of Evil* (New York: Palgrave Macmillan, 2006), 76 (hereafter cited as *CPE*); "To Be Called Beloved: Womanist Ontology in Postmodern Refraction," in *Womanist Theological Ethics: A Reader,* ed. Katie Cannon et al., 183–202 (Louisville, KY: Westminster John Knox Press, 2011) (hereafter cited as "Beloved"); and "Ethics as an Art of Doing the Work Our Souls Must Have," in Cannon et al., *Womanist Theological Ethics,* 35–50 (hereafter cited as "Souls").

social structures (institutions and organizations that embody the culture's patterns of meaning).[24] The racism that is endemic to our criminal justice system (social structures)—in our policing, in our politics, in our courts, and in our prisons—is part of a long history and pattern of oppression of persons of color (ethos) by powerful whites, whose "hegemonic imagination" (worldview) from slavery to Jim Crow to mass incarceration has considered persons of color inferior, even subhuman. This is one dimension of what Townes calls the cultural production of evil. "Exploring evil as a cultural production highlights the systematic construction of truncated narratives designed to support and perpetuate structural inequities and forms of social oppression" (*CPE* 4). Womanist ethics explores the lived realities of those who experience marginalization and oppression to uncover other narratives and ways of relating to challenge the systems that deny them their full humanity and justice.

A second, related element to bring to mind is what Townes calls "uninterrogated coloredness," which is "a complicated and interstructured set of social meanings that are always being transformed by political struggle" (*CPE* 75).[25] This is especially an issue for whites who do not see how whiteness is not colorless but is also a social construction; it shapes not only how they see brown and black persons in a negative light, "an unconscious color caste system on degrees of darkness and lightness" (*CPE* 64), but also allows them to ignore the extent of their power and privilege (*CPE* 60). When uninterrogated, whites see their values and beliefs (worldview), and their privileges (ethos) as normal; everything else is an exception. That is why when whites talk about race, they generally do not think about themselves (as members of the white race) but only about persons of color, often using negative stereotypes to suggest that the latter do not have the same moral qualities that whites have (*CPE* 74). These negative stereotypes have contributed to the racial disparities in our criminal justice system, where persons of color are stopped by police far more than whites, arrested at higher rates than whites, and six times more likely to be incarcerated and to experience longer prison sentences.[26]

Womanist ethicist Cheryl Kirk-Duggan calls the death penalty "a sophisticated, high-priced lynching, given the costs of appeals, housing, and the elaborate system designed to make this state-ordered, state-administrated act

---

[24] See, for example, Ruth Benedict, *Patterns of Culture* (New York: Mariner Books, 2013).

[25] Many people see the 2020 riots in cities across the United States in response to more African Americans being killed at the hands of police as an example of the interstructuring of oppression. The violence in the cities is a response to the racial and economic violence being perpetrated by those in power, violence that has become more evident with the disproportionate negative effect of the coronavirus on brown and black populations.

[26] See Sentencing Project, "Report to the United Nations on Racial Disparities in the US Criminal Justice System," April 19, 2018.

of violence a 'mercy killing.'"[27] That is why a crucial part of the sociohistorical history recalled by Townes, which is relevant to this case, is the history of
lynching in this country. She notes that with sanctions against racism lifted in
the period of Reconstruction and beyond, "Blacks within the United States
became the target of White frustrations" ("Beloved" 188). Whites, particularly
white men, were seeking to reassert and maintain their superiority at a time
when it was difficult to control where blacks lived and worked. Lynching
was one instrument used to demonstrate to themselves their power and to
intimidate and punish blacks. Black men could be lynched for any number
of reasons, including offenses such as rape and murder, or even as a result
of mistaken identity. Townes notes that the fear of lynching not only kept
blacks in their place, but also women in subordination to Southern white
men. "Lynching served as severe sanction against voluntary sexual relations
between African American men and White women. In addition, lynching
served to reinforce the hierarchical power relationships based on gender"
("Beloved" 189). Lynching also involved large segments of the population.
It was not simply done by individuals but involved mob violence—which,
Townes argues, became "the instrument to maintain segregation and solidify a
rigid caste division between racial groups," especially in a society that required
blacks and whites to live in close proximity. To highlight the precarious context
for blacks under such domination, Townes uses the words of Baby Suggs, a
character in Toni Morrison's novel *Beloved*: "And O my people, out yonder,
hear me, they do not love your neck unnoosed and straight."[28] (I imagine this
history is fresh in the minds of those African Americans who have called the
deaths of George Floyd and Eric Garner examples of a modern day lynching
at the hands of the police. Instead of a noose, the officers used a knee and a
chokehold, but the result was the same: the breath and the life were choked
out of them.) Today, Townes notes, the control is more systematic: "The nature
of structured social inequality in United States society is such that peoples
are confined or warehoused by choice or by condition" ("Beloved" 190).

Another way that cultures produce evil is when the "hegemonic imagination" creates images that play "with history and memory to spawn caricatures
and stereotypes" (*CPE* 7). As noted in the DACA case study in Chapter 5,
Townes argued that images of the "welfare queen" and the "black matriarch"
have been used by powerful elites to justify reductions to the social safety
net and to fuel racial animosity. In the context of our politics and criminal
justice system, the same could be argued of the image of the violent "angry
black man."[29] One such image that has contributed to the racially charged

---

[27] Cheryl Kirk-Duggan, *Refiner's Fire: A Religious Engagement with Violence* (Minneapolis: Fortress Press, 2001), xiv.

[28] Toni Morrison, *Beloved* (New York: Alfred A. Knopf, 1987), 88–89, quoted in
Townes, "Beloved," 186.

[29] See J. Hurwitz, M. Peffley, and P. Sniderman, "Racial Stereotypes and Whites'
Political Views of Blacks in the Context of Welfare and Crime," *American Journal of
Political Science* 41/1 (January 1997): 30–60.

politics of crime that continues to affect us today is the image of "Willie" Horton, shown as a threatening black man, used by the George H. W. Bush presidential campaign against Michael Dukakis to scare whites into believing that the Democratic governor of Massachusetts was soft on crime. William Horton[30] was a black murder convict who was convicted of raping a Maryland woman and stabbing her companion while on furlough from a Massachusetts prison, even though he had been sentenced to life without parole. While the furlough program was actually started by his Republican predecessor and eventually ended by Dukakis, it was not soon enough to stop the Bush campaign from using it against him. This image of the violent, angry black man has continued to harm a generation of African Americans who are arrested for "driving while black" or who are locked up because of its contribution to tougher sentencing laws supported by President Clinton and other Democrats to prove they are tough on crime, the impact of which disproportionately affected persons of color. Even when President Barack Obama sought to ease these tough sentencing laws and overhaul the criminal justice system in a bipartisan way, the "Willie" Horton episode made the task more difficult. Some also contend that the influence of this story can be seen in the tweets by President Trump against African Americans.[31] Townes calls all such images used to generate fear and encourage harsh penalties against persons of color "creations of the White imagination—its fears and its terrors and its stereotypes and its unilateral attempts at justice" (*CPE* 46).[32]

In response to this lived reality experienced by persons of color, Townes says we need counters to the white imagination "that will help us dismantle the stultifying and death-bringing stereotypes created by the fantastic hegemonic imagination that circumscribe our isness" (*CPE* 48). Womanist ethics contends that one way to challenge the cultural production of racism in our

---

[30] Horton was appalled by the way he was depicted by the campaign. "The fact is, my name is not 'Willie.' It's part of the myth of the case. The name irks me. It was created to play on racial stereotypes: big, ugly, dumb, violent, black—'Willie.' I resent that. They created a fictional character who seemed believable, but who did not exist." Quoted in Jeffrey Elliott, "The 'Willie' Horton Nobody Knows," *The Nation* 257/6 (August 23, 1993). Tali Mendelberg contends that [Bush campaign manager] Lee Atwater's reference to William Horton as "Willie" was typical of Southerners who refer to black men with "overstated familiarity" (Tali Mendelberg, *The Race Card: Campaign Strategy, Implicit Messages, and the Norm of Equality* [Princeton, NJ: Princeton University Press, 2001], 142).

[31] See Peter Baker, "Bush Made Willie Horton an Issue in 1988, and the Racial Scars Are Still Fresh," *New York Times*, December 3, 2018.

[32] A recent example of the use of the angry black man image occurred when an African American man calmly asked a woman in New York's Central Park to leash her dog as required by the park's rules. Instead of doing so, she decided to call the police to say that she was being accosted by an "African American man," a phrase she used repeatedly and with increasing intensity in her voice to try to get the man to stop filming the episode. The video went viral, and the woman ended up losing her job and apologizing for her actions (*New York Times*, May 26, 2020).

society, which is supported by a worldview or narrative that sees persons of color as dangerous and deems white lives as more valuable, is to recognize that the story "*can* be told another way. It can be told in such a way that the voices and lives of those who, traditionally and historically, have been left out are now heard with clarity and precision" (*CPE* 7). Townes finds such a counter-narrative in the collective experience and stories of black women. These stories provide the source for defining norms and values that are attended to in ethical deliberation. If we are seeking answers to how people should act in the face of structural injustice, womanist ethics looks at the values that helped the black community resist the horrors of slavery, Jim Crow laws, and ongoing racism, sexism, and classism, to see what can take us toward the vision of justice and wholeness that emerges from the Christian gospel.

One image Townes uses to expose the "willful oblivion" of uninterrogated whiteness is that of Sapphire, an image drawn from minstrel shows and electronic media. Townes says Sapphire "is malicious, vicious, bitchy, loud, bawdy, domineering, and emasculating . . . based on the oldest negative stereotype of woman: inherently and inescapably evil." While many have depicted such characteristics as problematic, Townes suggests that only such an evil stereotype or image can "destabilize and deconstruct a structural evil such as racism" (*CPE* 61). Sapphire was a black woman in charge; she had her own ideas and could articulate them clearly; she protected, cared for, and kept her family in line in every situation; and she chose not to relate to white culture in the way expected. She was fully human and could not be contained in the image of what blackness meant in the white imagination, thus posing a threat to their domination. Townes applauds these characteristics because they "are needed to untangle and demystify the intractability of racism. Being polite (dispassionate) about it has not worked" (*CPE* 62). In drawing from black women's narratives, she is not seeking to idealize or romanticize black women. Rather, she seeks a biblical justice that is inclusive of all persons. "A womanist social ethic that springs from Sapphire's steel-edged tongue must embrace all segments of society if it is to be thorough and rigorous and continue to push us into a critical dialogue that enlarges the boundaries of our humanness" (*CPE* 76).

A worldview that values the humanness of all, regardless of race, corresponds with an ethos that values right relationships among all. Townes's understandings of freedom, reconciliation, and justice are helpful here. Recall that the idea of liberation intends to "restore a sense of self as a free person and as a spiritual being" ("Souls" 39). It is the "God-presence" in each of us that provides a strong sense of the self and our right to being, giving each person worth and dignity. This gift of freedom opens the door not only to reconciliation and relationship with God but also the possibility of restoring relationship and harmony with others, through which we can work to build a more just social order, where each person's worth is recognized and respected (*CPE* 135). "Justice is the notion that each one of us has worth, and that each one of us has the right to have that worth recognized and respected. In short, justice lets us know that we owe one another respect and the right to our dignity" (*CPE* 135). This ethos suggests that Townes's view of justice is restorative, seeking to restore relationships among persons that have been broken by violence, whether personal or structural. She draws out the implications of this restorative view with her argument in favor of reparations that the dominant white society owe to persons of color because whites have gained their power and privilege on their backs, leaving many in poverty and despair (*CPE* 109). That is why simple criminal justice solutions to violence and crime—to build more prisons or enact tougher laws—are problematic for Townes; they lose sight of the underlying issues of drugs and poverty in the community that give rise to these problems and should be addressed to eliminate injustice ("Souls" 44). Moreover, an ethos that respects the God-given worth and right to dignity of every person and emphasizes reconciliation and restoration of relationships with others would call into question society's use of the death penalty in principle. In the case of the execution of Troy Davis, such an ethos would agree with progressive evangelicals that the appearance of prosecutorial misconduct along with the prevalence of class and racial discrimination perpetuate the evil in our criminal justice system. Instead, a womanist ethics conception of the common good means "having the social structures on which all depend work so that they benefit all people as we strive to create a genuinely inclusive and democratic social and moral order" (*CPE* 137).

Townes recognizes that achieving this systemic transformation in society will not be easy, especially for whites who have ignored their own racial construction and the privilege it has provided to them. Taking up the challenge to overcome racism and uninterrogated coloredness may even generate some pain and guilt as their worldview and ethos toward persons of color and about themselves implode. But they cannot let their guilt become a strategy for maintaining oppressive structures. "To counter this, a key goal is building a community in which you are willing to risk. This takes time, energy, and honesty" (*CPE* 77). Fortunately, we can see some of this investment of time, energy, and honest self-reflection in the response to the senseless killing of George Floyd at the hands of the Minneapolis police. Countless whites are reading and discussing books on racism and white privilege, such as *How to Be an Antiracist* and *White Fragility*,[33] to understand how this systemic evil was produced, its impact on persons of color, and their complicity in its creation. Whites are bringing their children to biracial protests and marches to educate them about the racial bias in the criminal justice system and beyond, becoming active allies rather than bystanders in the effort to eliminate racial injustice. Citizens and politicians of all races are using their voices to demand and enact change in the ways policing is done, outlawing chokeholds,

---

[33] Ibram X. Kendi, *How to Be an Antiracist* (New York: One World Books, 2019); Robin DiAngelo, *White Fragility: Why It's So Hard for White People to Talk about Racism* (Boston: Beacon Press, 2018).

removing no-knock warrants, mandating body cameras, and requiring police training on ways to de-escalate volatile situations.

Townes welcomes such protests and changes, but she cautions that this cannot be like what has happened so many times before, where the energy dissipates once the news cycle changes and the cameras are gone. Those seeking to dismantle the racist structures in our criminal justice system must make a "lifelong commitment to antiracist behavior, thought, and ideology," no matter how imperfectly they are able to live it out in the present (*CPE* 77). This is especially true for Christians who seek to live out God's call to resist injustice and to engage in actions that will bring about a just and loving social order that celebrates wholeness and community for all persons regardless of race and ends "the violence that circumscribes our lives" (*CPE* 58). By engaging in these "faith-filled responses . . . to dismantle the cultural production of evil," Christians "may meet the needs of those who may be the least of these or they may be folks just like many of us—blessed with resources and abilities and a divine mandate to use them with a spirituality that will not let go of that relentless sense of justice that can only come from a rock-steady God" (*CPE* 161).

RESOURCES

Discussion Questions

1. Does the prospect that the implementation of the death penalty may be flawed in some instances mean that we should abandon the death penalty as an option in our criminal justice system? John Jefferson Davis says it does not. Do you agree? If so, why? If not, why not?

2. The Christian ethical positions discussed above draw from readings in the same Bible but come up with different perspectives on the moral permissibility of the death penalty as an appropriate punishment for capital offenses. Which perspective do you think more accurately interprets the biblical record? Do you find that your own prior beliefs about the moral legitimacy of the death penalty influence your reading of the Bible, as Stassen and Gushee claim often happens?

3. Many students are against the death penalty not because they believe the penalty is too severe, but because they think it is too lenient. They contend that murderers should be incarcerated in very uncomfortable conditions for the rest of their lives to suffer and live with the guilt of their crimes. Do you agree with their judgment? How would the positions discussed above respond?

4. Stassen and Gushee and Emilie Townes contend that statistics suggest that both the criminal justice system and the implementation of the death penalty are skewed by race and class. Do you think this is the case? If so, is it because minorities and the poor are more likely to commit crimes? Is

it because of other social and economic factors, such as white privilege? If such bias exists, what can and should be done about it and its consequences?

5. Some claim that our criminal justice system is focused on punishment and not rehabilitation and restoration. What is the underlying conception of justice that contributes to this approach? Would a restorative justice model help to reduce the rate of crime, especially violent crime, in our society? If so, what might such a model entail? Would it reduce the escalation of violence that occurs between the police and persons of color?

Activities

1. Do an analysis of this case from the perspective of situation ethics. Compare and contrast the conclusions that model is likely to draw with those from the two perspectives in this case analysis. In what ways are they similar? In what ways are they different? Which approach, in your opinion, addresses the case most comprehensively?

2. Go to the local criminal court in your city, town, or county. Spend several hours in the open court and record what you observe. What do you note about the racial and class makeup of the defendants? How many have lawyers versus public defenders? Write up your findings, share them with the class, and discuss their implications.

3. Find a local church-related organization that provides ministry to inmates at the local prison. Arrange a visit to the organization to find out its mission and purpose and how it goes about its work. Focus on the values or beliefs that motivate the organization's work. Then make an analytical report on the organization, that is, a report that shows the connections between the organization's mission and its beliefs or values. Also include a critique of the organization from your perspective.

4. Review and analyze one of the films listed below. A good film review generally begins with an interpretation of what the reviewer thinks the central theme (or themes) of the film is. To do this, you might ask yourself, "What does the filmmaker want the viewer (me) to take from this film? What is the filmmaker saying about this theme (themes)?" State this clearly in one or perhaps two paragraphs. The remainder of the review should describe and discuss key scenes from the film that illustrate why your interpretation of the filmmaker's intent or theme makes sense. You don't have to discuss every scene in the film, but you should be sure to examine most of the relevant scenes and describe how they support your view. You may then touch on whether you think the filmmaker's efforts were successful. You should conclude the review with a summary of your argument and discussion.

5. Research the similarities and differences between retributive and restorative justice. Prepare a class presentation on the topic and illustrate how it might apply to the Black Lives Matter claims about racial injustice on the part of the police and in death penalty cases such as the Troy Anthony Davis case.

Readings

Alexander, Michelle. *The New Jim Crow: Mass Incarceration in the Age of Colorblindness*. New York: The New Press, 2012. This book highlights the many ways in which laws and legal maneuverings have led to the mass incarceration and disenfranchisement of African Americans, particularly men, creating what the author calls a reinvention of the Jim Crow period in the South.

Copeland, M. Shawn. *Enfleshing Freedom: Body, Race, and Being*. Second edition. Minneapolis: Fortress Press, 2020. Copeland demonstrates here how black women's historical experience and oppression cast a completely different light on our theological ideas about being human. This new edition incorporates recent theological, philosophical, historical, political, and sociological scholarship, and it engages with current social movements like #BlackLivesMatter.

Marlowe, Jen, and Martina Davis-Correia. *I Am Troy Davis*. Chicago: Haymarket Books, 2013. This book, by documentary filmmaker Jen Marlow and Troy Davis's sister, looks at the life of Troy Davis in Savannah, Georgia; the events surrounding his trial for murder of an off-duty police officer; and the two-decade struggle to prove his innocence.

Schieber, Vicki, Trudy D. Conway, and David Matzko McCarthy, eds. *Where Justice and Mercy Meet: Catholic Opposition to the Death Penalty*. Collegeville, MN: Liturgical Press, 2013. A collection of essays that highlight the Catholic opposition to the death penalty, this book includes topics such as methods of execution, the interconnection with race and class, and stories from families of murder victims and condemned inmates.

Stassen, Glen H., ed. *Capital Punishment: A Reader*. Cleveland: Pilgrim Press, 1998. This book brings together a variety of Christian ethical perspectives on the death penalty, both those in favor and those against.

Audiovisuals

A Life in the Balance: Examining the Troy Davis Case. Vimeo on Demand, 2013. Directed by Jen Marlowe and Laura Moye, this seventeen-minute, four-part video illustrates the questionable evidence used to convict Troy Davis as well as various efforts to have the verdict overturned or clemency granted.

Dead Man Walking. Metro-Goldwyn-Mayer Studios, 1995. This film, directed by Tim Robbins and starring Susan Sarandon and Sean Penn, highlights Sister Helen Prejean's efforts to provide spiritual counseling to a convicted killer on death row while also empathizing with the families of the killer and the victims. It illustrates the complexity of the death penalty for all involved.

Just Mercy. Warner Brothers, 2019. Directed by Destin Daniel Cretton and starring Michael B. Jordan and Jamie Foxx, this film follows a young Harvard Law School graduate who, instead of going to a lucrative law firm, chooses to move to Alabama to attempt to save the life of a death row inmate who was unjustly sentenced to die, even though most of the evidence proved his innocence and the only testimony against him came from a criminal with a motive to lie.

The Life of David Gale. Universal Studios, 2003. Directed by Alan Parker and starring Kevin Spacey as David Gale, this film raises questions about the implementation of the death penalty by demonstrating the possibility that an innocent man can be convicted of murder and executed by the state.

The Thin Blue Line. IFC Films, 1988. This documentary film, directed by Errol Morris, highlights the problems associated with the criminal justice system in Dallas County, Texas, when an innocent man is convicted of murder. The person was ultimately exonerated and freed.

The 13th. Kandoo Films, Netflix, 2016. This documentary, directed by Ava DuVernay, takes its name from the Thirteenth Amendment to the Constitution (which abolished slavery) and explores the intersection of race, justice, and mass incarceration in the United States. DuVernay contends that slavery has been perpetuated through the criminalizing of the behavior of blacks during Jim Crow; lynching; and the war on drugs that has led to mass incarceration of people of color in the United States. The film also examines the prison-industrial complex and the emerging detention-industrial complex, discussing how much money is being made by corporations from such incarcerations.

8

Church and State

In July 2012, Charlie Craig and David Mullins went to Masterpiece Cakeshop in Lakewood, Colorado, and requested that its owner, Jack Phillips, design and create a cake for their wedding. Phillips declined to do so on the grounds that he does not create wedding cakes for same-sex weddings—marriages that Colorado did not then recognize—because of his Christian beliefs. Phillips believes that his cake decorating is an expression of his art, a skill through which he seeks to honor God. Using those skills in the service of a same-sex wedding would amount to dishonoring God because it goes against God's intention of limiting marriage between one man and one woman. He would, however, sell them other baked goods, such as birthday cakes.[1]

Mortified, Craig and Mullins filed discrimination charges with the Colorado Civil Rights Division not just for themselves but for all LGBTQ persons who are discriminated against.[2] They alleged that the discrimination based on sexual orientation violated the Colorado Anti-Discrimination Act (CADA), which prohibits discrimination based on sexual orientation in a "place of business engaged in any sales to the public and any place offering services . . . to the public" (CADA, §§24–34–301 to -804, C.R.S. 2014). Under CADA's administrative review system, the Colorado Civil Rights Division first found probable cause for a violation and referred the case to the Colorado Civil Rights Commission. The commission then referred the case for a formal hearing before a state administrative law judge (ALJ), who ruled in the

---

[1] However, in June 2017, his wife refused to bake a birthday cake for a person who was coming out as transgender on her birthday because of her belief that gender was biological and immutable (see John Culhane, "The Cake Controversy That Just Won't Go Away," *Politico Magazine* [August 16, 2018]).

[2] See "'This Happens All the Time': Why a Gay Couple Took Their Cake Case to the Supreme Court," *Guardian,* January 18, 2018.

couple's favor. In so doing, the ALJ rejected Phillips's claim that requiring him to create a cake for a same-sex wedding would violate his First Amendment right to free speech by compelling him to exercise his artistic talents to express a message with which he disagreed and which would violate his right to the free exercise of religion. Both the commission and the Colorado Court of Appeals affirmed the ALJ's ruling. Phillips was ordered to change his wedding-cake sales policy to serve anyone regardless of sexual orientation and to educate his employees on the anti-discrimination statute. Instead, Phillips stopped selling wedding cakes altogether and, with the help of the Alliance Defending Freedom, a conservative Christian legal organization whose website describes it as "advocating for religious liberty, the sanctity of human life, freedom of speech, and marriage and family," appealed the ruling all the way to the Supreme Court.

In June 2018, the Supreme Court ruled 7–2 that the Colorado Civil Rights Commission in this case "violated the Free Exercise Clause" (*Cakeshop* 1).[3] However, the decision did not mean persons could use religious objections to discriminate against others in the face of generally applicable laws: "While those religious and philosophical objections are protected, it is a general rule that such objections do not allow business owners and other actors in the economy and in society to deny protected persons equal access to goods and services under a neutral and generally applicable public accommodations law" (*Cakeshop* 9). The decision affirms that Colorado can protect gays and lesbians from discrimination regarding the sale of goods and services to the public because widespread allowance to companies to stop selling to persons of homosexual orientation would amount to serious stigma against gay persons. Rather, the ruling argued, "Phillips was entitled to the neutral and respectful consideration of his claims in all the circumstances of the cases," which they argued the Colorado Civil Rights Commission denied him. In the transcripts the majority noted that at least one of the commissioners said that religious beliefs should not be carried into the commercial realm, which they thought suggested some hostility toward Phillips's religious beliefs. The hostility was exacerbated when this same commissioner argued that it was "despicable" that people would use their religious beliefs to discriminate against gays and lesbians, much like religion was used to promote slavery and the Holocaust. The majority argued that such language was a clear sign of hostility toward Phillips's sincerely held beliefs from a commission that was supposed to protect all persons from discrimination whether because of sexual orientation or religion (*Cakeshop* 13).

Justices Ginsburg and Sotomayor dissented with the ruling of the majority on two grounds. First, Ginsburg notes that the majority affirmed that the State of Colorado is within its authority to protect persons from discrimination based on sexual orientation. "The Colorado court distinguished the cases on the ground that Craig and Mullins were denied service based on an aspect

---

[3] *Masterpiece Cakeshop, Ltd. v. Colorado Civil Rights Commission*, 584 U. S. 1–8 (2018), https://www.supremecourt.gov (hereafter cited as *Cakeshop*).

of their identity that the State chose to grant vigorous protection from discrimination" (*Cakeshop* 7). The fact that Phillips might sell other cakes and cookies to gay and lesbian customers was irrelevant to the issue Craig and Mullins's case presented. What matters is that Phillips would not provide a good or service to a same-sex couple that he would provide to a heterosexual couple, which amounts to a violation of the anti-discrimination law. Second, Ginsburg takes issue with the majority's suggestion that because one or two commissioners made derogatory remarks regarding Phillips's sincerely held religious beliefs it was a violation of his free exercise. There were many levels of adjudication and no indication that those comments were influential in the decision by the other groups. Thus, Ginsburg concludes that the rulings "do not evidence hostility to religion of the kind we have previously held to signal a free-exercise violation" (*Cakeshop* 3).

ISSUES AND CONCERNS

This case raises several issues related to the relationship between church and state, religion and politics, in the United States. The First Amendment to the Constitution states: "Congress shall make no law respecting an establishment of religion, or prohibiting the free exercise thereof." The first part of the amendment is referred to as the *establishment clause* and the second as the *free exercise clause*. In the development of this amendment there was the awareness that government (state) and religion (church) were two distinct and separate institutions, and society needed to discern the appropriate boundaries between them. The search for those boundaries has provided much of the fodder for church-state problems ever since. As constitutional scholar Noah Feldman notes, "No question divides Americans more fundamentally than that of the relation between religion and government."[4]

There are some who think that the proper spheres are separate: religion in the private lives of individuals; the state in public lives. (This was implied in the case by the one commissioner who felt religious beliefs should play no role in the realm of business.) The nation's founders wanted to keep the institutions separate for the sake of the government and the church. Too much influence by the church over government, especially in the context of a religiously diverse society, can lead to instability in the state. History is full of evidence to support this claim (for example, wars over religion in Europe). Moreover, the founders wanted to protect the liberty of conscience that all citizens should have when it comes to religion. The freedom to believe and practice what one wants, if it does no harm to others, should be left untouched. Moreover, they felt that government influence on religion would pervert religion. It would force it to become something that it was not. So, the way to protect both institutions was to generate a "wall of separation"

---

[4] Noah Feldman, *Divided by God: America's Church-State Problem and What We Should Do about It* (New York: Farrar, Strauss, and Giroux, 2005), 5.

between the two, a term coined by President Thomas Jefferson in an official letter to the Baptists of Danbury, Connecticut, stating that the Constitution had "erected a wall of separation between church and state."[5]

From the church perspective, especially religious minorities, all persons should be able to worship and believe as they saw fit without interference either from government or from other religious groups, as had occurred in many states at the time. Moreover, they did not want to support (through taxes) ideas and institutions with which they did not agree. The best way to do this was to have government not support any of them—individual churches would find ways to support themselves. The government's role was to create a stable environment in which religious groups could thrive. Yet the boundary between church and state should be permeable enough to allow citizens to use their religious convictions individually or collectively to influence public policy.

The other issue that leads to church-state conflict, and that is central to this case, is the issue of authority. Who gets to set the standards for human behavior—government or religion? What happens when the standards conflict? According to the Gospel, Jesus said to "give therefore to the emperor the things that are the emperor's, and to God the things that are God's" (Mt 22:21), implying that each has its own sphere of operation. But problems arise when the state laws governing the behavior of religious practitioners conflict with the laws they feel come from their religious tradition. When this happens, what should the practitioner do? What should the government do? How one answers these questions depends upon how one interprets what is meant by the free exercise clause. Various notions have emerged at the level of the Supreme Court, such as that the state must have a "compelling" interest in restricting the behavior or a "reasonable" interest in doing so; and that all persons should follow generally applicable laws.

Kenneth D. Wald and Allison Calhoun-Brown contend that the Supreme Court's answers to the boundary and authority issues are mixed.[6] On the establishment or boundary issue, those justices they label as *separationists* advocate for a high wall of separation because government and religion will better achieve their ends if they remain independent of each other. Thus, at the institutional level they deny benefits to religious organizations, such as school funding or school prayer. *Accommodationists,* seeking to protect the nation's religious foundation, contend that religious institutions should be treated no differently than nonreligious groups when it comes to extending benefits. They should be treated in a nondiscriminatory manner, advocating for a benevolent neutrality with respect to religion, such as including religious schools in voucher programs and religious symbols in public displays that are inclusive. On the authority or free exercise question, separationists

---

[5] See Daniel L. Dreisbach, *Thomas Jefferson and the Wall of Separation between Church and State* (New York: New York University Press, 2002).

[6] See Kenneth D. Wald and Allison Calhoun-Brown, *Religion and Politics in the United States,* 8th ed. (Lanham, MD: Rowman and Littlefield Publishers, 2018).

permit most exemptions to individuals in their religious practices, especially when proposed laws target only specific religious practices or groups. Accommodationists deny most exemptions to individuals, especially when the practices go against generally applicable laws.[7]

The concern raised by the case study has been framed in this way: Can sincerely held religious beliefs, such as those held by Phillips, outweigh neutral laws that apply to everyone, such as the anti-discrimination laws in Colorado? The focus of the ruling in this case was on whether the state—the Colorado Civil Rights Commission—was respectful and neutral toward the sincerely held religious beliefs of Phillips in its ruling. The majority concluded that they were not. Had they demonstrated such neutrality and respect, the court might have upheld the ruling by the State of Colorado. Most advocates of the free exercise of religion would not be content with such a ruling, however. When the Supreme Court, in *Employment Division v. Smith*, first ruled that the First Amendment is not violated when neutral, generally applicable laws conflict with religious practices, they convinced Congress to pass and President Clinton to sign the Religious Freedom Restoration Act (RFRA 1993). The *Smith* case denied unemployment benefits to two Native American drug counselors who were fired by the state for testing positive for mescaline, the hallucinogenic compound in peyote, which they smoked as part of their traditional religious ritual. Because the rule against drug use was generally applicable to anyone and did not single out religious practitioners, the court ruled that the state's actions did not violate the free exercise clause. This standard differed markedly from previous cases (*Sherbert v. Werner*, 1963; and *Wisconsin v. Yoder*, 1972)[8] that required the state to have a "compelling interest" to interfere with

---

[7] Two Supreme Court precedents that were cited in this case were *Church of Lukumi Babalu Aye, Inc. v. Hialeah*, 508 U. S. 520 (1993) and *Employment Div., Dept. of Human Resources of Ore. v. Smith*, 494 U. S. 872 (1990). The former case rejected a city ordinance that was targeted to restrict animal sacrifice at a Santería church while allowing other animals at slaughterhouses to be sacrificed, and thus it was discriminatory and violated the church's free exercise. The second case rejected the claims of a person denied unemployment benefits because he was fired for failing a drug test administered by his employer, even though the drug use was part of his religious practice and not on the job. Because the rule was generally applicable to anyone and did not single out religious practitioners, it did not violate the free exercise clause.

[8] The *Sherbert* case involved a Seventh-day Adventist who was fired from her job at a textile mill when she refused to work on Saturday, her Sabbath, and whose subsequent application for unemployment compensation was denied by the state because she refused to accept available work, despite her religious reasons for doing so. The court ruled that there was no compelling state interest to violate her constitutional free-exercise rights. The *Yoder* case involved three Old Order Amish families who refused to send their children, ages fourteen and fifteen, to any formal school beyond the eighth grade because it went against their religious communal beliefs. The court held that the government's asserted interest in universal compulsory education did not justify such interference with the family's religious freedom.

a person's religious freedom. The RFRA restored the pre-*Smith* standard and prohibits the federal government and the states "from substantially burdening a person's exercise of religion even if the burden results from a rule of general applicability." To do so requires that the restrictions must further "a compelling governmental interest" and the government must use "the least restrictive means of furthering that compelling governmental interest."[9]

The unanimity of advocates for religious freedom begins to break apart when the issue is rights versus rights: the rights of a business owner to refuse service to customers or employees on the basis of religious beliefs versus the rights of persons who do not share those beliefs not to experience discrimination or be denied benefits. Neither party in the *Masterpiece Cakeshop* case wants to deny people their sincerely held religious beliefs. Craig and Mullins argue that if you are going to offer your services in the public sector, you cannot discriminate against a class of people whose identity differs from yours regardless of your religious beliefs. The rights of the individual to be treated fairly and equally in society outweighs one's religious objections, especially when those anti-discrimination laws are generally applicable.

Supporters of Phillips contend that the liberty of conscience that underlies the free exercise of religion must take precedence even in the economic realm. The Supreme Court gave some credence to that argument in its 2014 *Burwell v. Hobby Lobby Stores, Ltd.* decision. The Affordable Care Act required all employer-provided health insurance plans to cover FDA-approved contraceptive methods. When employers challenged the requirement on religious freedom claims, because the contraceptive methods might prevent a fertilized egg from implanting in the uterus—which they believed was a form of abortion—the Obama administration amended the rule to exempt religious and religiously affiliated employers but not secular, for-profit employers. Whereas federal courts were split on whether the exemption should apply to closely-held or family-owned for-profit employers for religious reasons, the Supreme Court ruled (5–4) as follows: "As applied to closely held corporations, the regulations promulgated by the Department of Health and Human Services (HHS) requiring employers to provide their female employees with no-cost access to contraception violate the Religious Freedom Restoration Act."[10] In particular, the majority said that while they assumed that HHS had a compelling government interest in requiring contraceptive coverage, it did not use the least restrictive means, such as a government-sponsored alternative provided to religiously affiliated organizations, which created the burden on the employer's free exercise of religion.[11]

---

[9] See H.R.1308, Religious Freecom Restoration Act of 1993, 103rd Congress (1993–1994). The Supreme Court later ruled that the part of the RFRA that applied to the states was unconstitutional and an overreach by the Congress. In response, some states have passed their own RFRA laws.

[10] See *Burwell v. Hobby Lobby Stores, Inc.* (573 U. S. 1(2014)).

[11] In the most recent case before the Supreme Court, *Trump Administration v. Pennsylvania*, the Trump administration is seeking the court to grant the administration's

Another concern raised in this case is whether people can be forced to participate in activities that violate their sincerely held religious beliefs. This is often associated with the concept of conscience clauses, where people engaged in a profession, such as medicine (doctors, nurses, pharmacists), are excused from providing a public service because it violates their consciences.[12] Phillips believed that using his artistic abilities to make the wedding cake for a same-sex couple amounts to forcing him to participate in an activity he believes is immoral. The owners of Hobby Lobby also claimed that requiring them to provide contraceptive coverage for their female employees, because they blocked a fertilized egg from implanting in the uterus, went against their religious belief that life begins at conception. Thus, they pushed to extend the concept of conscience clauses to the economic sector. The plaintiffs in both cases disagreed, arguing that expanding religious freedom exemptions in the economic sphere would undermine discrimination laws meant to ensure the individual rights of women, gays, lesbians, and others to equal treatment under the law. Craig and Mullins did not expect Phillips to attend the wedding service; nor did they ask him to write any message on the cake that would imply support for their marriage. The ruling in the *Hobby Lobby* case, many people argued, was tantamount to allowing for-profit employers to impose their religious beliefs on their employees. Interfaith Alliance leader Rev. Welton Gaddy argued, "The First Amendment is at its best when it is used to protect the rights of minorities from the whims of the powerful. Today's decision, which gives the powerful the right to force their religious beliefs on those around them, is a far cry from the best traditions of religious freedom."[13]

A final issue is whether religious ideology should influence the public sphere in its laws, its courts, or its politics. Many contend that the public realm should be secular and that religious motivations and arguments should play

---

rule that lifts the contraception mandate entirely from any employer—profit, nonprofit, privately held, or publicly traded—with a religious objection to covering birth control, as well as from any privately held employer that claims a "moral" objection. On July 8, 2020, the Supreme Court ruled 7–2 that the Trump administration had authority under the Affordable Care Act to promulgate rules exempting employers with religious or moral objections from providing contraceptive coverage to their employees. It will be interesting to see how this decision and the recent Supreme Court decision in *Bostock v. Clayton County, Georgia*, which ruled that discrimination against the LGBTQ community in the workplace is illegal, will influence future cases related to religious discrimination in the workplace. Many Christian conservatives are concerned that the ruling protecting the rights of gay and transgender workers could affect how conservative groups operate their own institutions.

[12] Some contend that the laws supporting conscience clauses started to grow in the wake of the Supreme Court's decision in *Roe v. Wade* (1973). Some states have also enacted them in the arena of education. See Claire Marshall, "The Spread of Conscience Clause Legislation," *Human Rights Magazine* [American Bar Association] 39/2 (January 1, 2013).

[13] Quoted in Michelle Boorstein, "Faith Groups Divided in Their Reaction to Court's Decision Affirming Religious Rights," *Washington Post*, June 30, 2014.

little to no role in our policies, especially since we are a pluralistic society. They most certainly should not dominate, because of the potential damage they might do.[14] Some argue for a middle ground. On the one hand, religious people should be able to bring their perspectives to the public realm, not only because it is a central part of their identity, but also because of the contributions they bring to the common good. However, they need to be aware of how they communicate those beliefs. As Senator Obama said in 2006:

> Democracy demands that the religiously motivated translate their concerns into universal, rather than religion-specific, values. It requires that their proposals be subject to argument, and amenable to reason. I may be opposed to abortion for religious reasons, but if I seek to pass a law banning the practice, I cannot simply point to the teachings of my church or evoke God's will. I have to explain why abortion violates some principle that is accessible to people of all faiths, including those with no faith at all.[15]

Many religious conservatives disagree, suggesting that because we are a Judeo-Christian nation, moral principles associated with that tradition should hold sway in the development of our laws and public policies.

SITUATION ETHICS

To analyze this case from the perspective of situation ethics, we should consider key assumptions made by Joseph Fletcher.[16] The key base point for him is the concrete situation or objective set of circumstances in which ethical decisions are made both by individuals and by society. Before one can know if one has done the right thing, or the loving thing, one must grapple with the situation at hand in all its complexity. As noted previously, Fletcher rejects legalism of any sort—whether the legalism of natural law or of scripture— that deduces certain rules or prescriptions that are universal and therefore must be applied in all cases. Fletcher would contend that while having such principles drawn from one's church or culture is important as a guide to one's actions, it is the situation or context that determines the right course

---

[14] See Christopher Hitchens, *God Is Not Great: How Religion Poisons Everything* (New York: The Hatchette Book Group, 2007).

[15] For the text of Senator Obama's speech, given at the Building a Covenant for a New America conference, Washington, DC, see "Obama's 2006 Speech on Faith and Politics," *New York Times*, June 28, 2006.

[16] For purposes of this analysis we draw from three texts by Fletcher: *Situation Ethics: The New Morality* (Philadelphia: Westminster Press, 1966) (hereafter cited as *SE*); *Moral Responsibility: Situation Ethics at Work* (Philadelphia: Westminster Press, 1967) (hereafter cited as *MR*); and *Humanhood: Essays in Biomedical Ethics* (Buffalo, NY: Prometheus Books, 1979) (hereafter cited as *HH*).

of action. The principles or rules may have a voice, but they do not have veto power. The right thing to do is the loving thing, after one has a clear sense of all the factors involved in the situation. Fletcher's conception of the moral agent affirms that the self is both personal and social, and thus any affirmation of one's freedom in a given situation comes with the expectation that one is using one's freedom responsibly and with a willingness to be held accountable for one's actions. In addition, Fletcher prizes personalism, which means that "people are at the center of concern, not things" (*SE* 50). When we treat people as ends, and not as things, then we are acting ethically. Finally, Fletcher affirms a relational theory of value in which good and evil, right and wrong, are dependent on the situation; nothing is intrinsically good or evil. The moral worth of one's actions depends on what ends one is seeking, the means one uses, the motive(s) for one's actions, and the consequences. If the end for an individual is love for one's neighbor, or for society doing the most good for the most neighbors, then the action is moral.

Fletcher writes a great deal about the relationship between freedom and order, morality and law, especially in the areas of sexuality, reproductive rights, and medicine. He acknowledges that moral values, both religious and humanistic, are a significant element that contributes to the making of law in a pluralistic society whose purpose is to make the consensus reached by the community regarding the common welfare, its social morality, effective. At that point, however, whatever the consensus regards as private "is not the law's business" (*MR* 111). "Only by means of distinguishing private and public (preserving privacy and responsibility and protecting the public order for the sake of justice) can we give life to the truth that freedom and order presuppose each other" (*MR* 108). He is not claiming religious or humanistic values can be separated from the public sphere: "On the contrary, ethics always limits individual or private freedom by subordinating it to the social or public interest—to neighbor-concern" (*MR* 105). But the public interest in a pluralistic, democratic society cannot be dominated by one metaphysical or dogmatic worldview. Rather, the laws must be generated by the consensus of the community to promote the greatest good for the greatest number, a utilitarian goal that from his Christian perspective becomes "the agapeic calculus, the greatest amount of neighbor welfare for the largest number of neighbors possible" (*SE* 95).

He recognizes that many religious moralists who have a law orientation desire a "one-faith, one-morality order" when it comes to such issues as contraception, abortion, or euthanasia (*MR* 106). For example, as we noted in Chapter 1, some Catholics and conservative evangelicals believe one or more of these is a sin and violates the natural law and God's law, which they claim is binding on all people. Society should enact laws to limit these practices. The problem is that they are relying on the teachings of their church to make the claim and not on the consensus of the community. Any attempt to enact one faith stance into law would be a violation of the First Amendment and religious freedom. Fletcher writes:

Sin is already divorced from crime in our pluralistic culture, and the only real sanction for criminal law is *the common interest*, public order, or the collective good. On this basis only may an ideologically free and pluralistic society frame its moral principles or judgments as to right and wrong and enforce its standards by legal weapons. Society has a right to *protect* itself from dangers within and without, but not to enforce a monistic and monopoly standard of personal (in the sense of private) conduct. (*MR* 106)

Lacking a democratic consensus on what is immoral would mean that instead of civil law we would be left with "tyranny, hypocrisy, culture lag, and bigotry" (*MR* 124).

Fletcher makes this distinction between public and private morality in his discussion of abortion laws and the Supreme Court's ruling in *Roe v. Wade*. Many religiously conservative individuals and groups believe that at conception the fetus is fully human and therefore ought to be protected from termination. Most are willing to accept abortion if conception is a result of rape or incest, or if the mother's life is in danger; but some still reject abortion, claiming that even in those circumstances the fetus is still an innocent person. Fletcher disagrees with claims about the fetus being a person. It is certainly alive and is human, but personhood requires rational capacity. "Before cerebration comes into play, or when it is ended, in the absence of the synthesizing or *thinking* function of the cerebral cortex, the person is nonexistent; or, put another way, the life which is functioning biologically is a nonperson" (*HH* 134). He notes that in the Supreme Court's *Roe v. Wade* decision the courts had affirmed a "postnatal" definition of a person, which means that full personhood emerges once a child is born. The reason for that, he contends, is "any other doctrine is necessarily only a matter of private faith or belief, and it is morally unjust to impose private beliefs upon others who do not share them. To do so violates the First Amendment of the Constitution which guarantees religious freedom and freedom of thought" (*HH* 137). For Fletcher, the ethical question is not whether we can justify abortion, but whether we can justify compulsory pregnancy, which is what outlawing abortion would mean. In his view to do so would be inhumane. Rather, compulsory pregnancy should be outlawed, "making the ending of pregnancies, like their beginning, a private or personal matter" (*HH* 138). Abortion may be a reason for regret but not for remorse, moral guilt, or criminal prosecution.

Fletcher makes a similar argument in support of the freedom of conscience to choose how one will die when in a terminal state with significant pain and suffering and in support of legal protections for medical personnel in treating such persons. When it comes to end-of-life decisions, many people believe that biological life is the highest good no matter the quality and that persons in a terminal state should be kept alive; and that anyone who assists in aiding their death should be susceptible to criminal penalty because they are "playing God." Fletcher suggests that such legal penalties are one more example of a religious perspective seeking to dominate what should be a personal decision. "Death control, like birth control, is a matter of human dignity. Without it, persons become puppets" (*MR* 151).[17] Moreover, medicine "has a duty to relieve suffering equal to preserving life" (*MR* 152). While he is optimistic that more states will pass right-to-die laws that legalize physician-assisted death,[18] he believes that other types of euthanasia that doctors already perform (indirect forms that most people support) should be safeguarded in laws to make sure that they are not guilty of any offense when easing patient suffering in the face of terminal illness. "Doctors would then have protection under the law, freedom to follow their consciences" (*MR* 150).

As a situation ethicist, Fletcher is sympathetic to the idea of granting a range of freedom of conscience on religious and moral matters that is as wide as possible because, from his perspective, situation ethics prizes freedom of choice. In fact, he argues, "when there is no choice, there is no possibility of ethical action. Whatever we are compelled to do is amoral" (*HH* 91). Considering this, and from his comments regarding religious freedom highlighted above, Fletcher affirms both the free exercise clause and the establishment clause of the First Amendment. He contends that in a pluralistic, democratic society a diversity of religious and philosophical perspectives is important. "For out of their rubbing together, their competition in the free market of ideas, truths and insights are revealed that would not have emerged in a monochrome culture. Many colors are needed in the democratic coat" (*MR* 106). People should have the freedom in their private lives to believe and practice the religion of their choice and not be forced to believe what others suggest they should. He writes, "It seems axiomatic that the law cannot rely upon a doctrine that its citizens are legally entitled to disbelieve" (*MR* 105).

However, the bulk of his discussion on the First Amendment focuses on the establishment clause, seeking to determine appropriate boundaries between religion and government. "Both religious and secular moralists, in

---

[17] The Terri Schiavo case provides an interesting example of the issues involved in the separation of church and state. Terri Schiavo suffered a brain injury that placed her in a vegetative state, with the doctors declaring the harm was irreversible. After many years her husband sought the removal of all life-support measures, including a feeding tube, so that Terri could die according to her own wishes. Her parents disagreed based on their Catholic faith and appealed for help from Florida's governor, Jeb Bush. The governor acted with the Florida legislature to pass "Terri's Law" in 2003, which gave the governor authority "to issue a one-time stay to prevent the withholding of nutrition and hydration from a patient under certain circumstances" and to intervene in this case. He had the feeding tube reinserted only six days after its removal in 2003. Eventually, the Florida Supreme Court ruled unanimously that "the law violates the fundamental constitutional tenet of separation of powers and is therefore unconstitutional both on its face and as applied to Theresa Schiavo" (*Bush v. Schiavo* SC04–925, September 23, 2004).

[18] As of this writing, nine states and the District of Columbia have legalized physician-assisted death or "medical aid in dying."

America's plural society, need to remember that freedom *of* religion includes freedom *from* religion. There is no ethical basis for compelling noncreedalists to follow any creedal codes of behavior, Christian or non-Christian" (*MR* 135–36). Religious people do not need the support of the civil law to follow their own religious convictions. If someone believes for religious reasons that heterosexual marriage is ordained by God, or that personhood begins at conception, then to be consistent they should not get married to a member of the same sex or use anything that would terminate an existing pregnancy. But they should not use government to impose their views on other members of society and deny them the opportunity to act on their own consciences. The state is not the secular arm of the church in the way it may once have been. "In matters of this kind there is great wisdom in the old adage, the best government is the least government" (*HH* 103). These are not matters to be decided by government fiat. Thus, Fletcher wants to erect a wall of separation between religious ideology and laws that people must follow, especially in areas that are more private than public.

Fletcher's understanding of situation ethics and his views on the relationship between church and state provide the backdrop for analyzing this case from a situation ethics perspective. First, we notice that the controversies in this case are often placed in the legalistic contexts of individual rights: Phillips and the owners of Hobby Lobby's rights to religious freedom, the rights of gays and lesbians not to be discriminated against, or women's reproductive rights not to be infringed. However, Fletcher contends that all "alleged" rights are imperfect and relative, reflective of the values individuals and societies support. When such rights and values conflict, as they do in this case, how do you determine which values to favor? He contends we do it based on needs.

> Needs are the moral stabilizers, not rights. The legalistic temper gives first place to rights, but the humanistic temper puts needs in the driver's seat. If human rights conflict with human needs, let needs prevail. . . . Rights are nothing but a formal recognition by society of certain human needs, and as needs change with changing conditions, so rights should change, too. (*HH* 90)

How does this assessment relate to this case? Surely there is a need underlying the right to free exercise of religion. Being free to follow one's conscience in religious matters enhances human dignity as the founders who placed freedom of religion in the First Amendment to the US Constitution recognized. If the matter were simply affecting the persons asserting their right to free exercise of religion, then there would not be much controversy. Instead, as the cases clearly indicate, we are trying to balance competing interests both for society in terms of the importance of generally applicable laws for social order and for the people who are being denied services and benefits in the public sector. Fletcher would agree with the assessment of Supreme Court Justice Goldberg in *Griswold v. Connecticut* that the rights of religion are not "beyond limitations" when the needs of others come into conflict with them (*HH* 128).

In a situation ethics approach Fletcher contends that "conscience makes decisions" (*SE* 153) and that "the decision must be made not only *in* the situation but also *by* the decider in the situation!" (*MR* 181). At first glance this would seem to support the decisions by Phillips and the owners of Hobby Lobby to deny service and benefits following their consciences. But Fletcher would raise the question of what we allow to inform our consciences. For Phillips and Hobby Lobby, what informed their consciences was a narrow, legalistic understanding of their conservative faith tradition, which asserts that marriage is between one man and one woman and that life begins at conception. Such legalism does not consider the consequences on others involved in the situation. For Fletcher, the primary ethical principle in any situation should be concern for people, which is central to the Christian gospel's message to "love thy neighbor as thyself" (*MR* 138). If neighbor love is not part of one's decision-making process, then one is not acting in a manner in accordance with the Christian gospel. By denying the same-sex couple's request for a wedding cake, Fletcher would argue, Phillips did not demonstrate neighbor-love and thus did not follow his own religious tradition on this. Instead, he chose to limit his sale of wedding cakes to opposite-sex couples to the exclusion of others. Phillips may not have intended harm in his refusal, but his indifference to their needs did insult the dignity of this gay couple, who felt mortified and embarrassed and who had had to withstand so much heterosexist discrimination in the past. Moreover, by adopting generally applicable anti-discrimination laws, the State of Colorado was seeking to protect the public interest, or in Fletcher's terms, providing the greatest amount of good for the greatest number of neighbors in their community, including gays and lesbians. In this way, it was protecting people from harmful action but also protecting them from the narrow religious understandings of others, which Fletcher says is part of the First Amendment's efforts to provide freedom *from* religion.

The same is true for the owners of Hobby Lobby. Fletcher would agree that they should be allowed to reject such contraceptive methods for themselves and to follow the dictates of their consciences for their own behavior. But they were acting in a public context and denying neighbor-love to women who need to make their own decisions regarding reproduction. Fletcher writes: "If there are people who believe that any of these things is wrong or sinful, let them conduct themselves accordingly. But let them not try to deprive their neighbors, who see it differently, of *their* freedom and responsibility. That is, let them not try to hold down the moral stature of others, which is measured by how much control we have over our natural processes—so that we can choose like people, not submit like sheep!" (*MR* 124). The Affordable Care Act, by mandating contraceptive coverage in health insurance plans, was seeking to extend significant health-care benefits to women of reproductive age to enable them to make their own choices about getting or remaining pregnant. In July 2020 the Supreme Court found in favor of expanding exemptions to the law to employers not only for religious reasons but for any moral objections. Thus the situation for women seeking to make reproductive choices—in a context where most people get their health-care coverage from their employers—could get worse.

FEMINIST LIBERATIVE ETHICS

Analysis of this case from a feminist ethics perspective requires that we bring certain central ideas to the fore. First is the centrality of relationship. For Beverly Harrison, there are no individuals who exist apart from relationship.[19] The ideal of autonomous individuals, who act above the fray, who assert their rights against all encumbrances by others, and who make decisions according to abstract ideals that are not muddied by lived experience, is a culturally male view. Instead, as human beings we are always already in relation to others—we never exist as isolated individuals apart from relationship to other people. Second, feminist ethics begins with the concrete experiences and lived realities in any situation to determine what the right course of action would be in any given social conflict, especially the experiences of those on the margins of society who lack social power. Third, we need a critical social and historical analysis of any social policies that have an impact on the well-being of persons and communities in order to discern where they have privileged some and disadvantaged others. Finally, feminist ethics understands justice as rightly related persons and communities under God, which from a biblical perspective is demonstrated through concern for the least well off, including their needs for supporting a life of human dignity. All these elements of feminist ethics play an important role in Harrison's perspective on the relationship between religion and society.

Harrison raises the question about what religion means and how it functions in society. Having clear answers on these questions might help to clarify why religious, ethical, and social policies in society are intricately interrelated. She notes that the word *religion* means "to bind," and that for those who are religious, this meaning illustrates a basic sense of their connectedness to God and to one another. A major function of religion for people who claim religious ties is to provide action guides for their adherents on religious and moral questions that lay out certain expectations for their behavior. In a pluralistic society, where there are people who follow many different religious

---

[19] For purposes of this analysis we draw from the following texts by Beverly Harrison: *Making the Connections: Essays in Feminist Social Ethics*, ed. Carol S. Robb (Boston; Beacon Press, 1985) (hereafter cited as *MC*); *Justice in the Making: Feminist Social Ethics* (Louisville, KY: Westminster John Knox Press, 2004) (hereafter cited as *JM*); and *Our Right to Choose: Toward a New Ethic of Abortion* (Eugene, OR: Wipf and Stock Publishers, 2011) (hereafter cited as *RC*).

traditions and others who have no religious tradition, following those guides may lead to conflict among them or even with the laws of society (*RC* 22). Should one obey or disobey a law that one perceives as violating one's religious commitments? This is the question of whose authority should take precedence over one's actions. Should one engage in direct political action based on one's official church teaching to change laws that accord with that teaching when such changes will inevitably restrict the behavior of others who do not agree with the teaching? This is the question of what boundaries should exist between church and state. In the case study we are exploring, those claiming a religious exemption from generally applicable laws argue that their religious beliefs should guide their actions and set the limits on government action to enforce the laws.

As a Christian ethicist, Harrison has some affinity for those with religious commitments seeking to engage in political discussions and to influence public policy and those who believe the boundary between church and state should be permeable enough to allow citizens to use their religious convictions individually or collectively to influence public policy. Whereas many seek to separate the public sphere of politics from the private sphere of religion and morality, she contends they are intimately related. The "personal is political," which means, for a Christian religious ethicist, that so is religion and politics, church and state (*RC* 5). She writes:

In any case, morality always enters into politics one way or another, and deep political conflict is always simultaneously basic value conflict about what constitutes human well-being. A moral analysis offers those engaged in political conflict an opportunity to both clarify and comment to others their goals and reasons for judgment. It also encourages self-reflective criticism and self-assessment. (*RC* 5)

For example, Harrison applauds the US Catholic bishops, who draw from their theological and ethical tradition to speak to issues of poverty (*Economic Justice for All*, 1996), capital punishment (*A Culture of Life and the Penalty of Death*, 2005), and peace and nonviolence (*The Challenge of Peace*, 1983), even though she does not necessarily agree with their views (*JM* 173). However, when religious-political conflict emerges, as it inevitably does when people engage in direct political action, the conflict should be resolved through persuasion, not coercion: "All advocacy of religious groups should be constrained by respect for others' rationality" (*RC* 19). This kind of dialogical discussion and communication is at the heart of what ethical and political deliberation is designed to do, even though it is not always put into practice.

One thing to keep in mind: feminist ethics is concerned with the concrete lived realities of people who are experiencing oppression. Often debates about religious freedom and freedom of conscience tend to be abstract or individualized rather than taking into consideration the messy happenings in the lives of people. The cases discussed above have been framed in terms of individual rights: Phillips's right to religious freedom and free speech versus the right of Craig and Mullins not to be discriminated against or denied services because of their sexual identity; and the right to religious freedom of the owners of Hobby Lobby against a government mandate that they provide contraceptive care to their female employees, which for many women is important for their own moral agency and well-being. Harrison would affirm that religious liberty and freedom of conscience are important values. But she contends that all rights are relational and that conflicts among them are often a result of a competition between different significant values.

The problem with an overemphasis on liberty or individual freedom when thinking about justice in this case is that it is nonrelational. It is an assertion of the individual over others. It generates a perception of a zero-sum relationship between liberty and equality. However, if we revise the notion to "equal liberty," then it has more of a communal ring to it. Harrison notes that a good society will maximize equal liberty, "but it will also never confuse it with privilege" (*JM* 23). This is at the heart of the *Masterpiece Cakeshop* case (and the *Hobby Lobby* case). They are arguing for their individual religious freedom not to be required to engage in certain activities. What they fail to recognize is the privilege they have in relationship to gays, lesbians, and women to whom they are denying services, whose lived realities often include discrimination, deprivation, and denial of their moral agency.

Part of the problem also, for Harrison, is that people who affirm the moral category of rights do not fully understand what rights are, in two ways. First, the claim that people have a right to free exercise of religion is not simply a legal claim. It is also a moral claim, as was clearly intended by the founders when they affirmed liberty of conscience in the sphere of religion. This is evident in the cases above because the claims in both relate to an exemption from generally applicable laws. Harrison argues that it is illogical to claim a right, outside of a contractual relationship, without granting that the claim belongs to all who fall into the category of being human. "If any of us is prepared to invoke anything as a human moral right on our own behalf, that very act implies the existence of a similar claim for every other member of our species" (*MC* 168). Second, she also notes that such rights are not simply a liberty, a demand to be left alone. Instead: "A right is relational and implies my claim to legitimately interfere with others should they attempt to restrain my action in certain specified ways" (*MC* 168). This means that if I assert a right to restrain others under specific conditions, I must acknowledge that they have a similar right to restrain me if my action infringes on them: "None who claim a right to discrete personal standing—that is, as 'an individual'— before the law could, on moral grounds, deny such standing to others of the same category" (*MC* 169). For example, the owners of Hobby Lobby indicate that they have the right to object conscientiously to providing contraceptive care that may prevent uterine implantation or lead to abortion. In this, they are affirming their moral agency. However, in doing so, they are denying the women in their employ the opportunity to use their own moral agency and to rely on their own consciences in determining whether to become pregnant or to terminate an unwanted pregnancy. The Supreme Court decision does not necessarily make any judgment on this when it notes that there are other avenues for the government to provide such contraceptive care, even though it ignores the broader reality that most people continue to receive their health care through their employers.

This issue of identity is also part of the dissent raised by Justice Ginsburg in the *Masterpiece Cakeshop* case. The denial of the service to a same-sex couple was based on their identity and their sexuality; it was a service Phillips did not deny to opposite-sex couples. The purpose of laws against discrimination because of sexual orientation is to recognize that they have the same rights as others. While Phillips's decision to stop selling wedding cakes to all couples may have eliminated discriminatory action on his part, it does not ultimately address the issue of whether he can claim his own religious exemption from generally applicable laws. However, as Harrison rightly asserts, this has not stopped the issue from continuing in the courts.[20] People will make First Amendment claims because there is no other recourse for people "who find their own religious practice or their theological convictions overridden by the law of the land" (*RC* 20).[21]

Harrison's perspective is that when laws conflict with her Christian understanding of justice and human well-being, she would be on the side of those who are being harmed or denied what they need for human dignity. While there are times when those who are in positions of privilege try to justify their privilege as somehow ordained by God, those on the margins in the current society "do not credit God with sanctifying widespread human bondage and oppression" (*MC* 246). Thus, the voices of the oppressed, of women who are subjugated because of a patriarchal society, of gays and lesbians who are discriminated against because of their sexual orientation, and of persons of

---

[20] In June 2019, the Supreme Court refused to hear a challenge by Sweet Cakes by Melissa in Portland, Oregon, which had also refused to make a wedding cake for a same-sex couple because it violated the company's religious beliefs; it was found to be in violation of state antidiscrimination laws and ultimately went out of business.

[21] Based on this line of thinking, one might assume that Harrison would support the claim of the owner of Hobby Lobby that his own theological convictions were violated by the Affordable Care Act's requirement to provide contraceptive care in health insurance plans. She might agree that providing the less restrictive means afforded to religiously affiliated employers would be a good solution. The issue for Harrison, however, is that this assertion of the employer's rights loses sight of the social context in which women, who seek to make their own reproductive choices, must rely on their employers for their health-care coverage. This is problematic given the efforts of religious and political conservatives to eliminate the ACA, and their propensity to deny any coverage to poor women to make their own reproductive choices.

color who are marginalized because of their race, must continually be attended to if the current situation is to be transformed.

One area where the relationship between church and state has come into conflict for the past forty years is over the reproductive rights of women versus the rights of a fetus, which is also part of this case study with its focus on freedom of conscience versus discrimination. Many pro-life persons are using their religious beliefs to develop policies and enact laws that restrict or even eliminate access to abortion services. Some even go so far as to criminalize anyone involved in the abortion process, including the medical provider and the woman. Harrison suggests that on the ethical principle of respect for human life, pro-choice and pro-life advocates agree. Where the controversy emerges is on a reading of the theological history of abortion. Contrary to what religious conservatives have argued, the theological history of Jewish and Christian traditions has made allowances for abortions. The absolute prohibition appears to be a more recent development. More problematic for Harrison, as a feminist ethicist concerned about the concrete realities of women's experience, is that those seeking to restrict access to abortion services on the basis of religious grounds fail "to reconstruct the concrete, lived-world context in which the abortion discussion belongs: the all but desperate struggle by sexually active women to gain some proximate control over nature's profligacy in conception" (*MC* 122). Abortion is not an abstract event; it is a concrete reality of the woman who faces a decision about whether to remain pregnant, a reality that may exist in an experience of economic injustice and sexual violence. Fetal life is important, but it is not the only value at stake. Non-coercion in childbearing is also a foundational social good (*RC* 17). Enforced pregnancy under these conditions violates a woman's bodily integrity and is a repudiation of her freedom, her moral agency, and her humanity based more on the misogynistic religious beliefs of others than on the sacredness of human life (*RC* 116). The irony here is that religious conservatives, such as the persons involved in the cases highlighted above, are the ones who want to restrict the state's ability to interfere with their religious and economic freedom. But to enforce compulsory pregnancy, which is what she argues eliminating legal abortion services entails, would result in greater government intrusions into people's lives (*MC* 125).

The debate over federal funding of abortion services in the Supreme Court case of *Harris v. McCrae* is the context in which Harrison discusses most clearly her views on the First Amendment's free exercise and establishment clauses. Her understanding of the free exercise clause is that a violation occurs when a given law "makes it impossible for one to conscientiously fulfill a religious obligation." An establishment clause violation occurs when "a given law constitutes direct governmental endorsement of a particular theological tradition" (*RC* 18). Her review of the case was that McCrae felt that God had wanted her to have an abortion and that the Hyde Amendment, which prohibited federal funding for abortions, infringed on her religious freedom because she was poor. She further claimed that because not all religious groups believe that abortion is immoral, the legislation had established one interpretation of fetal life belonging to a specific religious view, a position supported by some religious groups who filed briefs in support of her claim. The Federal District Court agreed with her on the free exercise claim. The majority in the US Supreme Court (5–4) overturned the decision but did it for technical reasons and evaded the question of religious freedom in the abortion debate. (The dissenting justices did raise the possibility that the restrictions of the Hyde Amendment did foist a religiously motivated, state-mandated morality on the politically powerless.[22])

However, as Harrison points out, and as has been happening ever since, future court cases will emerge, especially as states seek to generate more barriers to access to abortion services, and women who believe their faith proscribes abortion will appeal. But, she notes, other persons who say their religion does not proscribe abortion may make appeals based on the establishment clause. She concludes: "The more direct the involvement of churches in politics, the more likely it is that we will all witness frequent invocation of the First Amendment establishment of religion clause" (*RC* 19). She contends that the current anti-abortion efforts are directly related to a narrow articulation of our Christian heritage. Because of this, she argues that those Christians and non-Christians who differ are protected by the First Amendment because it "functions to prevent too-easy equations of particular religious groups' views with a general definition of the public good" (*RC* 19). In this articulation we see her raising the boundary issue, because the imposition of one group's religious views amounts to an establishment of religion. But she also sees the connection here with the issue of authority: "The prohibition of legal abortion will not only mean that many women must bear children against their will but that state power will be directed against the well-being and standing of women as moral agents" (*RC* 16).

So, what does she see as the role for Christian ethicists and churches in the interrelationship between church and state? For Harrison, the "critical intellectual task of theology is the serious one of re-appropriating all our social relations, including our relations to God, so that shared action toward genuine human and cosmic fulfillment occurs" (*MC* 245). Her conception of justice is committed to the common good and the creation of conditions that support human dignity and moral agency for all. Christians cannot be apolitical in the face of structures that continue to oppress wide swaths of humanity because of gender, sexual orientation, race, or class. In her view this should be the focus that religiously motivated communities bring to the public square rather than the narrow agenda around abortion, sex, and marriage that have dominated conservative Christian groups. A Christian feminist ethics on the relationship between church and state would seek to persuade

---

[22] See *Harris v. McCrae*, 448 U. S. 329 (1980).

likeminded citizens, religious or not, to bring their passion to concerns that matter most: overcoming the marginalization and subordination of women, gays, lesbians, and people of color. As Harrison notes, "Love in the pursuit of justice is effectual acting upon the longing to make right relation. And doing so does make for justice" (*MC* 26).

RESOURCES

Discussion Questions

1. Wald and Calhoun-Brown contend that the application of the First Amendment to religion raises issues of both boundaries and authority. Regarding boundaries, do people have the right to bring their religious views into the public arena? Or is the public square a secular space with a high wall of separation? Where would you draw the boundaries?

2. Regarding the issue of authority, should people be forced to participate in activities that violate their sincerely held religious beliefs if generally applicable laws require it? Or should they follow their conscience, even to the point of violating the law? What should be the consequence of doing so?

3. Part of the debate in this case is the suggestion that individual rights are absolute and that government should never infringe on them. Both Fletcher and Harrison contend that rights are relative, especially when they come into conflict. To resolve the conflict requires a fuller understanding of the situation and context in which the conflict emerges. What do you think about these positions? How do you think a society should resolve conflicts of rights versus rights?

4. Fletcher and Harrison both suggest that in a religiously pluralistic society, persons who are guided by their religious faith in debates about social policy should bring their religious beliefs to the table but be willing to engage in respectful dialogue with other views to seek some consensus, even if it means some compromises would have to be made. Do you agree with that argument? Why or why not?

5. One critical moral issue underlying much of the debate over the proper boundaries between church and state is the conflict between abortion and reproductive rights. The claim by both Fletcher and Harrison is that the belief that human life begins at conception is fundamentally a religious claim drawn from some people's faith perspectives. Not all persons of faith or persons of no faith agree with that belief. Do you think that a disputed religious claim should be the basis of laws that make abortion services illegal and demand criminal penalties against those persons, women and medical providers, who engage in the practice? Why or why not?

Activities

1. Stage a debate in class over which aspect of the First Amendment, the establishment clause or the free exercise clause, is the most applicable in this case. Be sure the arguments draw from the positions articulated in the Supreme Court cases and in the two Christian social ethical traditions discussed above.

2. Do an analysis of this case from the perspective of the two evangelical ethical traditions. What points of agreement do they find with situation ethics and/or feminist ethics? Where would they disagree? Share your analysis in a class presentation or in a written report.

3. Read one of the books in the reading list on religious and moral exemptions. Make an outline of the types of exemptions that have been allowed in the United States and the moral arguments for and against them. Make a presentation in class on their application to this case study.

4. Imagine that you are a female employee of Hobby Lobby and you found out that your health-care plan does not cover contraceptive care because your employer believes that some contraceptives are tantamount to abortion. You don't agree with your employer about this issue. What would you say to your employers to convince them to change their minds? In your answer, use practical, moral, and religious reasons to support your perspective.

5. Assume the role of a film critic writing for an online film blog. Compare and contrast two of the films on the list below to identify the filmmakers' perspectives on the issue of the relationship between religion and society, church and state. Assess how well they lay out their views and give them a rating, with 1 being terrible and 5 being excellent. Share your ratings with your classmates.

Readings

Feldman, Noah. *Divided by God: America's Church-State Problem and What We Should Do about It.* New York: Farrar, Strauss, and Giroux, 2005. Feldman traces the history of the debate over the separation of church and state, especially between legal secularists and values evangelicals. Feldman calls for a compromise, where the latter can have some symbolic public expressions of religiosity but with restrictions on government funding.

Haidt, Jonathan. *The Righteous Mind: Why Good People Are Divided by Politics and Religion.* New York: Random House, 2012. Evolutionary social psychologist Jonathan Haidt reviews the evolutionary and cultural developments that have led to the moral frameworks contributing to the political divisions between conservatives and liberals. He argues for moral humility on the part of both perspectives.

Merriman, Scott A., Sr. *When Religious and Secular Interests Collide: Faith, Law, and the Religious Exemption Debate.* Santa Barbara, CA: Praeger, 2017. This book examines the countervailing arguments in the religious exemption debate over the issues raised in this case and explains why this issue continues to be so heated and controversial in modern-day America.

Vallier, Kevin, and Michael Weber, eds. *Religious Exemptions.* Oxford, UK: Oxford University Press, 2018. The essays in this book raise questions about religious and moral exemptions to laws regarding discrimination, contraception, vaccination, and public health. The essays examine both the legal and moral issues that are part of this debate, such as questions of fairness and equal treatment.

Wald, Kenneth, and Allison Calhoun-Brown. *Religion and Politics in the United States.* Eighth edition. Lanham, MD: Rowman and Littlefield Publishers, 2018. In this book the authors contend that religion is a form of social identification that not only shapes our ideas about politics but also shapes the behavior of political elites and ordinary citizens, the interpretation of public laws, and the development of government programs.

Audiovisuals

Accidental Activist. American Family Association, 2013. This film, directed by Duane Barnhart, follows the tribulations of a family and business owner whose lives are turned upside down because the father signed a petition advocating traditional marriage, which others in his community described as a heartless act of bigotry.

Inherit the Wind. Stanley Kramer Productions, 1960. Directed by Stanley Kramer, this film dramatizes the 1925 Scopes Monkey Trial, concerning a Tennessee law banning the teaching of evolution in public schools, and highlights the controversy between religion and science.

One Generation Away: The Erosion of Religious Liberty in America. Echo-Light Studios, 2015. This documentary, directed by Ken Carpenter, explores seven cases of religious-freedom disputes throughout the United States, one of which is the *Hobby Lobby* case discussed above. While the film suggests that it explores both sides of the religious freedom debate, its focus is on what it perceives as the progressive marginalization of American Christianity from the larger culture.

Religulous. Thousand Words, 2009. This documentary, directed by Larry Charles and starring Bill Maher, is a satirical look at various beliefs espoused by fundamentalists regarding reason, science, and politics in an attempt to illustrate the dangers that religion poses to modern society.

The Handmaid's Tale. Cinecom Pictures, 1990. Based on the book by Margaret Atwood, this film, directed by Volker Schlöndorff, explores how every facet of people's lives, including their sexual and reproductive activities, might be controlled under a future repressive theocracy. It is also the basis of a Hulu series with the same name.

9

Violence

On January 2, 2020, the United States, using an unmanned aerial vehicle (UAV) or drone, targeted and killed a top security-and-intelligence commander, Major General Qassim Suleimani, who led the powerful Quds Force of the Islamic Revolutionary Guards Corps. The attack, carried out by an American MQ-9 Reaper drone, fired missiles into several vehicles leaving the Baghdad airport and killed several other officials from Iraqi militias supported by Iran in addition to General Suleimani. The attack was one of the possibilities the American military offered to President Trump in response to rocket attacks from an Iran-backed militia on an Iraqi base that housed Americans and killed an American contractor, attacks some Iraqi officials claim were perpetrated by ISIS rather than a Shia militia. The attack brought the United States to the brink of war with Iran, which retaliated by firing missiles into two Iraqi military bases where US military personnel were stationed. No one was killed, but over one hundred US servicemen suffered some brain trauma. While many were quick to condemn the Trump administration and its waffling on reasons for the attack, which ranged from the general's involvement in planning "imminent" assaults on US embassies in the region to payback for previous attacks he had orchestrated, the attack brought back into focus some of the ethical issues raised by the use of drones for targeted killing.

As Kenneth Himes chronicles, targeted killing is not new in human warfare. Targeted killing can be traced to the classical world of Greece and Rome in discussions of tyrannicide and assassination through modern-day Israel's formal policy of targeted killing in its fight against terrorists.[1] A most notable recent example of targeted killing through use of conventional

---

[1] Kenneth Himes, *Drones and the Ethics of Targeted Killing* (Lanham, MD: Rowman and Littlefield Publishers, 2016), chap. 2.

warfare—although aided by drones—was the killing of Osama bin Laden by the Obama administration. What is new is the use of remote or drone technology. Drones were first used to locate and identify suspected terrorists, who would then be targeted by missiles from ships or airplanes. However, the time lapse between identification and targeting sometimes allowed high value targets (HVTs) to escape. The CIA then added two laser-guided Hellfire missiles to the US's Predator drone to eliminate the delay between finding and killing a target, thus connecting intelligence collection and attack functions.[2] The first attempt at targeted killing took place in October 2001 against a Taliban leader in Afghanistan (who escaped). As the technology developed, the offensive capabilities of drones grew with the development of the much heavier Reaper drone, which specializes in combat and can carry Hellfire missiles and other munitions, making drone use for targeted killing of HVTs a staple in the American CIA and military arsenal in the so-called war on terror to this day.

Drones have been used for targeted killing in countries with which the United States is engaged in combat (Iraq, Afghanistan, and Syria) and in countries suspected of fostering militant Islamic terrorism (Pakistan, Yemen, and Somalia). While drone use began during the George W. Bush administration, their use escalated significantly during the Obama administration. President Obama claimed that doing so was "choosing the course of action least likely to result in the loss of innocent life."[3] This rationale was crucial at a time when the loss of American military lives as a result of the wars in Afghanistan and Iraq was beginning to weigh negatively in American politics. The American public was much more supportive of the use of unmanned drones to target and kill suspected terrorists with minimum civilian casualties than it was of placing more servicemen and servicewomen in harm's way.[4] Whereas President Obama moved toward more transparency about the secretive drone program during his second term, with an executive order requiring that civilian deaths from drone strikes be reported annually, the Trump administration has rescinded that executive order, reducing such transparency while increasing the number of drone strikes in Yemen and Somalia.[5]

Some other notable examples of drone use in targeted killing occurred in 2011 and 2013. President Obama ordered the targeted killing of Anwar Nasser al-Awlaki and his son, living in Yemen; they were US citizens believed to be involved in the planning and execution of terrorist activities. Five civilians were killed in Pakistan when they attempted to rescue militants who were

---

[2] James Igoe Walsh and Marcus Schulzke, *Drones and Support for the Use of Force* (Ann Arbor: University of Michigan Press, 2018), 12–17.

[3] See "Remarks by the President at the National Defense University," Office of the White House Press Secretary, May 23, 2013.

[4] Walsh and Schulzke, *Drones and Support for the Use of Force*, chap. 2.

[5] See "Executive Order on Revocation of Reporting Requirement," March 6, 2019; see also Daniel J. Rosenthal and Loren D. Schulman, "Trump's Secret War on Terror," *The Atlantic* (August 10, 2018).

targeted in a previous strike, a practice known as a "double tap," where a second attack is used to kill rescuers presumably because they are also fellow jihadists.[6] Also in Pakistan forty-two tribal leaders were killed when a drone fired four Hellfire missiles into their meeting, which was being held to resolve a mining dispute among the tribes. The attack was what is known as a signature strike, in which the identities of the terrorists are unknown but they are demonstrating patterns of behavior thought to be "signatures" of terrorists, which at times can include all military-age males in a strike zone.[7] In Yemen, twelve civilians traveling in a wedding convoy were killed and others wounded when a drone strike mistook them for a group of Al Qaeda militants—thus, some claimed, "turning a wedding into a funeral."[8] All four practices—the targeting of US citizens without due process, double tap, signature strikes, and collateral damage to innocent civilians—have raised serious concerns about the moral justification of the use of drone technology.

ISSUES AND CONCERNS

Several of those concerns emerged most recently in the case study above. One moral justification for any preemptive attack on a person or group, which is what targeted killing by drones entails, is that they pose an imminent threat to the United States and innocent persons. This was one of the rationales given by the Trump administration in its killing of General Suleimani. Historically, *imminent* has meant that an attack would take place in the immediate future. However, the Justice Department has revised that view to suggest that Al Qaeda and other terrorist organizations constitute an ongoing threat of attacks that could take place at any time, and therefore their members are always legitimate targets, even when no attack is taking place. This rationale leaves some to question whether such revisionist language is doublespeak reminiscent of George Orwell's novel *1984*.[9] Others, however, worry about whether mere membership in a group is sufficient warrant to be targeted for killing. Without any evidence that the targeted person is involved in direct participation in threatening activity, the attack is tantamount to summary execution.[10] While recognizing the ambiguity terrorist activity inherently

[6] Himes, *Drones and the Ethics of Targeted Killing*, 10.

[7] Arianna Huffington, "'Signature Strikes' and the President's Empty Rhetoric on Drones," HuffPost, July 10, 2013.

[8] Conor Friedersdorf, "The Wedding That a US Drone Strike Turned into a Funeral," *The Atlantic* (January 9, 2014).

[9] George Orwell, *1984* (London: Secker and Warburg, 1949). Himes suggests that this language reminds him of Alice in Wonderland, where Humpty Dumpty suggests to Alice that a word "means what I choose it to mean, neither more nor less" (*Drones and the Ethics of Targeted Killing*, 129).

[10] Kenneth Roth, "What Rules Should Govern US Drone Attacks?" *New York Review of Books*, April 4, 2013.

involves, they would contend that governments should have "substantial evidence" regarding the person's future involvement in attacks "in a manner that constitutes direct and active participation."[11]

The attack on Suleimani also raises the question of the tactical versus strategic benefits of drone strikes. In the short term, the use of drones for targeting killing of terrorists has proven effective in defusing the threat of Al Qaeda. Key leaders have been killed; its networks have been disrupted, thus hampering its ability to recruit new members; and its sanctuaries, where many attacks have been planned, are no longer safe havens. Drone warfare is cheaper financially, the threat posed to US military is minimized, and, as the targeting has become more precise, civilian casualties are less likely than in other military options.[12] Some contend that as one element of a counterinsurgency strategy, the use of drones has been an effective and an ethically viable option. Some go further to argue that the use of drones in the war on terror to minimize the risks to soldiers is morally obligatory. Emphasizing the principle of unnecessary risk, this view argues that it would be immoral to use means that would place soldiers in potential harm when other means, such as drones, would reduce that possibility.[13]

Others assert, however, that widespread use of drones within declared combat zones (Iraq and Afghanistan), and especially outside of them (Pakistan, Yemen, and Somalia), works against the broader strategy of counterinsurgency, which attempts to use political and humanitarian means, not just the military, to eliminate the larger issues that promote terrorism in the first place. Although the use of drones for targeting killing of suspected terrorists is meant to limit the violence they inflict, the United States has not been able to eliminate civilian casualties in their use. President Obama admitted as much in a 2013 speech, when he noted that while every attempt to minimize civilian casualties in drone strikes is taken, some civilians will be collateral damage and their deaths "will haunt us as long as we live."[14]

While the focus on the number of civilians relative to combatants killed, numbers that one writer says "are all over the map,"[15] is one aspect of the moral concern that "will haunt us" from the use of drones, the harm caused is more extensive; it includes the psychological, social, and economic impact on the persons and communities affected. The psychological toll includes the fear of the unknown that the constant buzzing of drones overhead elicits among the population, especially children. Family members of those killed become anxious and depressed over the loss of their loved ones. Extended family structures lose the social support and relationships the deceased provided. Parents are afraid to send their children to school, thus undermining their

---

[11] Himes, *Drones and the Ethics of Targeted Killing*, 125.

[12] Daniel Byman, "Why Drones Work," *Foreign Affairs* (July/August 2013), 4.

[13] Bradley Strawser, "Moral Predators: The Duty to Employ Uninhabited Aerial Vehicles," *Journal of Military Ethics* 9/4 (2010): 342–68.

[14] See "Remarks by the President at the National Defense University."

[15] Robert Wright, "The Price of Assassination," *New York Times,* April 13, 2010.

education. Normal efforts to aid others in response to a strike are disrupted by the possibility of double tap or signature strikes. Homes, where multiple families may live, are destroyed. Property destruction results in the loss of economic livelihood for the victims. While it is true that lethal harm is present in all forms of warfare, and that the precision of drone strikes may make the effects of these harms less severe, more consideration of these harms may lead perpetrators of drone strikes to reassess their effectiveness.

One result of these harms is that they have generated a great deal of resentment toward the United States and its allies within many of these countries. This resentment has been used by terrorist organizations to recruit new members from the families and communities affected by the strikes. "Every one of these dead noncombatants represents an alienated family, a new desire for revenge, and more recruits for a militant movement that has grown exponentially even as drone strikes have increased," wrote David Kilcullen and Andrew Exum, former advisers to General David Petraeus in Iraq and General Stanley McChrystal in Afghanistan, respectively.[16] For some, even the names given to the military and CIA drones—Predator and Reaper—carry a Christian apocalyptic tone. This reinforces the belief by some Muslims that the United States sees their use as a "righteous" response to terrorism, corroborating their fears that this "war on terror" is really a "crusade" against Islam, as was first suggested by President George W. Bush.[17]

The resentment against the United States is not limited to the countries where the strikes have occurred. Some home-grown terrorists have emerged within Western societies, including the United States, who point to what they see taking place in Islamic countries at the hands of the CIA and the military as the prime motivation for their radicalization. Faisal Shahzad, who attempted to set off a bomb in Times Square, pointed to a drone attack while he was visiting Pakistan as the basis for his actions, which he would continue, if released from custody, until the drone attacks stop in Muslim lands. Similarly, Dzhokhar Tsarnaev, the Boston Marathon bomber, claimed the victims of the bombs he and his brother planted were "collateral damage" in response to Muslims being killed in the Middle East.[18]

Another ethical concern is that the use of drones for targeted killing is a "moral hazard" in which people engage in risky behavior because they do not face the consequences of their actions.[19] One moral hazard arises when the use of drones and their improved precision and minimal risks to their operators lowers the threshold for lethal violence. The Obama administration

---

[16] David Kilcullen and Andrew McDonald Exum, "Death from Above, Outrage Down Below," Op-ed, *New York Times,* May 16, 2009.

[17] The Trump administration's ban on immigrants and refugees from countries with large Muslim populations has reinforced this belief.

[18] Fawaz Gerges, "Why Drone Strikes Are Real Enemy in 'War on Terror,'" CNN.com, June 21, 2013.

[19] John Kaag and Sarah Kreps, *Drone Warfare* (Cambridge: Polity Press, 2014), 108.

argued that its preference with terrorists was to capture them and hold them accountable through normal juridical processes. But some contend that targeted killing by drones and the use of a kill list have become a convenient substitute for capture and thus are encouraging unnecessary killing, especially in light of the controversy surrounding the indefinite incarceration of suspected terrorists at the facility in Guantanamo Bay.[20] Equally important is that such technological proficiency may lead to less deliberation about the legal and ethical issues involved. "We should not be seduced into thinking that technology can help us out of these legal and ethical decisions. In many cases, greater technological capability coincides with a greater difficulty in making responsible decisions."[21]

The clandestine nature of the drone attacks, particularly those done in the name of national security, leave them outside of the normal moral processes of what it means to wage war and not subject to military ethics or the Geneva Convention.[22] It has amounted to a secret war waged in the name of this country but without the moral deliberation that democratic societies usually demand of significant policies carried out in their name, although it is not clear how much the American public is interested in engaging in the moral and legal issues raised by drones.[23] As leaders of the Interfaith Network on Drone Warfare point out: "Democracies must debate and take moral responsibility for decisions to use violent force. By refusing to acknowledge most of its strikes, the CIA prevents civilian victims from receiving justice and conveys moral responsibility for killing on to an American people who have never been informed about this secret war, nor had their Members of Congress vote on it."[24] This was part of the issue with the drone strike against General Suleimani. Congress was not notified ahead of time of such a momentous decision, which would possibly bring the country to the brink of war with Iran, leading some congressional leaders to reassert that the constitutional authority to declare war rests with them and not the president.

The moral hazard of limited consequences for the use of drones in targeted killing could also lead us down a slippery slope to what many call endless war. Because of the low cost and limited risk to military personnel, the United States has started using drones against other lower-value targets where we would not have placed aircraft or special forces in harm's way. The point here is that the ease of using drones to eliminate any threat, not just those

---

[20] Scott Shane, "The Moral Case for Drones," *New York Times,* July 14, 2012.

[21] Kaag and Kreps, *Drone Warfare,* 12.

[22] The concern about the lack of moral deliberation on the part of the CIA led Colin Powell, former chairman of the Joint Chiefs of Staff and secretary of state, to argue that drones, which he favored in certain circumstances, should not be used by the CIA but by the military ("Powell: Pentagon Should Run Drone Program," Military. com, May 28, 2013).

[23] Kaag and Kreps, *Drone Warfare,* 126.

[24] Interfaith Network on Drone Warfare, Letter to Congress on CIA Drone Strikes, February 19, 2019.

who threaten the United States, may become commonplace. We risk that it could become "an endless cycle of perceived threat, drone strikes, inevitable collateral damage, and mutual animosity."[25] Just because they are cheaper and limit US casualties does not mean drones should be used in lieu of other options. One wonders if this was part of the calculation in the Trump administration's decision to use a drone strike to kill General Suleimani.

This points to another issue. Right now, the United States has the most drone capacity in the world. However, other nations are also purchasing and deploying them. What example is the United States setting in its use of drone strikes for these other nations? It is clear using drones against nations with anti-aircraft capability would be more difficult, but that is not the case with poorer nations, which would be extremely vulnerable to attack. The United States during the second term of the Obama administration did seek clearer guidance for its use of drones with an emphasis on only using them as a last resort, but only after it had already engaged in attacks on low-level targets.

Finally, some worry about the moral hazard done to drone operators in the form of moral injury; violating one's moral standards and values during a stressful situation such as war or violence can lead to cognitive dissonance between what one knows to be right and one's sense of oneself as a moral person. Such cognitive dissonance can generate deep wounds, which the morally injured internalize within themselves. Many soldiers have no issue with targeting a combatant who poses a direct lethal threat to them. However, drone operators, who operate thousands of miles away, are at no risk and may lose a sense of the moral justification of their actions. Moreover, they have often spent hours or days in surveillance of the targets and their families; they see them as human persons rather than as blips on a computer screen, as is often the case with aircraft pilots. After firing on the targets, they are expected to survey the area to be sure the target has been eliminated, thus seeing the effects of their actions on persons and communities with which they have become familiar. Once their shift is over, they go home to dinner with their families, which often generates additional cognitive and moral dissonance.[26]

NATURAL LAW ETHICS

Recall that in Chapter 1 we noted that while some in the natural law revisionist tradition find commonality with humanistic thinking on moral laws, Jean Porter seeks to articulate the specifically Christian beliefs underlying this tradition. Her discussion of a Christian view of natural law highlights two theological principles: the doctrine of creation and the image of God. Regarding the doctrine of creation, she writes that in response to their understanding

[25] Daniel Brunstetter, "Can We Wage a Just Drone War?" *The Atlantic* (July 2012).
[26] Adam Henschke, "Modern Soldiers Can Kill a Target on Computer, Then Head Home for Dinner—and It's Giving Them 'Moral Injury,'" ABC News [Australian Broadcasting Company], September 28, 2019.

of Paul's reference in the New Testament to the unwritten law of the Gentiles, the scholastics went on "to develop a view according to which the natural law is fundamentally a capacity or power to distinguish between good and evil; it is intrinsic to the character of the human soul as made in the Image of God, and therefore it cannot be altogether obliterated; and it is expressed or developed through moral precepts which are confirmed, as well as being completed and transcended, through the operation of grace" (13–14).[27] In other words, there are common inclinations that get reflected in various forms of laws and societal structures that develop. There is diversity in these, but they are all about achieving the same fundamental inclinations. "A given morality can thus be understood as a culturally and historically specific way of expressing the general social structures natural to us as a species" (*NR* 131). She suggests that the broad areas of convergence across cultures are what provide some consensus about moral questions, particularly regarding fundamental virtues and vices (such as a need to restrain violence or the undesirability of selfishness) (*NR* 132). What moral rules might persons with the capacity to discern good from evil develop in the context of restraining the violence perpetrated by drone strikes? A quick review of essays and articles written from religious, philosophical, and political perspectives discussing the ethics of targeted killing by drones reveals a common underlying ethical framework: the principles of the just-war tradition.

What is the just-war tradition? In the history of the Christian tradition, disciples of Jesus have wondered what to do in the face of violence. Early on, Jesus's admonitions to "turn the other cheek" and "love your enemies" led them to reject participation in armed conflict and adopt pacifism. Once Christianity became the official religion of the Roman Empire, many theologians sought to rethink this approach out of the desire both to reduce violence and to maintain a peaceful social order in the face of efforts to undermine it. Augustine (354–430 CE) was one of the first to articulate just-war principles. In the thirteenth century Aquinas made the connection between natural law and the development of the just-war tradition. Considering this connection, reviewing targeted killing by drones from the natural law tradition is important.

Critical reflection on the motives of nations before engaging in war is at the heart of just-war theory. Just-war theory seeks to reduce if not eliminate state-sanctioned violence in the world by forcing those who propose war to justify their actions in public according to specific principles. While various lists of these principles have developed over time, the two main categories are *jus ad bellum*, just-war principles to consider before engaging in war, and *jus in bello*, just-war principles to assess the conduct of war. In both lists the aim is to avoid or minimize violence and to promote peace.

The first principle of *jus ad bellum* is a *just cause*. Historically the just cause has been for defensive purposes, either to defend the nation against an

---

[27] Jean Porter, *Nature as Reason: A Thomistic Theory of the Natural Law* (Grand Rapids, MI: Eerdmans, 2005) (hereafter cited as *NR*).

imminent attack or to defend others who are being unjustly attacked. The second principle is that war must be a *last resort*. A nation should engage in war only after all peaceful means of resolving the conflict have been exhausted. Third, the war must be *declared by a competent authority*, usually a country or the international community. Fourth, *right intent* implies that the goal is to promote the justice and peace that were broken by acts of aggression, not out of self-interest or a desire for revenge. Fifth, the war should also have *a reasonable chance of success* in restoring the peace and ending the violence without prohibitive costs. The final criterion is *proportionality*, which alludes to the means used so that the costs of using them are proportional to the ends being sought—restoring peace or the balance of power necessary for that peace.

Proportionality also comes into play in the principles of the conduct during the war (*jus in bello*). The force must be appropriate—not excessive—to restore justice and peace, a line that many have claimed was crossed in the nuclear bombing of Hiroshima and Nagasaki by the United States in 1945. In addition, those engaged in war must target only combatants and avoid harming civilians to the extent possible.

All the Christian ethical traditions discussed in Chapter 1 engage to some degree the principles of the just-war tradition. They agree that the goal is to limit violence as much as possible so that social order is peaceful and enables the common good and the flourishing of all. They affirm that love and justice are part of this tradition, particularly love for one's neighbor and justice for those who have been victimized (in the sense of restoring the order that was broken and restoring people to their natural rights, not in any sense of vengeance or punishment). Although Porter does not fully develop insights into just-war theory, her allegiance to the scholastics, particularly Aquinas, requires us to apply the ideas developed in her discussion of natural law to this case.

What do these criteria suggest about the moral permissibility of the use of drones for targeted killing? While the initial attacks on Al Qaeda and the Taliban in response to the 9/11 attacks on the United States appeared to meet the principles of a just war, the continuation of the so-called war on terror raises questions about whether this is still the case. The revision of the term *imminent*, away from a defensive stance to an offensive position that supports preemptive action against any perceived terrorist threat, no matter how small, anywhere in the world, fails to meet the principle of a just cause. It is difficult to claim that a preemptive drone strike can be justified in the name of defending a nation or innocent persons against an imminent attack. Moreover, whereas the Obama administration initially created guidelines that sought the capture of terrorists to bring them to justice, or killing them only as a last resort, the development of a kill list, and the ease of drone technology to do so, suggests that the aim is no longer their capture with due process but their killing, which violates the criterion of last resort. The same failure to meet this criterion could be argued with the targeting of General Suleimani. The Pentagon offered other options to respond to the death of the American contractor, but President Trump chose what to many seemed like the extreme one—not a last resort but seemingly a first resort. Moreover, the Trump administration's suggestion that the targeting of General Suleimani was payback for previous attacks he orchestrated against US embassies and forces indicates that the intent was revenge, not peace. The secretive nature of the drone program and the expansion of drone strikes to lower-value targets and to areas outside the declared war zones raise questions about the criterion of declaration by a competent authority, especially as Congress suggests the administration's efforts undermine Congress's constitutional authority to declare war. While HVTs have been eliminated, Al Qaeda networks have been disrupted, and no new terrorist attack has taken place on American soil, we seem to be in the state of an endless war, with new enemies emerging, raising questions about the war having a reasonable chance of success. The cost of the war effort has reached the trillions. As noted earlier, although fewer Americans have been killed in the war effort because of the drones, the psychological, social, and economic impact on civilian populations has generated resentment and contributed to the recruitment of new terrorists. Regarding proportionality, given that drone technology has developed more precision with fewer civilian casualties and reductions in US military deaths, the use of drones appears to meet this criterion. However, noncombatants continue to be part of the collateral damage done—damage that is more than just civilian deaths.

The second theological conviction Porter affirms, the notion of the image of God, is also crucial in this discussion: "Human beings are images of God in a more distinctive sense, sharing in some way in divine capacities for self-determination and providential care" (*NR* 135). All persons, however marred by human sin, reflect God's image. In addition, Porter argues that the image of God also affirms the importance of human agency and the human person "as a free and self-determining agent . . . enjoying certain powers on the basis of his or her capacities for choice and self-direction" (*NR* 359).

While Porter does not specifically address the relationship between the image of God and targeted killing by drones, she does talk about the natural law approach to torture, which has relevance for this discussion. For her, torture is seen as "a fundamental assault on human dignity."[28] This violates God's command to love one's neighbor. More important, torture is an assault on the image of God that is present in all persons, even those "who exercise their rational freedom in sinful and destructive ways" ("Torture" 348). Inflicting great physical and emotional pain on persons with the aim of breaking their spirit is problematic because it undermines the inherent dignity of all persons. While it is true that sometimes individuals are required to sacrifice their private good for the sake of the common good, this is not the case in torture; nor, I would argue, is it in the case of targeted killings by

---

[28] Jean Porter, "Torture and the Christian Conscience: A Response to Jeremy Waldron," *Scottish Journal of Theology* 61/3: 340–58 (hereafter cited as "Torture").

drones. "The good of the soul, the integrity of the image of God within the individual, his or her capacities for faith, hope, and love—no considerations of personal or national security, nor even the possibility of widespread loss of life, can justify an assault on these" ("Torture" 351). The application to the case at hand seems most appropriate when considering the impact of these strikes on the persons and communities they affect.

Porter also speaks about the impact of torture on the person who commits the acts of torture. We cannot insulate ourselves from the effects of our actions ("Torture" 352). "Still, killing another human being is potentially corrupting even when it is justifiable—that is one of the reasons why it is so difficult, and yet so necessary, to sustain a sense of moral boundaries, reinforced by a sense of military honor, even on the battlefield" ("Torture" 352). The same could be said of the potential moral injuries suffered by those who operate the drones that target and kill the terrorists and inflict damage on innocent civilians and their communities. We need to provide appropriate spiritual and moral assistance to the operators, even when the attack is morally justified.

Porter also illustrates the problem with the secretive nature of the drone program for targeted killing. "There are certain classes of acts which are regarded as justifiable only if they are carried out by an agent of the state, on behalf of the common good" ("Torture" 353). The state is a publicly constituted authority. Some of the moral wrestling with drone strikes is that they do not follow normal processes that are under democratic control. The presence of a kill list kept by the president or military leaders suggests that they can judge that the other does not deserve to live. She suggests this is a demonstration of pride and is dangerous. "Not only can we not reliably make these judgments about one another's lives—the attempt to do so is itself corrupting, in so far as it encourages us to overlook the manifold limitations of our judgments, the way in which they can be skewed by our self-interests and our fears" ("Torture" 354). This is especially problematic in the case of signature strikes, where so-called common terrorist behaviors are the reasons for killing people; it is even worse in the case of double-tap strikes. That is why they need to be more public and done in the name of the "overarching claims of the community rather than the determinations of one individual standing in relation of self-legitimated authority over the other" ("Torture" 354).

Just like the exposure of the torture at Abu Ghraib had a negative impact on the individuals doing the torture, it also cast doubt on the moral integrity of the nation, giving rise to further terrorist activities in response. The same is true regarding the targeted killing by drones done in the name of national security. There must be ways to place limits on the power of the president, the CIA, and the military to conduct these strikes, one of which is "the institution of ideals of due process and the rule of law under the auspices of an independent judiciary" ("Torture" 355). We cannot sacrifice justice for the sake of security. Especially as other countries develop the technology to use drones for targeted killing, we may find ourselves in the same position where their self-interest or their kill list has a comparable result. The impact will be an increase in insecurity and the relinquishing of our own claims to be a just society. Porter writes: "To the extent that the enactments of a given society are unjust, it inflicts a grave wrong on all its members, and not only those who are victimized by the injustice in question" ("Torture" 356). This applies not only to torture but "to any kind of injustice sanctioned in the name of collective security" ("Torture" 356).

HISPANIC LIBERATIVE ETHICS

Exploring this case from Hispanic liberative ethics requires that we follow Miguel De La Torre's hermeneutical circle—observing, reflecting, praying, acting, and reassessing—beginning with observations he makes on the state of war in the United States. The first thing De La Torre observes is that the making of war has generally been for the benefit of the dominant group to ensure that most of the world's resources are available to its members. He contends that "those on the periphery of power are seldom consulted, even though they are disproportionately on the receiving end of the violence of war" (113).[29] He highlights as an example the Iraq war, in which President George W. Bush engaged the world in a war under the pretense of weapons of mass destruction, weapons that were never found. That did not stop the United States, because it found other rationales for ousting Saddam Hussein—democracy, freedom, and oil. While wealthy contractors made money, the soldiers—many of whom come disproportionately from low-income families—and the Iraqi civilians paid the price with their lives. "There is something morally reprehensible about asking our young to die for empty slogans."[30]

A second observation is that the United States commits a great deal of resources to the military, spending more on its defense appropriations than the next fourteen nations combined. The problem, as President Eisenhower noted many years ago, is that the connections between the defense industry's desire for profit and its influence over politicians affect negatively not only foreign policy, but also lead to stagnation in the economy by taking resources away from those industries that meet society's needs for health care, education, and infrastructure. Quoting Eisenhower, De La Torre writes: "This world in arms is not spending money alone. It is spending the sweat of its laborers, the genius of its scientists, the hopes of its children" (*DEM* 105). Moreover, in addition to those for its own use, the United States is the largest exporter of weapons around the globe, generating a great deal of instability on the global stage.

Third, while use of drones for targeted killing may mean that fewer US military personnel are placed in harm's way, such emphasis on efficiency does not overcome the ethical problems their use creates. One ethical issue De La Torre raises, which was mentioned earlier in the chapter, is with the

---

[29] Miguel De La Torre, *Doing Ethics from the Margins*, 2nd ed. (Maryknoll, NY: Orbis Books, 2014) (hereafter cited as *DEM*).

[30] Miguel De La Torre, "Rhetoric Kills," EthicsDaily.com, June 30, 2006.

targeted killing of two US citizens, Anwar al-Awlaki and his son, without due process. No US court reviewed the evidence of the government's claims against al-Awlaki, and his son was never accused of terrorist activities. The Obama administration's actions as accuser, judge, and executioner are a slap in the face to all those who take seriously the freedoms and rights guaranteed by the Constitution. Another ethical issue, also mentioned above, is the moral difference between those actively engaged in terrorist activities and those who are sympathizers to their cause, who are also targeted by such tactics as signature strikes and double taps. When even conservative estimates of civilians killed as a result of collateral damage are added to the mix, the moral problems associated with the use of drones for targeted killing become greater (*DEM* 103).

De La Torre also observes the moral hazard of what happens when other countries develop drones to the same degree that the United States has. He writes: "Our unilateral killing of those whom we call 'terrorists' anywhere in the world without some type of global consensus has created a precedent for other nations to follow suit" (*DEM* 104). For example, when a US surveillance drone landed accidentally in Iran, the Iranians boasted that they had broken the code encryption and copied the technology. While the United States says Iran doesn't have the capacity to create and deploy drones, De La Torre wonders what would happen if they sold the technology to the Chinese. Would they develop drones for targeted killing of persons they deemed terrorists, such as the Dalai Lama, who they claim is a "terrorist in disguise"? The possibility for such proliferation of drone warfare would be irresponsible.

When engaged in reflecting, the second step of the hermeneutical circle, De La Torre highlights other issues and raises important questions. First, the war on terror continues to divide the world into the binary of good and evil, which makes war inevitable, especially as we continue to maintain international structures that make war possible and profitable. Because those in power get to define what good and evil are, they also decide the definition of terrorism and what actions are acceptable or unacceptable in the battle against it. Is the use of violence in the form of targeted killing or torture against terrorists justified as an acceptable means to punish their actions and to promote freedom and democracy? The United States has said yes to both, some even suggesting that it is a moral imperative. De La Torre understands that some violence may be necessary, but he notes that there is a difference between killing someone as part of an offensive strategy and defending others against harm from an oppressor. Many of the targeted killings by drones thousands of miles away can hardly be perceived as responses to an imminent threat. Moreover, the deaths of innocent civilians as part of the collateral damage of these strikes suggest that the real oppressor in this context may not be the terrorists but those who ordered the strikes. However, he warns that even if justified, the use of violence "forever changes a person and a society" (*DEM* 112), a concern he shares with Jean Porter. Given the moral injury many drone operators and other military personnel have experienced during this war on terror; and the way the civilian casualties from these strikes undermine the humanitarian elements of our counterinsurgency strategy to eliminate the larger issues that promote terrorism, there is cause for such concern.

Another question De La Torre raises is about the possibility of waging a just war from a Christian perspective in this day and time. The answer to that question, like the previous one, depends upon the social location of those seeking to justify it. Most Christian leaders and ethicists condemned the Iraq war and declared the targeting killing of General Suleimani unjust. Others disagreed, arguing that both actions met the just-war criteria. Why the difference in perspective? De La Torre proposes that the reason is because they inhabit different institutional, political, and ideological social locations that are inherently biased, not objective, and represent "the subjective views of those applying the just-war theory" (*DEM* 106). The subjective nature of the perspectives is why De La Torre concludes that, from a Christian perspective, he would much rather recognize the evil that war is and ask God's forgiveness than try to distort the gospel message of love by justifying it using just-war theory (*DEM* 113–14).

The same is true when it comes to the use of torture, euphemistically known as "enhanced interrogation techniques," to gain information from terrorists. The George W. Bush administration defended the use of such techniques as waterboarding and emotional abuse, arguing they are legal and effective. De La Torre, like Porter, argues that such treatment calls into question our moral sensibilities: "The *imago Dei* of the enemy must be recognized at all levels of conflict, for the enemy is also created in the image of God and thus has dignity and worth" (*DEM* 114). De La Torre agrees with the assessment of torture by former Senator John McCain, a victim of torture during the Vietnam war, who commented in response to a report on those techniques: "What I learned . . . confirms for me what I have always believed and insisted to be true—that the cruel, inhumane and degrading treatment of prisoners is not only wrong in principle and a stain on our country's conscience, but an ineffective and unreliable means of gathering intelligence" (*DEM* 109).

Moreover, debates about national security and just war often have little connection to those who experience oppression, but instead seem more concerned with maintaining empire, which many see as the prime motivation for the continuation of the war on terror. For the marginalized, violence is already a reality perpetrated by unjust institutions and extremes of inequality. De La Torre writes: "Ethical debates concerning what makes a war just may have validity among ethicists of the dominant culture, but for the masses that live under the strain of racism and classism, such debates are irrelevant" (*DEM* 114). What is relevant to their security is the cost of preparation and participation in war, which means less money available for the resources that the poor and marginalized really need both in the United States and abroad. He quotes the 1994 UN Human Development Report to illustrate his point:

In the final analysis, human security is a child who did not die, a disease that did not spread, a job that was not cut, an ethnic tension that did not explode in violence, a dissident who was not silenced. Human security is not a concern with weapons—it is a concern with human life and dignity. (*DEM* 115)

To stand in solidarity with the marginalized requires that, in justifying violence, we include all the costs associated with it—not only physical and psychological damage done to combatants and civilians alike, but also the material deprivation it inflicts on the poor.

The third and fourth steps of De La Torre's hermeneutical circle, praying and praxis, explore the biblical and theological basis for the use of violence and the actions taken in response. The biblical witness is mixed. There are many examples in the Hebrew Bible of the Israelites using violence at the command of God, such as the command to kill everyone and everything in Jericho once the walls of the city fell, actions that were repeated in the European colonization of the Americas, and which we might call crimes against humanity. "The Hebrew's (European) dream of religious freedom and liberation became the Canaanite's (Native Americans) nightmare of subjugation and genocide" (*DEM* 116). However, given the Christocentric nature of Hispanic ethics, the biblical example of Jesus is the most relevant when discerning the use of violence. De La Torre acknowledges that Jesus's statements to turn the other cheek and to pray for one's enemies suggest that he abhors violence, while at the same time acknowledging that those who become his disciples are likely to face violence on his behalf. "I have not come to bring peace, but a sword" (Mt 10:34). On the basis of these statements De La Torre concludes that violence "should never be accepted as a necessary evil, nor should it be rejected as antithetical to Jesus," noting the violence he used in the cleansing of the temple and attached to the day of judgment (*DEM* 116). The concern for him is making a distinction between the use of violence by the powerful to maintain their privilege and the violence used by the oppressed or on their behalf to bring about justice and abundant life. The targeted killing by drones and the collateral damage inflicted on innocent people are clearly more aimed to maintain privilege than to promote justice.

De La Torre suggests that there are two choices for Christians seeking to address the injustice of oppressive structures: participate in the use of violence or advocate nonviolent resistance. Some liberation theologians, he notes, have found ways to legitimize violence. They make distinctions between the violence of the oppressor, which maintains a system that does institutional violence to the marginalized, and the violence of the oppressed who are seeking to liberate themselves from their oppression. The question for them is not if Christians should use violence, but rather, "Do Christians have a right to defend themselves from the already existing violence?" (*DEM* 117). The answer for them is yes. They recognize that while all forms of violence may be evil, not all decisions to use violence are unethical. Rather, "persons making a preferential option to love the oppressed may very well find themselves harming the oppressor" (*DEM* 118). In this case violence is seen as a defensive action trying to protect the humanity of the innocent. Doing nothing or remaining silent in the face of the violence of oppressive structures would make one complicit in the violence. "History has demonstrated that denouncing unjust social structures is simply not enough, for those accustomed to power and privilege will never willingly abdicate what they consider to be a birthright" (*DEM* 118). It is difficult to see how the violence associated with targeted killing by drones or torture can be seen as protecting the innocent.

The second choice facing Christians in the face of violence is nonviolent resistance. Those who advocate this perspective act out against oppression but refuse to use the tools of the oppressor. De La Torre rejects any call for nonviolence by those who are in positions of power and privilege as attempts to maintain the status quo. Instead, he highlights the examples of several key figures involved in nonviolent movements. Martin Luther King Jr., a leader in the US civil rights movement, is a prominent example. In response to racism and classism King advocated confrontation with these unjust structures using nonviolent means, which he saw as the embodiment of the Christian ideal of love. The hope was that by engaging in protests and other actions that resisted injustice but still respected the humanity of the oppressor, the movement would provide a path for all to live in a more just society as members of the "beloved community." Engaging in violence by and for the oppressed only encourages greater violence on the part of the powerful, resulting in a never-ending spiral of hatred and violence (*DEM* 119). De La Torre also highlights the work of Nobel laureate Adolfo Pérez Esquivel, who argues that Christians should model their actions after Jesus in their efforts to overcome injustice even in the face of violence. Violence, no matter the source, is an attack on humanity and ultimately on God (*DEM* 120). These same principles have been at work in the heart of those Christians who have protested the development and use of drones for targeted killing.

This affirmation of the sanctity of life is an important element for De La Torre, one he does not think Christians support in all cases but which should be central to reassessing our approach to the use of violence even if justified. "To truly be pro-life is to believe that all life, created by God, has worth, dignity, and purpose; therefore, no human, under any circumstance, has the right to play God and terminate any life" (*DEM* 120). The implication here is that no emphasis on national security or freedom or democracy should take precedence over the sanctity of life. Any decision regarding the use of violence, whether the targeted killing of suspected terrorists or the killing of an oppressor, must demonstrate respect for the dignity of all persons that is fundamental to the Imago Dei that dwells within them.

RESOURCES

Discussion Questions

1. The Justice Department has changed the rationale for attacking potential terrorists from an "imminent" threat to membership in a terrorist organization. Do you agree with this change? Why or why not?
2. Both natural law ethics and Hispanic liberative ethics raise issues with the application of just-war theory in the use of torture and the use of drones for targeted killing, suggesting that their use violates the principle of just cause and denies the image of God that exists in all persons, including one's enemies. Do you agree with their claims? If not, what challenge would you make to them?
3. The CIA claims that the increased precision of targeted killing by drone strikes all but eliminates the collateral damage of killing civilians. What do you think about their claims? Is this the only collateral damage being done to civilian populations? What would Porter or De La Torre say to this claim?
4. De La Torre contends that some violence may be necessary, but he notes that there is a difference between killing someone as part of an offensive strategy and defending others against harm from an oppressor. Are the targeting killings by drone strikes in places like Pakistan or Yemen about maintaining empire or creating justice for the people of these countries? Why or why not?
5. Do you think the United States has a moral obligation to join with international leaders to limit the proliferation and use of drones in warfare, as they have done with nuclear weapons? What role do you think Christians and other religious persons should play in facilitating such discussions?

Activities

1. Do an analysis of this case from the progressive evangelical ethics tradition. Compare and contrast the conclusions drawn from that tradition with the two perspectives in this case analysis. In what ways are they similar? How are they different? Which approach, in your opinion, addresses the case most comprehensively?
2. Gather a group of students to watch one or more of the films or documentaries suggested below that raise questions about the use of drones for targeted killing. Hold a discussion on what the group thinks the ethical stance being taken by the filmmaker(s) is on this issue? Do you agree or disagree? Consider how Porter or De La Torre would respond to the filmmaker. Record the discussion and share it with other classmates.
3. Have a debate over the following statement: *It would be immoral to use means that would place soldiers in potential harm when the use of drones*

would reduce that possibility. Have teams research possible responses to this claim and provide time for each group to make its response.

4. Research the concept of moral injury, which many soldiers and drone operators have experienced in the US war on terror. *Soul Repair* in the "Readings" list below is a good resource. How is moral injury defined? What are the psychological and ethical effects on persons who experience it? What can Christians do to bring about healing and reconciliation to them, their families, and their communities? Write a report or presentation to share with the class.

5. The Interfaith Network on Drone Warfare is a coalition of faith-based organizations working to raise awareness about the moral concerns and consequences of the US government's increasing use of drone warfare. Visit its website and write a report that analyzes its religious and ethical framework and the implications for its work in ending drone warfare. Compare its arguments with those of Porter and De La Torre.

Readings

Brock, Rita Nakashima, and Gabriella Lettini. *Soul Repair: Recovering from Moral Injury after War.* Boston: Beacon Press, 2013. The authors tell the stories of four veterans of wars, from Vietnam to our conflicts in Iraq and Afghanistan, who reveal their experiences of moral injury from war and how they have learned to live with it. They also explore its effect on families and communities, and the community processes that have gradually helped soldiers with their moral injuries.

Himes, Kenneth R., OFM. *Drones and the Ethics of Targeted Killing.* Lanham, MD: Rowman and Littlefield Publishing. 2016. Himes traces the role of the use of drones in the war on terror and highlights the historical, political, personal, and moral implications of targeted killing through the use of unmanned aerial vehicles (UAVs).

Kaag, John, and Sarah Kreps. *Drone Warfare.* Cambridge: Polity Press, 2014. In this book the authors engage the political, legal, and ethical dimensions of UAVs. They argue the United States has an important role to play in developing international agreements to control the use of drones in the future.

Walsh, James Igoe, and Marcus Schulzke. *Drones and Support for the Use of Force.* Ann Arbor: University of Michigan Press, 2018. In this book the authors use their research on Americans' support for drone technology to raise questions about the implications for democratic control of military technologies.

Woods, Chris. *Sudden Justice: America's Secret Drone Wars.* New York: Oxford University Press, 2015. This book by an investigative journalist explores the secretive history of the US use of armed drones and their key role not only on today's battlefields but also in a covert targeted killing project that has led to the deaths of thousands.

Audiovisuals

Drone. VoltFilm, 2014. This documentary, directed by Tonje Hessen Schei, follows people on both sides of the use of drone technology. The unique access to drone victims in Waziristan is juxtaposed with drone pilots who struggle to come to terms with the new warfare. The film covers diverse and integral ground: the recruitment of young pilots at gaming conventions; the redefinition of "going to war"; the moral stance of engineers behind the technology; the world leaders giving the secret "green light" to engage in the biggest targeted killing program in history; and the people willing to stand up against the violations of civil liberties and fight for transparency, accountability, and justice.

Eye in the Sky. Raindog Films, 2015. This film, directed by Gavin Hood, highlights the moral, political, and personal implications—for the operator as well as the commanders ordering the strikes—for the use of drones in targeting terrorists within civilian areas.

Good Kill. IFC Films, 2014. Directed by Andrew Niccol, this film highlights the psychological and moral toll that drone warfare has on pilots and their families when faced with challenges of collateral damage on civilian targets.

National Bird. Ten Forward Films, 2016. This film, directed by Sonia Kennebeck, follows the journey of three military veterans who felt guilty over their participation in targeting killing and who seek to break the silence around the secret US drone war.

The Religious Community and Drone Warfare. Interfaith Network on Drone Warfare. Vimeo, 2020. In this short film by George McCullough faith leaders give their moral and theological perspective on a range of issues: the history of drone warfare, the situation of drone operators, the secrecy of the drone program, "killing one terrorist and creating 10 terrorists," civilian deaths, the need for international agreements controlling the use of drones, and providing real security for the United States.

Unmanned: America's Drone War. Brave New Films, 2013. This documentary, directed by Robert Greenwald, investigates the impact that US drone strikes have around the globe. The film reveals the realities of drone warfare—the violation of international law, the loss of life, the far-reaching implications for the communities that live under drones, and the blowback faced by the United States.

Index